Belgium in the
Great War

By the same author

Belgium in the Second World War

Belgium in the Great War

Jean-Michel Veranneman

Pen & Sword
MILITARY

First published in Great Britain in 2018 by
Pen & Sword Military
An imprint of
Pen & Sword Books Ltd
Yorkshire – Philadelphia

Copyright © Jean-Michel Veranneman 2018

ISBN 978 1 52671 660 6

The right of Jean-Michel Veranneman to be identified as Author of this work has been asserted by him in accordance with the Copyright, Designs and Patents Act 1988.

A CIP catalogue record for this book is
available from the British Library.

All rights reserved. No part of this book may be reproduced or transmitted in any form or by any means, electronic or mechanical including photocopying, recording or by any information storage and retrieval system, without permission from the Publisher in writing.

Printed and bound in the UK by TJ International Ltd, Padstow, Cornwall.

Pen & Sword Books Limited incorporates the imprints of Atlas, Archaeology, Aviation, Discovery, Family History, Fiction, History, Maritime, Military, Military Classics, Politics, Select, Transport, True Crime, Air World, Frontline Publishing, Leo Cooper, Remember When, Seaforth Publishing, The Praetorian Press, Wharncliffe Local History, Wharncliffe Transport, Wharncliffe True Crime and White Owl.

For a complete list of Pen & Sword titles please contact

PEN & SWORD BOOKS LIMITED
47 Church Street, Barnsley, South Yorkshire, S70 2AS, England
E-mail: enquiries@pen-and-sword.co.uk
Website: www.pen-and-sword.co.uk

Or
PEN AND SWORD BOOKS
1950 Lawrence Rd, Havertown, PA 19083, USA
E-mail: Uspen-and-sword@casematepublishers.com
Website: www.penandswordbooks.com

Contents

List of Maps	vii
List of Plates	viii
Words of Thanks	xii
Note on place names	xiii
Introduction	xvii
Prelude The Fall of Fort de Loncin	xx

PART I   NEUTRAL BELGIUM — 1

1 Waterloo and All That — 3
2 Leopold II, Brialmont and Ordinary Politicians — 6
3 The Flemish Movement before 1914 — 15

PART II   BRAVE LITTLE BELGIUM — 19

1 Crisis — 21
2 Invasion — 29
   2.1 First Blood: Cavalier Fonck and the Visé Bridge — 31
   2.2 The Bloody Harvest of August 1914: Visé, Andenne, Aarschot, Dinant, Louvain and other Places of Infamy — 33
   2.3 Resistance of the Forts of Liège and Namur — 43
   2.4 Haelen: The Battle of the Silver Helmets — 48
   2.5 Antwerp — 55
   2.6 The Battle of the Yser River — 59
3 Stabilization: Mud and Misery, Dogs and Rats, Flies, Lice and Ice — 67
   3.1 In Flanders Skies: Of Camels and Pups, SPADS and Fokkers — 76
   3.2 Off Flanders Coast: Bruges, Zeebrugge and the U-Boats — 84

4	King Albert, his Bavarian Queen, a Post Office and a Saintly Address	89
	4.1 Peace Feelers	98
	4.2 The *Frontbeweging*, the Flemish Movement at the Belgian Front	104
	4.3 Belgians Abroad, or Where Agatha Christie Found her Inspiration	110
5	Out of Africa and around the World	112
	5.1 The African Campaign	112
	5.2 The 'Auto-Cannons' from Russia to New York and Bordeaux	123
6	Occupation	125
	6.1 Feeding the Belgians: Of Ships, Sealing Wax, Cabbages and Kings	129
	6.2 Enslaving and Robbing the Belgians: Plundering and getting rid of Competition	131
	6.3 Dividing the Belgians: The *Flamenpolitik*	134
7	Resistance: A Merchant Navy Captain, Edith Cavell, Gabrielle Petit, a White Lady, a Cardinal, a Burgomaster, a Professor and others	138
8	Belgium and the Propaganda War	154
9	Liberation: The Emperor's Battle and the King's Flanders Army Group	162
10	Liberation Politics	170
	10.1 Chaos in Brussels	170
	10.2 Lophem	170

PART III   AFTERMATH   173

1	Disappointing an Immense Minister	175
2	Settling Accounts and the Leipzig Farce	189
3	Cleaning up, Rebuilding and Remembering	192

Notes	196
Bibliography	208
Index	220

List of Maps

1. The campaign of 1914   57
2. The Battle of the Yser   65
3. The East African campaign   119
4. The final offensive, 1918   166
5. Annexations   184
6. League of Nations mandates   185

List of Plates

Leopold of Saxe-Coburg-Gotha, first King of the Belgians.

Leopold II, second King of the Belgians.

Brave Little Belgium: the sketch in *Punch* that helped to sway British opinion.

Lancer Fonck, the first Belgian casualty of the Great War.

Belgian soldiers in their 1914 uniform, with dogs of the now extinct Belgian mastiff breed.

The strategic Visé bridge over the Meuse River, which was blown up by the Belgian army before the Germans arrived.

The historic centre of Louvain (Leuven), completely devastated by the Germans.

Plan of Fort de Loncin, typical of a Brialmont-type fort.

General Leman, in his Napoleonic-style uniform.

The mammoth 420 mm German naval Krupp gun, adapted to demolish the Belgian forts from a safe distance.

One of the gun turrets of the Brialmont forts pre-war.

Effects of the 420 mm shells on one of Loncin's turrets.

Haelen: Belgian Lancers hold a barricade against an attack by Mecklenburg Dragoons.

Haelen: the German cavalry charges.

King Albert of the Belgians holds a medal parade.

Two of the beautiful German helmets that are to be seen in large number at the Haelen Museum.

Haelen: the monument the Germans erected close to Yzerwinning Farm.

List of Plates   ix

The 'Goose's foot' at Nieuport.

Contemporary drawing of hand-to-hand fighting during the Battle of the Yser.

Aerial view of the 'Goose's foot' in Nieuport, where the drainage canals converge that were used to flood the 'German' bank of the Yser River.

The Kaiserliche (Imperial) Marinekorps was responsible for defending the coast, from the front to the Dutch border.

The Kaiser visits his troops at the front in Flanders.

Stabilization. Endless watching over the desolate, inundated front.

The 'Trench of Death' on the bank of the Yser River has been preserved.

Madam Tack and her donkey Paula would bring sweets to the soldiers.

Albert I, King of the Belgians, in the new khaki uniform introduced in 1915.

Bavarian-born Queen Elisabeth; her loyalty to her husband's country never wavered.

The Sainte Adresse government in exile in France.

Belgian Henri Farman 20, early in the war.

Famous balloon buster André de Meulemeester, with his Hanriot Dupont biplane.

Spad XI two-seater, of the type King Albert sometimes flew across the lines.

The Belgian Congolese *Force Publique* during the campaign in German East Africa.

The 'auto-cannons' and their colourful CO.

The 'auto-cannons'.

Cardinal Mercier.

Brussels Burgomaster Adolphe Max.

Gabrielle Petit, who was executed as a spy by the Germans.

The Tir national shooting range in Brussels, where many executions took place.

The Belgian army at the battle of Merksem.

Before evacuating Belgium, the Germans systematically plundered and destroyed.

The final offensive.

Portrait of King Albert that hangs at the entrance of the Belgian ambassador's residence in London.

Belgian troops occupying Aachen, Germany.

The large cemetery at Poelkapelle where 1,722 Belgian soldiers are buried.

The Ijzertoren (Yser tower) monument in Dixmude.

The monument to the dead at Warsage village, where the Germans executed a number of civilians in August 1914.

Stocks of shells found in the fields by farmers and waiting to be destroyed.

In peace sons bury their fathers.
In war fathers bury their sons.
Thucydides, Greek historian, *c*. 460–400 BC

Words of Thanks

The author would like to mention several historians who have inspired him. Of course, Henri Pirenne is the premier Belgian historian and lived through the whole of the Great War, indeed suffering exile in Germany, writing extensively about it and other subjects after the war. One of the best contemporary Belgian historians was Jean Stengers of Brussels University (ULB). The author had the privilege to be taught by him, as he was also by Professors John Bartier and Jacques Willequet. He was fortunate to be able to discuss the period and particular episodes with Professor Francis Balace of Liège University, Professor Etienne Rooms, Dr Chantal Kesteloot of the *Centre d'Etudes de la Seconde Guerre Mondiale (CEGES)* in Brussels and Professor Van Goethem of the Dossin Barracks Memorial and Antwerp University. Historian Professor John Rogister FSA, FRHistS, kindly read the work. My daughter-in-law Ana Carolina Lopes Ferreira da Silva drew the maps, while Pierre Lierneux of the Brussels Royal Army Museum (now the War Heritage Institute) and Daniel Brackx, who has an extraordinary collection of aviation pictures, helped me with plates representing planes. Last but not least, Lieutenant Dobbelaere of the Poelcapelle Unexploded Ordnance Disposal unit (SEDEE/DOVO) of the Belgian army gave us an extremely interesting tour of the facilities there.

To them and to many others who ceaselessly encouraged him the author would like to express his sincere gratitude, with special thanks to his patient wife Maria, who accompanied him to wrecked forts and former battlefields.

Author's Note

At the publishers' prompting, the author has not interrupted the text with notes. They are cued by superscript number in the text and grouped together at the end of the main text. They usually refer to points that are of minor importance or are not directly part of the history of Belgium during the First World War, but may be of interest to the reader. Others are bibliographic references of sources used.

Note on place names

A traveller to Belgium today might be puzzled when trying to find directions to some of the places named in this book. For example, someone driving in the Flanders region, the northern part of the country, will look in vain for road signs telling him where the road to Mons is. That city, where the British fought a famous battle in August 1914, is now referred to as Bergen. Most English speakers will have heard of Ypres, but might be excused for not realizing that the old medieval city is now known locally as Ieper. Without going into the complicated language politics of modern Belgium, now a federal construction where language groups enjoy large autonomy, suffice it to say that before the First World War many place names had been 'francised' – for example the names for what the British know as Ypres, Passchendaele or Furnes, had been pronounced locally in a way that is closer to the spelling now in use. However, contemporary maps showed the 'French' spelling and that logically enough has stuck in the military history literature. To help the English-speaking reader a glossary with the principal place names follows. The rule adopted in the text has been to retain the English name for very well-known places, like Brussels, Antwerp, Ypres or Bruges. For the lesser known like Haelen, Passchendaele, Ploegsteert or Nieuport the name best known to English speakers through the military history books has been kept. The glossary should help when trying to find directions or look at modern maps or use a GPS.

The best-known version to the English speaker is always placed first and is the one used in the text. It is usually followed by the name used locally today. When a place name is mentioned for the first time in the text, its modern spelling is written in brackets if it differs from the one that is best known to English speakers, like Passchendaele (Passendale).

Some are the same in all languages and thus are not repeated. Practically no names in Wallonia, the southern French-speaking part of Belgium, have changed since 1914. These (like Charleroi or Dinant in Wallonia or Hasselt in Flanders) are not listed in the glossary. Louvain, Liège, and Brussels are also known differently in German and the German version is mentioned in the glossary.

Aerschot, Aarschot
Alost, Aalst
Antwerp, Antwerpen, Anvers
Bruges, Brugge, Bruges
Brussels, Bruxelles, Brussel,
Bikschote, Bixschote,
Dunkirk, Duinkerke, Dunkerque (France)
Dixmude, Diksmuide
Eeclo, Eeklo
Furnes, Veurne
Gete, Gette (river)
Ghent, Gent, Gand
Liège, Liège, Luik (Dutch), Lüttich (German)
Lophem, Loppem
Louvain, Leuven, Löwen (German)
Luxemburg, Luxembourg, Luxemburg (Dutch and German)
Lys, Leie (river),
Mons, Bergen,
Namur, Namen,
Passchendaele, Passendale
Pervyse, Pervijze
Poperinghe, Poperinge
Scheldt, Schelde, Escaut (river)
Selzaete, Zelzate
Steentraete, Steenstraat
Termonde, Dendermonde
Tongres, Tongeren
Thielt, Tielt
Nieuport, Nieuwpoort
La Panne, De Panne
Lille, Rijsel (France)
Lier, Lierre
Thorout, Torhout
Poelcapelle, Poelkapelle
Roulers, Roeselaere
Lombartzyde, Lombaertsijde
Merckem, Merkem

Visé, Wezet
Keyem, Keiem,
Yser, Ijser (river)

The German city of Aachen is known in French as Aix la Chapelle and as Aken in Dutch.

This book is dedicated to the memory of Robert V. At the outbreak of the Great War he had just graduated from the Royal Belgian Military Academy. Young Second Lieutenant V. fought at the Battle of Haelen, a Belgian victory, took part in the two sorties from Antwerp and the retreat to the Yser River, where his unit, *4ème Régiment de Ligne* was heavily engaged. After stabilization of the Front there he remained, with little news of his family in occupied Belgium. He heard that his father, whom he had last seen before the war, had died.

In the final offensive which was to liberate Belgium, in October 1918, Major V. was seriously wounded in the legs. Though he resumed his duties and married the young lady who had patiently waited for him, this wound was eventually to kill him in 1926. Therefore I never knew him, but those who did were unanimous in their praise of his courage, leadership, kindness and good humour.

Robert V. was my grandfather.

Introduction

At the date of writing, a century has passed since the outbreak of the First World War. All the protagonists have passed away. The last Belgian soldier, Emile Brichard, died aged 104 in 2004. He had served in the army medical corps in the Great War. Lazare Ponticelli, an Italian immigrant and the last French soldier to have fought in that war died in 2008, aged 118. Erich Kästner, a retired judge, probably the last surviving German soldier of that conflict, died in Germany in 2008, at 107. Charles Künz died at the same age in 2004, but since he hailed from Colmar in the disputed Alsace Lorraine, I do not know which side he fought on. I had the chance to meet and befriend the last British soldier of the Great War, Harry Patch, who was severely wounded in Flanders and who died aged 111, in 2009. I am very proud to have pinned on his chest the Belgian medal of Knight of the Order of Leopold, awarded him by H.M. the King of the Belgians. Through Harry, it was all the British and Commonwealth soldiers who fought, were wounded or killed when fighting for Belgium as well as for their own king and country that were thus honoured by my country.

Except for a thin slice of territory west of the Yser (Ijzer) River, between the sea and Ypres, Belgium was entirely occupied by the Germans from October 1914 until the end of the First World War. The suffering of the Belgian people, which made such a vivid impression on Americans, British, Canadians, and Australians at the time has now been largely forgotten. The invasion was accompanied by mass executions, arson and wanton destruction. Nearly six thousand civilians were killed in the first weeks of the conflict. Over two million terrified Belgians escaped to the Netherlands, France, and Britain.

In the nineteenth century, after Britain, Belgium was the first country to develop a metallurgic industry, in part thanks to an Englishman called John Cockerill who saw the potential of the coal seams in the Sambre and Meuse valleys. Liège, Mons, and Charleroi developed into prosperous industrial cities. The first railway on the European continent after Britain's linked Brussels to a small city to its north in 1835. By 1914, Belgium had become a major exporter of steel products as well as manufactured goods like rolling stock, locomotives, rails, textiles, as well as chemicals and other goods which were sold as far away as Russia, China, Egypt or Brazil. It ranked among the most prosperous countries in Europe. Indeed, immediately after the American Civil War the two countries' industries were on a par and rivalled each other for third place in size of balance of payments, after Britain and France; a little known fact! Most of the trade passed through Antwerp, which developed into one of the largest ports in Europe and through which hundreds of thousands of immigrants left for the United States and South America, not only from Belgium but also from Germany, Switzerland and Eastern Europe. It also served to import goods, mainly copper and tropical agricultural products from Belgium's large colony in Central Africa, the Congo.

When it was invaded, Belgium was cut off from its supplies of raw material and its export markets and subjected by the Germans to heavy 'war taxes', illegal fines and requisitions. As Germany began increasingly to feel the effects of the Allied blockade, the occupiers started to exploit Belgian resources, including labour. The thousands of summary executions of August 1914 were followed by other calamities. Hunger, deprivation, unemployment, censorship, arbitrary arrests and deportations, conscription of workers, confiscation of metals needed for the German arms industry, dismantling and destruction of Belgian factories and the administrative division of the country became the lot of the Belgians. It was an unprecedented arrangement between the USA, neutral Netherlands and Germany that allowed in American foods to save Belgian families from starving. The people have not forgotten.

Belgians know they owe their freedom to the enormous sacrifices the French, British, Commonwealth and American troops made on their soil twice last century. Many, very many of those young men now rest forever in Flanders Fields. The Belgians have not forgotten that either. If Belgium is attached to a closer integration of Europe it is in large part because it lived through two cruel and oppressive occupations, brought about through no fault of its own during two of the many wars between their neighbours which for centuries more often than not were fought on Belgian soil: at Sluys, Fontenoy, Seneffe, Ramillies, Oudenaerde, Fleurus, Neerwinden, Waterloo, Ypres, Zeebrugge, Bastogne and many others. European integration has had the merit of putting an end to such conflicts.

The author in his previous career as a diplomat often noticed how little is known outside its borders of the role Belgium played in the First (and in the Second) World War. Remarkably few books in English have been written about it. Therefore he has tried to write a factual, objective report of those momentous events, which left no family in his country unaffected (his own being no exception).

Many books, probably thousands, have been written about the First World War, as is also the case for that which erupted in 1939, but they tend to give a very partial view, in both senses of the word. They tell the story of this or that battle, this or that country's involvement, some important developments or aspect: the war at sea, propaganda or the economic aspects, diplomatic endeavours and so on. Rarely do they give an *overall* picture and they are too often based only on sources originating in one of the belligerent countries. The tendency is rather to stick to what happened in this or that country, usually that of the author, and the sources tend to be monolingual. Often propaganda or some degree of mild nationalism is also present: our politicians and generals were all competent, our soldiers were always courageous and victorious and behaved properly. The present work is indeed a relation only of what happened in Belgium, or about this country in those fateful years, but it also contrives to contribute to the general history of that terrible conflict, during which, according to Ian Kershaw, Europe went to hell and back.

Prelude

The Fall of Fort de Loncin

On 15 August 1914, at 1710 hrs,[1] a tremendous explosion shook the earth about 10 km north-west of Liège in eastern Belgium. Not unlike a volcanic eruption, lumps of soil, shreds of metal, blocks of masonry and concrete the size of barns were slung sky high, whole metal gun turrets were popped out of their bases like champagne corks and catapulted into the air, some to land upside down, others to fall back hundreds of metres away. Some 250 Belgian soldiers were killed instantly. The explosion was heard in Maastricht in neutral Holland and in Aachen, Germany, even as far away as Cologne. The left magazine of Fort de Loncin, hit by a 420 mm shell, had just blown up and now there was nothing to stop or slow the Kaiser's troops on their way to France. However, this was almost two weeks behind the careful plans of the German general staff and those twelve days may well have lost Wilhelm II the Great War.

Colonel Naessens, the CO of Loncin, hailed from a Flemish family living outside Bruges, where he was born in 1864. His uncles were former French Foreign Legion veterans and when very young he had known an old Waterloo veteran. Naessens became an NCO in the artillery in 1884 and studied after hours to become an officer. He was made a second lieutenant in 1889 and sent to Fort de Barchon outside Liège. In 1907, he was given command of Fort de Loncin, another of the forts protecting Liège. A charismatic leader he became popular with his men, his unorthodox training methods notwithstanding. A true leader, he knew how to keep up morale both in tedious peacetime and under the stress of siege. When war broke out the entire garrison took a voluntary oath never to surrender, an oath they were to keep. And all reservists showed up, without exception, some coming from as far as northern France. Thus the garrison counted 550 men: more than half of them were to perish during the siege.

Compulsory national military service was being introduced in Belgium. Apart from the purely military aspects it had the unexpected effect of improving relations between the two language groups in the country, since lots of young Flemings were being sent to serve in Wallonia. Naessens, himself a Flemish officer, in a minority not to say an oddity at the time, did his bit by encouraging Walloon soldiers to invite Flemish soldiers for meals at their homes when on leave, not a few Flemings eventually marrying their colleagues' sisters. Among his young officers was a Second Lieutenant Derousseaux, later destined to play a role in the Second World War. (By then a general he was sent as an intermediary to the German lines on 27 May 1940, to enquire about armistice conditions.)

Completed in 1888 and built in a triangular shape, Loncin was part of the ring of Belgian forts protecting Liège and designed to deny an invader, in this case Germany, access to the vitally important road and railroad from Liège to Brussels. At the points of the triangle were 37 mm guns to protect the fort itself and in a central redoubt were the heavier guns, two 210 mm heavy mortars which could fire into low ground that could not be reached by direct fire, two 150 mm guns and two more of 120 mm. The large moats could be kept under crossfire, as could the entrance gate. The neighbouring village church towers and hilltop chateaux were linked by telephone lines and observers kept watch 24/7, prepared to correct the fort's fire. An infantry company was attached to the fort for sorties.

Colonel Naessens was aware that intensive spying by Germans in mufti was going on just before the war and not much escaped the thorough German reserve officers, busy sketching and noting anything of interest for the future invaders. After the forts had surrendered they would confide to the Belgians that their staff maps were far more precise and detailed than the Belgian ones. Some living in Liège were caught red-handed, but as long as war was not declared Naessens had to resist the temptation to put them against a wall. (He would later resort to unconventional warfare himself with his *Bande à Bonnot*, the 'Bonnot Gang' as we shall see.)

On 7 August the first fire by the fort's heavy guns, loaded with shrapnel calculated to spread over a certain area, fell on a German column just as it reached a railway crossing and was signalled by the observation posts. Each 210 mm carried 1,360 shrapnel balls and the result was devastating. The next day an aeroplane was spotted preparing to land at Ans field and several staff motorcars were approaching to meet the passengers. There again withering fire killed most of the German officers including a promising young colonel, as German General von Emmich would later tell Lieutenant Modard, in charge of the fort's guns, von Emmich sportingly congratulating the Belgian on the accuracy of his gunnery calculations.

A while later, two German officers approached under a white flag and demanded the fort's surrender. They were given a negative answer and told not to bother to try again.

After he narrowly escaped a raid at his downtown HQ, the Liège garrison commander, General Leman took refuge at Fort de Loncin and was to stay there until the end. He brought with him the captured colours of the 89 Mecklenburg Regiment.

Slowly at first and with the guns firing on them steadily increasing in calibre, continuous fire was directed at the fort, the German observers 'walking' the impacts from turret to turret and progressively but surely turning the fort into rubble. Sometimes several guns were timed to fire simultaneously at the same spot, increasing the damage inflicted. The fort's own observers were spotted and dispatched, the telephone lines cut so the fort had to fire blindly, like a wounded beast lunging at the hunters around it. The occupants of the fort were going through hell. Twice the chimneys of the generators became obstructed, stopping the air conditioning which then had to be operated by hand-turned cranks. Sergeant Albrechts and his three men died, suffocated at their post while refusing to retreat from where they operated the crankshafts. All had bound handkerchiefs over their mouths to keep out the dust falling from the roof after each impact. Some soldiers just played cards, sitting on ammunition boxes and keeping a tally of the heavier shells landing – these made the whole fort shake and large parts of the gallery roof collapse, killing many. The rate of impact was calculated to be twenty-seven a minute. Lights went out.

On 12 August, at 1600 hrs, the super-heavy Krupp 'Grosse Bertha' 420 mm Kurze Marine Kanone, whose existence had been kept secret, was finally in place and fired its first shot at the fort from a Belgian army training field at Bressoux, a village 9 km away, while the guns of the fort could only fire at a maximum rage of 8.5 km, a fact the Germans obviously knew. Each shell weighed 931 kg and was as tall as a short man, as one of the fort's garrison members saw when he found one unexploded in a gallery. After twenty-four hours of various types of artillery fire, the delayed fuse of the nineteenth 420 mm shell exploded in one of the fort's magazines, containing 12 tons of explosive. The fireball went up 60 metres high, blew a 30-metre-wide and 6-metre-deep crater and hurled pieces of masonry, concrete and armour plate 30 cm thick, broken like china, sky high, to rain down in a circle 100 metres in diameter. A 'nuclear' smoke plume rose to the sky. An estimated 250 Belgians were killed instantly, others were buried alive or blocked by debris, unable to move and in excruciating pain. The survivors, some terribly burned, were surprised suddenly to see blue sky, as part of the roof collapsed. The fort's CO, Colonel Naessens and the CO of the Liège garrison General Leman, both survived but were knocked unconscious. The German fire paused for a few minutes, then the assault was resumed. Some officers, NCOs and men made a brave stand in a corner of the north moat. They were shot down to the last man. Other dazed Belgian soldiers scurried out from under the debris, trying to find help. The Germans, having overrun the surface of the fort in a skirmish line and no longer being fired upon, started helping them. One German officer saw a Belgian officer helping General Leman and gave him some water from a field canteen. When Colonel Naessens regained consciousness he was lying in a military hospital controlled by the Germans. It had apparently been set up in a school, because someone had scribbled with chalk on a blackboard: *Le Fort de Loncin ne s'est pas rendu!* ('Fort de Loncin did not surrender!') Some Belgian soldiers were pinned under pieces of debris too heavy to move and the Belgian and German medics could only administer morphine to relieve their agony. Others had to have a limb sawn off to be freed. Some forty others, unhurt, managed to flee and rejoin the Belgian army in the field.

The German high command paid homage to Loncin's brave defence: General von Emmich visited General Leman in the Liège military hospital, saluted and congratulated him. Naessens was allowed to keep his sword.

Leman wrote a moving letter to his king and former pupil at the Belgian military academy, stating he had fulfilled the task he had been given to hold Liège to the utmost. He was taken to Germany as a POW, but later released and arrived at the Belgian front in his outdated 1914 dark blue uniform (the rest of the army had switched to khaki in 1915), to be congratulated and decorated by King Albert.

Several of the Belgian soldiers missing are still buried under the rubble at Loncin, now declared a national necropolis. In 2007 the Belgian army explosives disposal unit SEDEE/DOVO removed 4,000 shells and 143 tons of ammunition. They also found twenty-five corpses of which four could be identified by medals, a wedding ring, a pistol, and the button of a regiment not normally stationed there.

Fort de Loncin can still be visited.[2]

A century later one is impressed by the site, by the destruction resulting from the cataclysmic explosion and by the knowledge that there are bodies still there unaccounted for. It is a moving sight. One of the 57 mm guns has been restored and is fired every year on the exact anniversary and hour of the explosion, always in front of a crowd of visitors.

Near the access postern a stone bears the inscription paraphrasing that of the Spartans after Thermopylae: *Passer-by go tell Belgium, go tell France, that here 550 Belgians have been sacrificed for freedom and the salvation of the world.*

Part I

NEUTRAL BELGIUM

1

Waterloo and All That

Belgium only became an independent and sovereign nation state in 1830, although the people that now live within its borders had long had common rulers. Most of the territories of the countries that today form Benelux were united by conquest, inheritance or purchase during the Hundred Years War, by the Dukes of Burgundy. After a few generations the lord of the counties of Flanders and Holland, the duchies of Brabant, Hainault and Luxemburg and so on, had become one and same person – among others Philip the Good, and then his son Charles the Bold. Their wealth was larger than that of the kings of England and certainly than that of their ruined and beaten cousin the king of France. The Flemish painting school (Van Eyck, Memling, Van der Weyden) flourished, especially in Bruges, an important and rich port where wool from England and Scotland was woven into cloth and exchanged for wines and wheat from France, olive oil from Italy, spices from the Portuguese colonies in Asia, wood, pelts and leather from the Baltic and so on. In the fifteenth century, the realm of what is now roughly the three BENELUX countries was inherited by the Habsburg kings of Spain and the Reformation took hold, more so in the north which became the independent protestant Dutch Republic, than in the south which remained under Catholic, Spanish Habsburg control. In 1713 at the Treaty of Utrecht (that also gave Gibraltar to Britain) the Southern, until then Spanish, Netherlands were transferred to the Austrian Habsburgs. Rule from faraway Madrid and then Vienna, together with a large degree of self-government granted by these sometimes nominal rulers and the fact that the ruling power, until 1792 was *not* a neighbouring country, thus preventing simple annexation, were all factors that gave the Belgians a sense of belonging together. When the French revolutionaries invaded in 1792, burning down cathedrals and chateaux, they were welcomed only by a limited number of politically motivated sympathizers, won over to the ideas of the French Revolution. That sympathy evaporated when Republican and then Imperial France annexed Belgium and drafted young men for faraway wars in Spain and Russia that made no sense to them.

After Napoleon's final defeat at Waterloo outside Brussels, the powers gathered at Vienna tried to glue Belgium and Holland back together as a buffer against France. The kingdom of the Netherlands was thus created, to this day the official name of what is also known as Holland. The arrangement however did not last more than fifteen years, and an alliance of Catholic and liberal Belgians revolted against the protestant and conservative Dutch in 1830. The powers were at first reluctant to see the kingdom of the Netherlands collapse, the more so when the Belgians were soundly defeated by the returning Dutch army. However, French diplomatic skill by Talleyrand and Lord Palmerton's sense of realism worked out a compromise whereby Belgium became an independent country that had strict neutrality imposed on it by the Treaty of London in 1839. Moreover, a German-born British Prince, Leopold of Saxe-Coburg-Gotha, widower of Charlotte, heiress to the British throne,[1] was sworn in on 21 July 1831 as first king of the Belgians (not of Belgium), while the constitution, rather progressive for the times, strictly limited his powers. This constitutional monarchy was a first in continental Europe but closely resembled that adopted shortly before in Paris with the French king, Louis-Philippe (though the French arrangement would last only eighteen years).

Leopold I had been an army officer fighting Napoleon and it was hoped he would provide the fledgling Belgian army with a competent leader, as was indeed proven a few years later, since the Dutch did not give up until 1839. However, in the early 1830s, France was still seen as a potential threat to, and invader of, other countries in Europe and seeing their anti-French barrier collapse with the Belgian Revolution, the British, Prussians and Austrians negotiated with the wily French Foreign Minister Talleyrand a compromise whereby Belgium became independent but neutral. But Belgium had to give back some strategic territories to Holland, making sure the strategic port of Antwerp could not menace the English coast and Prussia and Austria could reconquer Belgium and attack France through Holland, whose government would welcome their troops in if the French invaded again. These were territories where the mainly Catholic populations had sided with Belgium in what is now the south of the kingdom of the Netherlands, including the cities of 's Hertogenbosch and Maastricht and the surrounding provinces (Noord Brabant and Limburg), the south bank of Scheldt River linking Antwerp to the sea, as well as what is now the independent Grand Duchy of Luxembourg, where a Prussian garrison was stationed (this had been removed however by 1914). They were to play an important role at the

Versailles negotiations, when (some of) the victorious Belgians would claim them back.

The fact that both banks of the Scheldt estuary were Dutch and neutral also made it impossible for the Royal Navy to attack Antwerp or reinforce it by sea, whoever occupied it. This of course from 1914 to 1918 was Germany, a fact certainly not anticipated by the British Admiralty in 1839!

These arrangements proved sound for exactly a century, as Belgian neutrality was respected by both sides during the Franco-Prussian war of 1870, but King Leopold II took great care to mobilize the Belgian army, at that time strong, well organized and, in proportion to the size of the country, second to none in Europe. It was deployed along the borders. However, the fact that Prussia and France respected Belgian neutrality may have had dire consequences, as an important sector of the Belgian political establishment and public opinion took to thinking this might last forever, became complacent and allowed the defence effort to lapse round the turn of the century, a time when the rest of Europe, especially France and the now unified Germany, were creating huge conscript armies, well equipped with modern armaments.

By 1914 Europe was a very different place. Germany had united under the Kaiser and Bismarck in 1871 and was the rising power on the continent, while France mourned the loss of Alsace and part of Lorraine. The famous *Schlieffen* plan to invade France obviously rode roughshod over Belgian neutrality. When an amended version prepared by General von Moltke was put in practice in August 1914, Berlin did not expect the small Belgian army to resist and even offered financial compensation for any damage in the event that free passage was allowed. As we shall see, this was denied.

2

Leopold II, Brialmont and Ordinary Politicians

Leopold II succeeded his father, Leopold I to the throne in 1865. His reputation in the English-speaking world could hardly be worse and even some Belgians agree he was a scoundrel. However, an historian should look at facts not at contemporary propaganda, whose effects still stick. A few years ago, an American author published a book on Leopold II which enjoyed widespread sales. In this work he claimed that in Central Africa, where at the turn of the century Leopold II had set up a personal colony, the Congo Free State, a mass extermination took place. The Congo Free State had no official link with the Belgian government but the king's (mostly) Belgian agents allegedly caused ten million people to lose their lives, thus making Leopold II guilty of a worse mass murder than Hitler's of the Jews, and a death toll almost comparable to the total military deaths on the Western Front during the First World War! The 'projection statistics' made in the book, however, do not stand up to scrutiny since no census taking was carried out in the region until much later, in the 1920s. The entire population of the Congo River basin at the time of Leopold's Congo Free State might not even have attained that total.

The figures were based in part on the erroneous mathematics of the British-born American explorer Stanley, who worked for Leopold, and partly on a projection for the whole country from the loss of life sustained in riverbank villages that had been visited and which were more populous than the country inland. Leopold II's agents present in the region at the time were far too few to commit or even organize a massacre of such scale, that would have deprived them of a large part of their valuable workforce. Nevertheless, even if the number of ten million deaths is based on sloppy research and vastly exaggerated, it is indisputable that indigenous populations in central Africa as a whole did suffer heavy losses, their lack of immunity to imported diseases also playing a very important role. It should be noted that on the whole, and judged by modern eyes and minds, these were very hard times indeed for African, Asian or Native American populations. British repression of the Indian Mutiny or of the Zulus and Boers, French interventions in their African colonies (like the now forgotten Voulet-Chanoine 'infernal column' in Chad) and Madagascar, German repression of the Herero revolt in today's Namibia or the Portuguese destruction of Gugunhana's kingdom in Mozambique were all contemporary, to name only a few examples.[1] If expeditions by the Argentinean and Chilean armies against native populations in the south of their continent, or the way that most of the native North American nations were 'made to disappear' in part by destroying the bison herds on which the Plains Indians depended, do not qualify as genocide, one wonders what does.

In 1864–7, Leopold II sent a contingent of about 2,000 Belgian soldiers under the command of Colonel van der Smissen to help bolster the Mexican Empire where Napoleon III had installed a brother of the Emperor of Austria to rule, whilst the US, in full Civil War were incapable at that time of enforcing the Monroe Doctrine. Kept on the throne by a large French army, Maximilian of Mexico was married to Leopold II's sister Charlotte (named after their late mother, the Princess of Wales and wife to Leopold I). Once abandoned by the French, Maximilian's Central American Empire collapsed and he himself was tried and executed in 1867 at Querétaro, on the orders of the Mexican republican ruler Benito Juarez. Empress Charlotte was in Europe by now and collapsed into madness whilst visiting the Pope in Rome. Leopold II arranged for her to spend the rest of her long life in a chateau outside Brussels.[2]

Belgian Politics 1880–1914

Apart from the growing language dispute discussed in the next chapter, three political issues dominated Belgian internal politics in the late nineteenth century and up to the First World War: education, voting rights, and national military service. The first, though very bitter, need not concern us here, the second we will come back to later because the war brought radical change. The third question, of who should serve in the armed forces, was very contentious. In these years the Catholic party was dominating political life and usually had a comfortable majority in parliament, though its supremacy was challenged by the Liberals, who were close to the masonic lodges and who had adopted the ideas of the French Revolution. The other upcoming challenger was the fledgling Socialist party which grew apace with the increase in industrialization and mass migration from farms to industrial suburbs.

King Leopold II and his successor realized the small Belgian army had been strong enough in 1870 to deter French or Prussian violation of Belgian neutrality by the fact their numbers, however reduced, would have tipped the balance to the detriment of the violator, and in favour of the country that respected Belgian territory. However, demographics and the introduction of long national services lasting years in both France and Germany changed that radically. While the Belgian army remained small, the French and (now) German army had become behemoths of several million soldiers each with thousands of guns, and by the end of the century King Leopold II and his more enlightened advisers realized the Belgian army could no longer offer any credible deterrent to an invasion. There had been a few scares during Napoleon III's reign (1852–70), because lots of French political refugees, including the poet Victor Hugo, were causing him trouble from Brussels, some even conspiring against his life, while he dreamed of restoring the borders his uncle had had in the north – that is, re-annexing Belgium to France. Following the nationalistic principles his uncle had introduced to Europe, Napoleon III had rather foolishly allowed, even encouraged German unification, which was far from being in his country's interest. Now Bismarck's policy was to prevent a new war with France, where the loss of Alsace and Lorraine in 1871 was deeply felt and resented. With the gradual rise of German power after 1870 a Prussian/German invasion of France via Belgium, at first unlikely, became more conceivable. Kaiser Wilhelm II threw out Bismarck, and his own mercurial character and love/hate relationship with his grandmother Victoria's country started to influence German foreign politics.

To prevent and deter these two neighbours from using its territory as their battlefield, Belgium had to do two things: strengthen its army and built credible static defences, i.e. forts to hold an invader at bay or at least slow him down until help could arrive. To increase the number of soldiers under arms and expand it from a small professional army to a credible body in proportion with the German and French armies Leopold II could only change the draft law, which until then was a curious lottery system: every young man of military age had to draw a lot, but if his lot was to serve he or his family could, if they were able, pay someone to take his place, usually a fellow from a poor background. This obviously made for mediocre recruits and limited numbers and the method had to be changed. However, two political parties strongly opposed the introduction of a general draft: the powerful Catholic party because they wanted to prevent the depravity of drink and prostitution the Christian young men would be exposed to outside their barracks, while the Socialist party opposed it out of pacifist principles. It was only on his deathbed in 1909 that Leopold II could finally sign into law a comprehensive draft law (one man per family), later extended to include all fit young men in 1913. This would have increased the army to about 350,000 men but came too late for the necessary reorganization (drastic increase in number of officers and NCOs, training, building of barracks, acquisition of armament, etc.) to be ready by August 1914 and the Belgian army was definitively not ready when war came.

The other defensive/deterrent measure was the building of rings of forts, first around Antwerp, where it was envisaged the Belgian army would eventually retire in a national redoubt if invaded by either France or Germany, and possibly that Britain might provide reinforcements by sea. Next came Liège and Namur as defensive positions, the former against an invasion on the Aachen-Liège-Brussels axis, and Namur against an attack from France along the Meuse and/or Sambre river valleys. The idea was that if an invader could be held long enough, first in open combat by the land army and then in one of these city-fortresses, the other guarantor(s) of Belgian neutrality would have the time to come to their aid. General Brialmont, a brilliant military engineer, was tasked first to study, then to design and supervise the building of the three defensive rings of forts. The expense involved met strong opposition and, in the case of Antwerp, a vigorous campaign by the local population against the destruction of civilian property they would bring about. The time lost because of such resistance was to cost them dear when Germany invaded.

With a few exceptions, Brialmont chose triangle type forts with a central redoubt containing magazines, officers' and other ranks' sleeping and washing quarters, kitchens, bakery, pantry, and so on, as well as the main artillery battery of 210 mm guns, designed to, say, interdict the passage of a railway bridge over the Meuse River. There were also guns of lesser calibre, 150 mm and 120 mm, complicating the supply of ammunition. Most guns were supplied by Krupp of Germany or Le Creusot in France, while the steel armoured covers protecting them were made in Liège by Cockerill Works. At the points of the triangle the 57 mm Nordenfeldt quick-firing secondary artillery was located, to defend the fort itself against any hostile approach. First the bases were dug out to house the underground magazines and drinking water tanks, then the horizontal galleries were tunnelled out, and finally the whole was given a several-metre-thick earth and concrete cover, into which the heavy, battleship-like gun turrets were sunk. These were attached to counterweights and retracted flush with the surrounding steel ring and the concrete top, hoisted up only when ready to fire and immediately lowered again to reload. Access was via a chicane, with a rolling floor that could be taken away and kept under fire, one method being simply dropping grenades through a small diagonal sloping tunnel. A counterscarp, a large ditch 6 metres deep and 8 metres wide was supposed to impede the enemy infantry from reaching the fort triangle itself; these large ditches being kept under fire by light artillery, mortars and machine guns firing in enfilade into them. Some of these defensive inward firing posts were arranged in two decks, so that if enemy artillery collapsed the walls of the ditches and/or caused the field of fire to be obstructed by debris, the upper deck could still be used to fire at the enemy. Retractable searchlights were mounted on top of the forts. At some points, the walls had been thinned out and tools pre-positioned to allow offensive sorties or eventual escape.

There were mainly two types of fort, large or small, and of course their location was determined by topography, fields of fire, possibility of having observation posts linked by telephone to correct the fire, objects to be covered by fire and so on. It was even arranged that they could fire at each other to dislodge enemy infantry that might have managed to creep on top of them. The twelve forts of the Liège Fortified Position and the nine of Namur were located at about 5–7 km from the city centres and 3–4 km from each other.

Fort de Loncin, outside Liège and controlling the Liège-Brussels road and railway and which merits special attention because of its stubborn defence described earlier, is located about 7 km west of the centre of Liège, in the direction of Brussels, the road to which it kept under fire. The garrison comprised about 500 men.

The fort was of the larger type, forming a triangle whose base was 300 m long, with sides measuring 235 m.

Work at Loncin outside the village of Ans, took 10,000 workers three years to complete, during which time ten fatal accidents occurred. A French firm was responsible for the rough works, using sand and big pebbles from the Meuse River, mixed with cement to form the concrete. About 300,000 tons of cement, stone and bricks were used and three million tons of earth moved by a specially built small railway, as well as tons of wood planks for the forms on to which the concrete of the galleries was poured. The concrete was found to have been badly mixed in some places, with too much water added allowing the stones to sink, or it was allowed to partly dry overnight or on Sundays, causing it to crack when new concrete mix was poured later – cracks which can still be seen today. From the air, one could only see a large triangle formed by the ditches; from the surrounding land, next to nothing. Apart from the cracked concrete, which let in rainwater, there were other defects: the heavier guns had a maximum range of 5,700 m, which at the time of construction, the end of the nineteenth century, was enough to keep the artillery of potential enemies at bay. But by 1914, Germany's Krupp and Austria-Hungary's Skoda had developed super-heavy guns of 420 mm and 305 mm which could fire from a far greater distance, safely outside of the range of the fort's guns, and pound them into submission. The heavy Krupp guns that reduced Fort de Loncin to rubble first fired from the village of Mortier about 15 km away. In fact, the Belgian forts were obsolete by the start of the Great War, though they were still to play an important role.

One other seemingly trivial flaw at Loncin, corrected at later-built forts, was the absence of latrines in the central redoubt. As the garrison was prevented by enemy fire from using the unprotected latrines outside the redoubt, a terrible stench soon developed in the summer heat of August, which was insanitary and bad for morale.

Born in 1881 and after attending Catholic schools, including the Jesuit College Saint Michel in Brussels, which still exists, Robert V. [the author's grandfather] joined the Royal Military School in Brussels in 1900. He took the officer's oath on 14 February 1903, at the rank of second lieutenant and joined 4ème Régiment de Ligne, an infantry unit where he was to spend his whole career. During the riots in the industrial suburbs his Regiment was deployed to keep law and order.

The Pre-1914 Economic Boom

In the late nineteenth century, Belgium, especially Wallonia, experienced an extraordinary economic boom. A combination of rich coal seams in the Liège and Charleroi-Mons areas, low taxes, dynamic entrepreneurship, active research and development of new methods of producing high quality steel and chemicals, a flexible banking system, a dense and efficient railway and canal network, the efficient and well-located port of Antwerp and low wages saw the spectacular development of the coal and steel, glass and chemical industries. Prominent chemist, industrialist and inventor Ernest Solvay regularly organized international meetings of scientists in Brussels, to which no less than Rutherford, Marie Curie, Max Planck, Einstein, and many others, would come. Belgium sent a polar expedition on the ship *Belgica*, which spent the 1898 Antarctic winter south of the polar circle, a historical first. Among the crew were future polar explorers Frederick Cook and Roald Amundsen.

Immigration from the rest of Wallonia and from poorer, rural Flanders to these regions saw the development of new industrial towns with lodgings built to accommodate the miners, steel workers and their families, not unlike what was happening in the British Midlands or in the German Ruhrgebiet at the same time. Commercial activity doubled between 1900 and 1913 and Belgium saw itself raised to fifth rank among the world's industrial nations in output and an incredible fourth in volume of exports, before Italy, Russia or the United States. Chemicals, non-ferrous metals, steel railways, locomotives, rolling stock and tramways for example were exported to Russia, Spain, Egypt, China, Brazil, Argentina and elsewhere. A complete prefabricated steel opera house was shipped to Costa Rica and steel mills built in St Petersburg. The Cairo and Tashkent tramways were all manufactured in Belgium and the Paris metro was started by a Belgian entrepreneur, as was Heliopolis, a whole new suburb of Cairo. In and around Liège thriving small arms, hunting guns, motorcar and motorcycle industries also developed.

This all came at a price, however. Wages in Belgium were among the lowest in Western Europe in real purchasing power, the workers lived in deplorable conditions and the industrial suburbs turned into squalid, unhygienic shanty towns, where alcoholism was rife. Women and children worked too, for dismal wages, until 1886 when this was banned, and riots which had to be put down by the army broke out in Liège and Mons in 1886 and 1893. Between 1845 and 1847, Karl Marx was in exile in Brussels, where he wrote his famous Manifesto, before being expelled and moving on to London. The Belgian Socialist Party was founded in 1885 and several Belgians, like Jules Destrée, who questioned the very existence of Belgium, Emile Vandervelde, who would sponsor a bill in parliament to limit the sale of alcoholic beverages, Edouard Anseele, who founded a workers' cooperative in Ghent, Camille Huysmans, later burgomaster of Antwerp and speaker of the parliament, would play a prominent role in the *Internationale Socialiste* which had its secretariat in Brussels, where meetings were held with Keir Hardie from Britain, Jean Jaurès from France, Karl Liebknecht and Rosa Luxemburg from Germany, as well as delegates from Russia, Austria, Italy, Spain and elsewhere.

Belgium had universal male suffrage, but the well-educated and wealthy were allowed up to three votes each. In 1914, power was held by Baron de Broqueville and his Catholic Party. Not unnaturally in the years of boom, accompanied by misery in the industrial suburbs, the socialists saw in universal suffrage (one man, one vote, at least for the male citizens) a means to further their cause by increasing their votes. Equally predictably, this was resisted by the then dominant parties, the Catholic and the Liberal, who invoked all sorts of arguments like possible demagoguery and subversion.

It should be noted that Prince Albert, the future king, caused a scandal in posh Brussels drawing rooms by ostensibly saluting the Red Flag one day when passing on horseback a '*Maison du Peuple*'³ and there was an exchange of letters between his uncle Leopold II and himself in which he drew the then monarch's attention to the fact that his role as a future head of state would be finished if the Regiment he was serving in was called to quell the riots and he had to order his men to open fire. His uncle's answer was uncompromising: 'You will do as you are ordered by your commanding officer!'

Leopold II died on 17 December 1909, after reigning for forty-four years, a very unpopular man both at home and abroad. Prince Rupprecht of Bavaria, brother-in-law of the new queen of the Belgians and wife of Albert I attended the funeral. He was later to command a section of the German army in Flanders. Leopold II's family life had been disorderly to say the least: he had married Archduchess Marie-Henriette of Austria, cousin of the Austro-Hungarian emperor Franz Josef, and had made her a sad, unhappy woman, had treated his legitimate daughters appallingly (they sued to annul his will) and had several mistresses and two illegitimate sons. The Belgian government forced him in 1908 to give up the Congo Free State as his personal possession, making it a Belgian colony, after which most abuses ceased, and the territory was then governed certainly no worse and possibly better than the French or British African colonies. He had amassed a huge personal fortune, part of which he kept in a foundation for his own use, or to build or supervise the building of architectural embellishments in Brussels and the rest of the country, which are still to be seen. A dynamic and inventive man, more so than the Belgian politicians who were his contemporaries, at a time when kings had a more active role than today he played an important part in Belgium's economic boom. His vision of international affairs was sound, especially the dangers his country faced, and subsequent events were to prove him right. He had managed to keep his country out of the 1870–1 Franco-Prussian war. In 1904, when in Berlin on an official visit he was astonished to hear Wilhelm II promise him parts of northern France if Belgium sided with Germany in the 'coming and inevitable war between France and Germany,' as the Kaiser said. So unsettled was Leopold he put on his helmet of the Hanoverian Dragoons Regiment, of which he was Colonel-in-Chief, back to front when being driven away. The same promises, including even the important French city of Lille, were made by the Kaiser and General von Moltke to his successor Albert I in 1910, in similar circumstances, Moltke's description of the overwhelming might of the German army being tantamount to direct threats if not blackmail.

Appalled by what he had heard, Albert answered that these territories had been French for a very long time (since Louis XIV) and discreetly informed the French via his ambassador in Berlin.[4]

Leopold II was not spared suffering: his beloved son and heir, also Leopold, died young in 1869, after an accident from which he never completely recovered, followed in 1891 by his nephew and new heir apparent Baudouin, elder brother of the future King Albert. He had had several mistresses and married one on his deathbed. The Belgian press, sometimes relaying the British press, who had severely and sometimes exaggeratedly criticized the actions of his agents in the Congo Basin, had attacked him viciously and repeatedly on this and other subjects. As the great Belgian historian Henri Pirenne wrote: 'What he had done for his country (a lot), he had done without his country's support.'

3

The Flemish Movement before 1914

Though it was given a substantial boost by the events taking place on both sides of the front during 1914–18, events we will study, it would be wrong to assume the Flemish Movement started during the First World War.

It should first be noted that what evolved into the Dutch language was spoken in an area roughly comprising the whole northern half of Belgium and the Netherlands, this since the collapse of the Roman Empire, when invasions by Germanic tribes left a stronger imprint there than in the south of that area, where Latin evolved into French and other Latinate languages, like Walloon and Picard. The Dutch language, which is akin to German and closer to it than English or the Scandinavian languages, was certainly spoken there from the twelfth century. However, during the seventeenth century French became the international and diplomatic lingua franca, as English is today, and was spoken for example at the courts of Prussia and Russia. During the reign of Louis XIV and his successors, French cultural influence especially in literature, theatre and philosophy (Corneille, Racine, Rousseau, Voltaire) was dominant. The educated classes all over the European continent followed the trend and the southern Netherlands, later to be known as Belgium, were no exception. Until the French Revolution, language was not considered so important as it has become in recent times, precisely under the influence of the ideas and principles of 1789, spread across Europe by the French troops of the Republic and Napoleon: political liberalism and its 'bastard child' nationalism, according to the Austrian writer, Stefan Zweig. One (over-centralized) nation-state, with one people speaking the same language (not always though), one economy, one currency, one set of laws, later one education system and so on. After the French Revolution, loyalty to one's sovereign was substituted by loyalty to one's nation.

Belgium in fact had existed under different names and with different boundaries from, say the late sixteenth century, when the United Provinces (what was later to become BENELUX) split into a northern, protestant part that became the independent Holland and the southern Catholic Low Country that Spain and later Austria at first maintained under tight control.

Gradually given a larger degree of autonomy and self-rule by their distant rulers in Madrid and Vienna, the Belgian homelands evolved into a self-sufficient and integrated entity, though often invaded by its neighbours who continued to fight their wars on its soil. I was astounded some years ago to hear an Oxford professor and relatively well-known author declare on the BBC that Belgium was a part of Holland and a part of France glued together. Nothing could be further from the truth, as Dutch-speaking Flanders and French-speaking Wallonia *never* were *separately* part of France or the Netherlands. The oft-made point that Belgium was created as a buffer state in 1830, to check the northward expansion of France carries more weight. The fright Napoleon had given Europe by escaping from Elba and reclaiming the French throne until finally defeated at Waterloo outside Brussels, prompted the Powers to glue back together the southern and northern Netherlands (Belgium and Holland), which was intended to keep France within its pre-1789 revolution borders. But what bonded together the new kingdom of the Netherlands proved to be no superglue either. Only fifteen years later the Catholic, mostly French-speaking Belgians, in league with those who had adopted French liberal ideas, revolted and threw out the Dutch, who, though benign occupiers compared to most, had made silly mistakes like trying to re-impose the Dutch language by coercion in education, law courts, the army and so on. This was resented by the Walloon and French-speaking Flemish educated elites and the Dutch king's clumsy and uncompromising behaviour made a bad situation worse.

Naturally, when Belgian independence was formally achieved by treaty in 1839 the French speakers in both Wallonia and Flanders had their *revanche* and dominated the country, where all but elementary education – that is, the courts, political life and so on – was in French. A young promising Fleming from a poor background had to learn another than his mother tongue to go to school and university, to become a doctor or a lawyer. The army was also officered by French speakers, though those officers living in Flanders were usually bilingual. Not surprisingly the tendency of the language spoken by peasants and other uneducated folk to split up into local patois was accentuated. A small tenant farmer living outside Bruges would have had difficulty in understanding an Antwerp dockworker.

Romanticism, especially historical romanticism is also a by-product of political liberalism and surprisingly in the second half of the nineteenth century Flemish writers including Henri (Hendrik) Conscience, curiously the son of a French officer in Napoleon's navy stationed in Antwerp, wrote books reminding the Flemish of their glorious past in the Middle Ages, especially the Battle of the Golden Spurs on 11 July 1302, when militias from Bruges, Ghent and Ypres defeated an army of French knights. Though it did not have a long independent status like Scotland, Bavaria or Catalonia, medieval Flanders was indeed a flourishing and highly developed region at the crossroads of Europe, where the merchants of the above-mentioned cities and later Antwerp thrived in the commerce between Britain, the Baltic, France and Portugal. Flemish painting developed to the superb standards we know.

In the 1880s, other Flemish writers like Stijn Streuvels, together with newspapers and book lending societies appeared, which caused a renaissance of Flemish collective feeling and accompanying resentment against the French speakers and French cultural influence, now seen as smothering the aspirations of the Flemish people, who were at the time mainly rural and much poorer than their fast industrializing, more affluent Walloon compatriots. Efforts were made to reunify the language spoken by all Flemings, introducing Dutch words where French ones were used, standardizing spelling, grammar and above all pronunciation. A whole new literary school grew up, and many creative Flemish writers and poets would attain fame in the years between the wars, some of them having fought at the front. Father Guido Gezelle from Bruges wrote delicate poems in the local patois.

Still, the two most famous Belgian writers of the period, Nobel Prize-winner Maurice Maeterlinck and Emile Verhaeren, though Flemish, wrote in French.

Fast-growing Germany, not seen at the time as a menace, but culturally and linguistically closer to the Flemings was seen as a counterweight to the overwhelming French influence. The Flemish Movement, aspiring to oversee the legitimate cultural right of the Flemings to enjoy education and see justice administered in their own language, also wanted to distance itself from French cultural and political influence and regarded Germany and Holland as counterweights (without coming under German or Dutch influence though). Some Dutch and German politicians, especially the Pangermanists[1] and associated writers played a role in the Flemish *ontvoogding* (emancipation) movement but never was there a serious will to see Flanders annexed to either neighbour, except during the two German occupations, and even then with only a minuscule following. Interestingly, there was also a *Wallingant* movement in Wallonia and their calls to be re-attached to France were louder and still have not disappeared today although always very marginal.

Part II

BRAVE LITTLE BELGIUM

1

Crisis

News of the assassination at Sarajevo of Archduke Franz Ferdinand and his wife made international headlines, but few Belgian readers could have guessed how the events that followed would affect their lives, changing their country completely and for ever, and leaving it devastated. The ensuing Great War was the worst calamity to befall Belgium since the Spanish invasions of the sixteenth century, though the territory that is now Belgium has known so many invasions and wars both before and since. A funeral service for the archduke was held at St Jacques sur Coudenberg church in Brussels, close to the Belgian royal palace and Austro-Hungarian Ambassador Clary received the mourners' condolences.

However, at that date in June 1914 when the heir to the throne of Austria-Hungary was assassinated, there was more public interest in another crime recently committed in Paris. The wife of a prominent politician had shot dead in his office the editor-in-chief of the leading newspaper *Le Figaro*, who had violently attacked her husband, Minister of Finance Joseph Caillaux. This had ruined at least temporarily her husband's political career. Some have speculated that since Caillaux was a moderate in relations with Germany and that there had been a chance he would lead France's next government, the crisis that followed Sarajevo might have had a different outcome.

The network of alliances dividing Europe in 1914 has been described often enough and is not really the subject of this book. Suffice it to say that Russia, having seen its eastward expansion thwarted by a severe defeat by Japan in 1905 and being held in check in its southward expansion by Britain's defence of India (the so-called 'Great Game'), St Petersburg started looking towards the Balkans and the old dream of controlling Constantinople/Istanbul with access to the ice-free 'blue seas'. There it clashed with Austro-Hungarian expansion in the Balkans. Add to this the increasing unease Britain felt at seeing the German navy rapidly transformed from Bismarck's coastguard into an effective rival to the Royal Navy (this when the small British army was overstretched all over its colonial empire), and last but not least the ever present longing of a large part of French opinion to reconquer Alsace Lorraine, and you have the ingredients for a confrontation between two blocs who had almost come to blows before, during crises between France and Germany in Alsace, and more particularly because of clashing colonial rivalries, notably over Morocco.

In 1852 and 1863, trade agreements between the Zollverein, the German Customs union and Belgium were concluded, strengthening relations. In 1867, Leopold II's brother, the father of the future King Albert married into the Hohenzollern German imperial family. From 1898, the volume of German trade through Antwerp surpassed that of Britain and a colony of forty thousand Germans lived in the great Flemish port city, often intermarrying with families in the Rhineland, with which close ties were kept.

However, as early as 1861 Prince Albert of Saxe-Coburg, Leopold I's nephew and the consort of Queen Victoria, had written to Lord Clarendon, the Secretary of State for Foreign Affairs, that he thought Bismarck wanted to offer Belgium to France in exchange for acquiescence to Prussian expansion in the rest of Germany, thus robbing Peter to pay Paul. At about the same time Bismarck offered Napoleon III the parts of Belgium and Switzerland where French is spoken. When the 'Iron Chancellor' engaged in his *Kulturkampf*, a campaign against the mighty German Catholic church and was severely criticized in the Belgian press, he called Belgium a 'Jesuit's nest'. The building of the Brialmont forts in Liège were also seen unfavourably in Berlin for obvious reasons, although criticism abated somewhat when forts were also erected around Namur, a measure clearly intended to dissuade an invasion from France.

In the years after the 1870 Franco-Prussian war, when France had had to give up Alsace and Lorraine, the fact that Belgian neutrality had been respected in that war had led Belgian public opinion into a false sense of security and belief that neutrality would be preserved again in the next conflict. However from the 1890s, during the various crises between France and Germany in the early nineteenth century and especially when a serious international crisis developed during the days following Sarajevo, several voices from the German cousins of the Belgian Royals, from King Carol of Rumania, who was Albert's brother-in-law, and even from a German diplomat in London, warned Belgium that the 'miracle of 1870' would not be repeated and that if it came to war between Germany and France, Belgium would not be spared. King Carol even gave very precise information on the German plans. This came on top of the tactless proposals made by Kaiser Wilhelm II to both King Leopold II and Albert about northern France being offered as a 'gratuity', mentioned earlier.

On 29 July 1914, as the black clouds of war were gathering menacingly, the Permanent Office of the Socialist International called an exceptional meeting in a circus ring in Brussels to try to keep peace. Keir Hardie came from London, Karel Kautsky, Rosa Luxemburg and Hugo Haase from Berlin, Jean Jaurès and four other delegates from Paris, Pavel Axelbrod from Russia, Angelica Balobanov from Italy and of course, the Belgians Vandervelde, Anseele and Huysmans were present. The hall was packed and most of those who spoke, especially Jean Jaurès (who was assassinated in Paris just a few days later) gave moving speeches in favour of peace, but both Jaurès, who felt unwell and Rosa Luxemburg were pessimistic in tone. Haase was very critical of his own government. Rosa Luxemburg's fate was to be summarily executed in 1919.

On 30 July 1914, Bethmann-Hollweg offered the British ambassador in Berlin his promise to respect Belgium if Britain would not enter the war. This was interpreted in London as confirmation of Germany's intention to invade Belgium and violate its neutrality. In the years and months preceding the outbreak of the war, a number of German officers in mufti, including Ludendorff, who was to play a leading role in the siege of Liège, had reconnoitred the areas around that city, also those of Namur and Antwerp – the approach routes, the places where invading troops from the east were more likely to be ambushed, the bridges and fords and so on. Some were members of the large German colony in Belgium who were reserve officers.

On 31 July 1914, two Belgian policemen/border guards (in fact Gendarmes) Bouko and Thill went to Aachen in mufti to see for themselves what to make of the rumours of large troop concentrations in the old imperial city, just over the border. They noted the presence of large numbers of soldiers belonging to other units than the ones normally stationed in Aachen and hurried back to report. The Gendarmerie was a paramilitary police force, organized along military lines but attached to the minister for Home Affairs and the Justice minister. It was later merged with the government criminal police and is now known as the Federal Police.

Also on 31 July, Germany proclaimed *Kriegsgefahrzustand*, a state of danger of war, one step short of actual mobilization (*Mobilmachung*). On the same day Belgium mobilized its army, one day before the Germans and French, as General Galet, the king's former teacher and now adviser counselled him, not waiting for the French to do so. Brussels also declared it would defend its fortresses Namur and Antwerp, to dissuade respectively France or Britain from preventatively occupying them, which a secret clause of the 1839 treaty allowed them to do, and further, the Belgians queried London, Paris and Berlin about their respect of Belgian neutrality.

French Ambassador Klobukowski's answer was unambiguously positive.

The German Ambassador von Below had served in Peking during the Boxer war, in Sofia during the Balkan wars, and kept a metal ashtray on his desk that had been shot through by a stray bullet, assuring his visitors that after what he had been through in these previous postings he did not see what untoward events could happen to him in a backwater like Brussels, and looked forward to a long quiet, uneventful mission! His answer was late and ambiguous.

On 1 August 1914, Albert, whose mother was Princess Mary of Hohenzollern, wrote a personal letter to Kaiser Wilhelm II, the text of which his wife Elisabeth of Bavaria helped him translate into perfect German, looking up some words in the dictionary. To no avail it appeared.

The Austrian writer Stefan Zweig, who happened to be in Brussels left that day, on the last train to Cologne.

Also that day, German troops occupied the neutral Grand Duchy of Luxembourg, like Belgium a neutral state and important for its rail and road communications to France and Belgium. Belgian intelligence became aware that of the million and a half German soldiers concentrated between Aachen and the Swiss border, the vast majority, about 800,000, was massed at the Belgian/German border – an ominous sign indeed.

On 2 August 1914, on the rather unconvincing pretext that French troops had already invaded Belgian territory in the Meuse valley, Ambassador von Below presented his ultimatum. Germany requested free passage through Belgian territory and, if unopposed, would pay for possible damage. The Belgian Council of Ministers, presided over by King Albert, unanimously rejected the German proposal. The same day, in accordance with article 68 of the Belgian Constitution, King Albert took up effective command of the Belgian armed forces and called a council of ministers, later extended to a crown council, which included former cabinet ministers and other prominent personalities. A row developed between the two senior generals present, General de Selliers de Moranville, Chief of the General Staff, who urged a defensive posture, while firebrand deputy General Baron Louis de Ryckel, influenced by French ideas of *offensive à outrance*, loosely translated as 'attack is the best form of defence' prevailing in the French officers' corps, wanted to *piquer dedans*, or 'get in there'! Wiser counsel prevailed and King Albert, as Commander-in-Chief, stopped this hare-brained scheme, which might have disorganized the German military juggernaut for a (little) while but would have wasted valuable troops. General de Ryckel was given 'other tasks'.

On 4 August, Belgium made a solemn appeal to the ambassadors of France, Great Britain and Russia to cooperate as guarantors for the defence of its territory and called for a 'common and concerted action' to maintain the independence and integrity of Belgium. Sir Edward Grey assured the Belgian ambassador in London that Britain would help Belgium with all its might. As will be seen later this was premature, because the London cabinet had not yet reached that decision.

The same day King Albert, clad in his superb old-style uniform of a lieutenant general, with a black dolman pinned with his main decorations, a feathered two-pointed hat, white breeches and shiny black riding boots, rode to the Belgian parliament, his family following in open horse-drawn carriages. To the House he made a moving speech that every Belgian schoolchild has since learnt (or used to learn), saying that never in its existence as an independent state had Belgium faced such a threat, recalling the courage of the Flemish militia at the battle of the Golden Spurs against the King of France in 1302 and that of the burgers of Franchimont when they attacked the troops of the Duke of Burgundy in 1468. The conclusion was that a country that defends itself will not perish, it inspires respect from all.

Patriotic fervour was intense in both Flanders and Wallonia. Belgians felt more humiliated that their country could be considered a pushover than aggrieved at seeing their country invaded through no fault of theirs, by a country they had no quarrel with. The offer of compensation which may have been added by Berlin as an afterthought was taken as particularly offensive: 'Do they really think we could be bribed?' German shops were sacked, and cafés ceased to serve German beer.

In fact, the German ultimatum created a terrible dilemma for Belgium: if it accepted, apart from violating its treaty obligations of neutrality it would certainly have been dragged into the war anyway and would have been treated by France and probably Britain as an enemy state. If it refused, it faced a destructive war with Europe's strongest military power, with all the consequences thereof. On the other hand, Belgian resistance would and did win France and Britain precious time.

The gold and foreign reserves were transferred to vaults in Antwerp and after addressing Parliament, King Albert immediately left for Louvain (Leuven), where the campaign headquarters of the army would be. The royal palaces in Brussels were transformed into field hospitals.

Contrary to later popular belief, in London, where minds were concentrated on Home Rule, it was by no means a foregone conclusion that Britain would go to war if Belgian neutrality was violated by Germany attacking France through Belgium. It should be noted that France, Britain and Russia and their allies had no great qualms about violating Greek neutrality later in the war, by landing large troop contingents in Salonika and Corfu as well as interfering in Athens' internal political affairs.

In fact a large part of the British establishment and the City were not in favour of intervention in Belgium. Even in his time Gladstone seems to have had his doubts about it and said he did not feel the 1839 Treaty did compel Britain to go to war under all possible circumstances. And if it had been France invading Belgium in 1870, Britain's reaction might well have been not to lift a finger. In 1914, however, it might have depended on the scale of the invasion and probably the determining factor was who would be holding the port of Antwerp – though in fact the port did not play the strategic role it was traditionally given because the Dutch, who held both banks of its access river, the Scheldt, forbade its use. There was however in London a strong pro-French lobby, who in concert with the dynamic, able and enthusiastic French ambassador Paul Cambon (whose brother was ambassador in Berlin) had encouraged the Entente Cordiale, and more importantly the discreet preparatory discussions between French and British military officers, including on the spot visits to northern France to study what should be done if Germany attacked France. The go-ahead for this seems to have been given by Prime Minister Asquith when, in 1912, a mission by Lord Haldane to try to come to a naval holiday agreement with Germany failed.

Invasion of Belgium by Germany was a necessity, because the French had built a strong line of defence along their 1870 border with Germany, including stout fortresses at Verdun, Toul, Épinal and Belfort, and because otherwise the enormous manpower Germany had built up by increasing the length of its military service could not be put to use for lack of space to deploy it. Germany also saw itself as having no choice but to attack France in force, since otherwise Saarland, Ruhr and the Rhine Valley would be occupied by the French army.

The French, whose war plan (Plan XVII) called for a headlong attack to reconquer their beloved Alsace Lorraine, could not of course stand idle if the German army came through Belgium *en masse* to attack their army at its back, but it was in their political and military interest not to be the first to violate neutral Belgian territory – it gave them the moral high ground and they otherwise might have lessened the chances of a British intervention on their side.

As regards Britain, it was undecided about what to do if Germany invaded Belgium. *Entente cordiale* agreements were not very clear and some of the British establishment and the City opposed intervention in Belgium even if Belgian neutrality was violated. Ambassador Cambon now made moving appeals to remind Downing Street that the French Atlantic coast was completely defenceless against a German naval attack since, according to the *Entente cordiale* arrangements, its defence had been entrusted to the Royal Navy while the bulk of the French fleet was withdrawn to the Mediterranean to protect troopships voyaging from North Africa to mainland France. Indeed, the French naval officers of the few light vessels left at Boulogne and Calais, preparing for an attack by the mighty German Fleet they anticipated facing on their own, actually wrote farewell letters to their families. This seems to have been the wake-up call for Asquith. Some changes at the Foreign Office, both of the secretary himself and the permanent under secretary, the senior civil servant serving under him, also helped further the cause of a British military intervention. It is worth mentioning that Lord Esher, famous for his behind-the-scenes influence over political, military and diplomatic affairs during these years was married to the daughter of Sylvain van de Weyer, the first Belgian ambassador to London and one of the members of the Belgian national congress that founded the country.

The Schlieffen/Moltke plan now started rolling, yet even with years of preparation the logistical problem of marching almost two million German soldiers from their normal stations, or peacetime dwellings if they were called-up reservists, entraining them, shunting the trains to the right stations, detraining, feeding and accommodating them for the night, and then marching them on to the border was simply mind-baffling. The railway specialists of the German army could tell exactly how many axles of passenger carriages for officers, boxcars for other ranks, flatbeds transporting guns or mobile kitchens (their crews already at work on the trip), cattle trucks for horses, crossed the huge Hohenzollern Bridge over the Rhine in Cologne every minute. It was said that when a young officer joined the railway corps he would either quickly go mad or be marked out for quick promotion. Once unloaded, troops had to be matched with their officers and equipment, trains had to be sent back for more troops, coals and water provided for the locomotives and so on. The whole process worked like a well-oiled machine, but once started could not be stopped. In fact, the sheer size of the conscript armies of 1914 was one of the factors of the inevitability, length and bitterness of the Great War. When at a certain point Wilhelm II got cold feet and asked if the whole thing could not be paused, to give peace and negotiation a last chance, it is said Moltke answered in tears that it simply could not be done, imagining his beloved troop trains crashing into each other…

In Belgium some locomotives were allowed deliberately to crash into each other, as the Belgians started sabotaging, blowing up and collapsing bridges and tunnels on the railway lines from the German border to Liège.

2

Invasion

Soldiers and other animals

At the beginning of 1914, Belgium had a population of around 7.5 million and a small regular army of 43,000 men, with another 115,000 trained reserves. It was organized in six infantry and one cavalry divisions and would remain so until the end of the war. The total number during the summer and autumn of 1914 seems to have reached 200,000, as about 40,000 volunteers enlisted after hearing of the invasion. Equipment and arms were lacking however, and the *Garde civique*,[1] also mobilized, was incorporated in the army since the Germans, not recognizing their status as combatants had hanged some of their members. Of the total army number, 117,000 were in the field army, the rest in garrisons.

Each division of the field army was divided into three brigades of two regiments, each with three battalions of a variable number of companies. This made for about 18 infantry battalions per division, and 70 field guns of either 75 mm or 105 mm caliber in each division, plus auxiliaries, supplies etc. The individual weapon was the Mauser bolt action Model 1889 and there were also Hotchkiss and Maxim machine guns, but too few, far fewer in proportion than the German infantry regiments possessed. Some of these were drawn by Belgian mastiff dogs, also used to pull milk carts at the time. (The breed subsequently went extinct, but has been revived by breeding.) Though horsedrawn field artillery was reasonable in quantity and training, apart from the fixed guns on the fortresses, Belgium had no heavy artillery. Some had been ordered with Krupp in Essen but, unsurprisingly, delivery had been delayed by the crisis and they would not be available to the Belgian army during that fateful summer. Communication was another weak point as orders had to be transmitted by motor cyclists or requisitioned motorcars, or by pigeons – which were to prove very useful throughout the war. Brussels is probably the only city in the world where a monument to the military carrier pigeon was ever erected.

Each active peacetime regiment was to split up and give birth to another 'clone' regiment in wartime, for example *4de Linie* gave birth to *24ste Linie*, half the officers and NCOs transferring to the new unit.

Thousands of horses already belonged to the cavalry and horsedrawn artillery and supply regiments and thousands more were requisitioned from farmers, but as is well known eventually played a far less significant role in the conflict than was generally anticipated. As for aircraft, there was one squadron of 12 planes, and trials to fire machine guns from them had been carried out north of Antwerp.

Belgian uniforms, ranks, denomination of units and regulations were largely inspired by the French army, since the Belgian army had been trained after independence in 1830 by French and Belgian officers who had fought under Napoleon. Some Polish officers who had been in the Russian army also joined in the 1830s, after one of the many unsuccessful revolts against the Tsar. There were (and still are) *Régiments de Ligne* who were regular infantry, *Grenadiers*, *Carabiniers* infantry, and *Guides*, *Lanciers* and *Chasseurs à Cheval*, all cavalry. The *Grenadiers* and *12e de Ligne* were the elite infantry regiments, the former being the unit where members of the royal family usually served and the latter having strong links with the city of Liège. Another infantry regiment, *4e Linie* kept traditional links with the city of Bruges, where it was long in garrison.

The initial deployment in early August 1914 was, in accordance with the neutrality posture:

- one division at Liège to protect against a German invasion and supporting the forts around that city by occupying the terrain between the forts;
- one around Namur against a French invasion;
- one around Ghent, officially to deter a British landing on the Belgian coast before it had been formally asked for, in fact, as with Namur, to forestall any German accusation of breach of neutrality;
- one around Antwerp, in the long planned national redoubt;
- and the rest in general reserve, the cavalry division acting, as was the practice in all armies in those days, as a scouting force.

Thus, all four directions from which an invasion could have come were covered and Belgium waited scrupulously until Germany had effectively violated its neutral border to call for the other guarantors of the 1839 treaty to come to its aid. Next, the Belgian army reinforced its eastern border by creating a centrally based concentration around Louvain (Leuven), where King Albert set up his GHQ to repel the German invasion.

Morale, discipline, motivation and training were variable, good in some units, less so in others. There was a dearth of trained officers and NCOs due to the sudden large increase of enlisted, called-up men, after the law on general compulsory military service was introduced in 1913. An exceptionally good core of officers, trained at the famed Brussels Ecole Royale Militaire, together with King Albert's insistence on tough, disciplined training, explain the good account the Belgian army gave of itself in the summer and autumn of 1914; something none of the neighbouring countries expected, certainly not the Germans. The German ambassador in Paris, before leaving for home had scoffed, 'The Belgians will line up on the roads and present arms to our troops!' In fact, the Belgian army proved very effective in defensive combat, intelligently using terrain obstacles, or half-demolished buildings and improvised barricades, inflicting serious losses on green German troops foolishly sent forward in thick throngs against well-defended positions. Belgium's defenders proved able to absorb serious punishment without flinching.

During the whole war, a total of 267,000 men served in the Belgian army, of whom by 1918 about 54,000 had been wounded and 14,000 killed. During the war, some were killed, wounded and declared unfit, or discharged for other reasons, while young men came of age and were drafted in the small unoccupied country, also a significant number managed to escape from internment camps in the Netherlands or joined crossing the Belgian/Dutch border (at great peril as we shall see), more living in Allied or neutral countries being drafted, and Luxemburgers and other non-Belgians volunteering. All these more than compensated for the losses.

2.1 First Blood: Cavalier Fonck and the Visé Bridge

Between 30 July and 3 August, the Belgian Gendarmerie close to the border at Aachen reported huge contingents of German cavalry and cyclists detraining in and around the old imperial city. On 31 July, the German border guards at both the Dutch and Belgian borders with Germany were replaced by army personnel and the borders closed with chains, no vehicles being allowed through either way.

On 2 August, *Maréchal des Logis* (Cavalry Sergeant) Pfeiffer of the Belgian Gemmenich frontier post walked up to the border with cigarettes, which he offered to German soldiers he knew well and chatted to them. He found out they were also aware of what troop movements were taking place on the Belgian side, namely about the Belgian *Lancier* (Lancers) Regiment which was patrolling the area.

On 4 August at 0805 hrs, the first German cavalry patrol crossed into Belgium at Gemmenich. Told by the Belgian Gendarmes at the border that they were crossing into neutral territory, the German officer answered he knew that well enough, but that the French army had already violated Belgian neutrality elsewhere. The Gendarmes withdrew towards Liège and were then ordered north to Visé. Two German divisions of 60,000 men started leaving Aachen towards Liège and Visé, in an attempt to seize the bridges over the Meuse there, as well as those between these two cities. At 1000 hrs they passed the peaceful villages of La Calamine and Henri Chapelle (where a huge American Second World War cemetery is now to be found), but quickly realized when seeing the first felled trees and upturned carts barring their way that this would not be the walkover they had been led to expect. At Thimister-Clermont 70-year-old Théodore Pauchenne was harvesting hay and was screamed at by a German officer who told him to help remove the obstacles. Not understanding German, he was immediately shot dead, the first of many Belgians who were to lose their lives in the coming years. Half an hour later a German cyclist patrol ran into Belgian Lancers on horseback. They opened fire and 21-year-old Cavalier Antoine Fonck fell, the first Belgian military casualty. A white marble monument now stands to the memory of Fonck at the exact spot where he died, at Thimister-Clermont on the road from Battice.

On forced marches, German troops reached Battice, on the main Aachen–Liège road at 1230 hrs. Finding the city completely deserted, they smashed the doors and start plundering, especially the wine cellars.

The first objective of the German *Handstreich*, or 'sudden attack' was to capture the vital Meuse bridges, whose possession was essential to the execution of the Schlieffen/Moltke plan. Thus, they rushed on to Liège and to Visé on the Meuse River, an important communications hub where roads and railways cross the Meuse and each other, about halfway between Liège and Maastricht in the Netherlands, just before the Meuse reaches the Dutch border. However, when they arrived at Visé they found the Meuse bridges blown by the Belgian *12ème de Ligne* infantry Regiment who had taken up defensive positions on the other side of the river. At that moment the Gemmenich Gendarmes, wearing their uniform bearskin hats arrived on bicycles from Liège. Gendarmes Bouko and Thill were killed by shots to the head after a brief exchange of fire, but not without having each expended most of their ammunition. (A monument to their memory was built in Visé's main square, at the post office. It was removed by the Germans in 1942 but has been recently replaced.) In the afternoon, rifle fire was exchanged between Belgian and German troops across the Meuse and the Germans started assembling river barges to build a makeshift bridge. Their effort was shot to pieces by the guns of Fort de Fléron, the closest to Visé of the Liège ring of forts. Realizing the crossing of the Meuse would be opposed, contrary to what they hoped, German troops now started brutalizing the civilian population, the first of many examples of civilians being shot or bayoneted.

German reconnaissance just north of Visé however discovered a ford on the Meuse at Lixhe, just skirting the Dutch border, whose neutrality they had orders to strictly respect, but which was out of range of the Fléron guns. A pontoon bridge was built there with barges and German troops started pouring over to the western bank of the Meuse. General Brialmont had recognized this possibility and strongly advocated the building of an extra fort there. This never happened, for lack of funds, and Brialmont predicted: 'You *will shed tears of blood because of that* [my italics].' After the war, in the 1940s, this weak spot was recognized and the big Fort of Eben Emael was built to cover the whole area.

Ironically, four and a half years later, it would be precisely at Visé and Lixhe that defeated Kaiser Wilhelm II would arrive to seek and be granted asylum in the Netherlands, precisely where his troops had first violated Belgian neutrality and killed the first military and civilian Belgians.

2.2 The Bloody Harvest of August 1914: Visé, Andenne, Aarschot, Dinant, Louvain and other Places of Infamy

Real atrocities and propaganda

In 1914 Germany enjoyed a good image in Belgium, especially among the elite. This might sound surprising when one knows what followed, but the impressive progress German industry had made at the turn of the century, its social security system, at the time the most advanced in Europe, and more than anything else the achievements of its academic world forced admiration. So much so that when promising young men were considering studying abroad it was often Germany's outstanding universities they went to. Relations with France, whose cultural influence was very strong indeed because of the common language, were good, but the anticlerical measures taken there at the turn of the century had alienated part of the largely very Catholic population. Britain was also admired, but the Boer War had seen widespread sympathy expressed for the two small Dutch-speaking republics (Transvaal and the Orange Free State) crushed by the London government for obviously purely economic motives, especially in Flanders, as in the Netherlands. The strong anti-Belgian propaganda waged in Britain against the colonization of the Congo, denouncing partially verified abuses but also seen as inspired (and financed) by rival economic interests based in Liverpool, had left their mark. On the whole, Germany, which had a large and active colony in Antwerp and used that port extensively for its exports, was probably the most esteemed among Belgium's larger neighbours.

The hilly region that separates Aachen from Liège in the Meuse valley, north of the Ardennes, is called the Pays de Herve. It is covered with pasture that produces excellent milk and cheese. Pears, apples and cherries are grown. In the woods, where wild boar and deer can be seen, specially trained horses with broad hindquarters and feathered legs are still used today to pull the felled logs through the trees to the waiting carts. Quiet rivers flow from here into the Meuse. The green, peaceful landscapes where these lines are written were shattered three times in thirty years: 1914, 1940 and 1944, and plenty of demolished forts, monuments and military cemeteries still dot the landscape or are to be found on hilltops, village squares, or outside local parish churches. They remind us of the fury, sacrifice and suffering by many from several nations in this corner of Belgium, very close to the Dutch and German borders.

August is traditionally the month for reaping the harvest. The German army of August 1914 could have been called the Grim Reaper indeed, as in this region and others in Belgium it left about 7,000 civilians dead, including women and small children, and not sparing the elderly. Some of the victims were educated people, lawyers or doctors or members of the clergy, some had even studied in Germany. Most were simple souls who did not understand what was happening to them until it became all too obvious, as they stood trembling against a wall, their families looking on crying.

As will be discussed in Chapter 8 (Belgium and the Propaganda War), the 'German atrocities' in Belgium in August 1914 were disputed and continued until quite recently to be dismissed as Allied propaganda, even by some in the US, Britain and less surprisingly in Germany, or at least explained away by reference to the need to wipe out *francs-tireurs* (irregular 'free-shooters'). Some of the stories were without doubt exaggerated, but that a large number of Belgian civilians were summarily executed by the German army in August and September 1914 is an undisputed and historically proven fact. In the years immediately before the 2014 commemorations, serious historical investigation based on irrefutable written evidence such as local population records and coroners' reports for the months in question in all cities, villages or boroughs known to have been affected, was organized by two Belgian universities, one in each language region of the country. They sent out teams of researchers and came up with complete lists of names, ages, dates and places of demise, and a summary of the events that took place in each of the cities or villages. This was published under the title *Villes Martyres*, by Professors Axel Tixhon and Mark Derez. It makes impressive reading.

Trends can be established:

1. When war broke out the Belgian government, in particular the Home Affairs Ministry and all municipalities made insistent appeals to the population to refrain from hostile acts, and certainly extremely clear and insistent exhortations under no circumstances ever to fire on German troops. Firearms were to be deposited or got rid of. This was announced in the newspapers and posted on bills all across the country.
2. Among the German soldiers there existed an obsession with *francs-tireurs* of the Franco-Prussian war of 1870, during which French irregulars effectively waged a guerrilla war behind the Prussian lines. This must have been discussed at length in German officers' messes and barracks before 1914.
3. It was not always on the day(s) the first German troops invaded a town that the worst outrages occurred. In fact, they usually took place several days later.
4. There was almost always a link between Belgian army resistance and abuses against the local civilian population: when the Belgian forts defending Liège fired at German troops trying to cross the Meuse or repulsed a German attack with heavy losses, reprisals quickly followed, and likewise when the Belgian army made successful sorties from Antwerp where it was besieged.
5. In practically every instance German officers in charge, far from moderating their troops, were seen to condone, encourage, organize or even conspire to let their men believe there were actually *francs-tireurs* operating, to justify summary executions of civilians, burning down of cities, looting and arson.
6. German soldiers involved were usually green troops who could in some cases genuinely have thought they had been fired upon by civilians when in fact they had been attacked by regular Belgian army troops concealing themselves in civilian houses. Belgian army uniforms, some of whom (the *Carabiniers*) wore a sort of black top hat as uniform headdress, could have been mistaken for civilians.

7. In a city, when gunshot reports echo against the walls it is sometimes difficult to determine from which direction you have been fired at. This is especially true for troops that have never been fired upon in anger and find themselves in unfamiliar surroundings.
8. Most of the outrages were committed under the influence of drink, the German troops having looted wine cellars in practically every case where abuses occurred.
9. Many official German regimental campaign records mention the presence of *francs-tireurs* though there were in fact extremely few, so in some cases German soldiers might well have been misled into believing it. Some reports of *francs-tireur* incidents made their way into the German press, which the soldiers then read. When the incidents were reported to have happened in places they had been in, yet had seen nothing, they might believe that nevertheless such a thing had taken place 'because it is written in the newspaper' – an often-verified sequence of events.

On invasion day, 4 August 1914, Battice, a small city on the way between Aachen and Liège, was burned down and the first civilians were shot, apparently after a firefight between Belgian army *Lanciers* firing in ambush from houses and German Hussars. The same day summary executions occurred at the small village of Warsage and the crossroads hamlet of Berneau next to it, on the way between Aachen and Visé. Two men were hanged and nine executed by firing squad as spies because they had stopped to watch, out of sheer curiosity, a huge staging camp the German were building just a few kilometres before Visé. At Blégny, a peaceful mining town some kilometres south, the burgomaster, the parish priest and two brothers were placed against the church wall and summarily executed. In total, 19 executions took place at Blégny-Trembleur, 33 at Battice, 118 at Soumagne. Barchon, Mouland, Magnée, Romsée, Olne – the list of villages in the region where such executions took place goes on and on. At the middle-sized city of Herve that gives its name to the region there were 108.

All through these August days, the red wave of summary executions spread over Belgium: not only in the Pays de Herve, but also much further south in the Semois river valley that skirts the French border, at small villages called Tintigny, Ethe and Etalle, firing squads executed 71 civilians of all ages; at Rossignol alone 100 people lost their lives. The burgomaster of Cornesse was executed. In other cases hostages were taken, then released the next day in the absence of any *franc-tireur* activity. In France, over the border, the same atrocities took place and evidence of all this was sometimes recorded in the personal journals kept by German soldiers, found in their possession when they were captured later in the war.[2]

Back in **Visé**, between Liège and the Dutch border, when the first German troops had to retreat after finding the bridges on the Meuse blown on 4 August, they did wreck a few houses but the real outrages only began several days later, on 18 and 19 August. They constitute typical examples of both revenge taken on civilians because of a military setback and the *francs-tireurs* obsession. A brewer who had had his wagons requisitioned was summarily shot, as were several bystanders. Twenty hostages were taken of whom eighteen were executed. A retired policeman was hanged. In the days following, German troops from the *Pionier* (Engineers) *Regiment 18* from Koenigsberg in East Prussia[3] recently arrived, started shooting civilians at random and burning houses, as well as the large gothic-style church of St Martin, which was gutted. The priceless reliquary of St Hadelin, dating from the first millennium, had been safely hidden away, but some other precious artefacts were lost, and the church reduced to a shell, as were hundreds of the houses.[4] Bands of drunken German soldiers roamed the streets, sometimes shooting at each other, breaking into houses, brutally evicting the inhabitants and setting the dwellings on fire after having looted them, especially looking for drink. A man called Désiré Duchène, aged sixty-six and almost blind, was bound to a tree and executed by three consecutive rifle salvoes, after which a bottle was broken over his head. In total, 42 civilians, aged between 9 and 66, were killed at Visé and another 300 were taken to Germany under escort, there to languish in camps for no reason for months. The city was left to burn for two weeks and 586 houses were destroyed, along with the city hall, the medieval church, a school and an old folks' home.

During the weeks of August and September the bloody trail extended all over Belgium: in the Meuse valley at **Andenne**, south of Visé, one Leutnant von Bülow, cousin of a former chancellor of Germany and serving in the Imperial Guards Uhlan Regiment was shot. After this, the Germans went on a drunken spree during which neither women nor small children were spared, sometimes being gruesomely executed with axes. Out of 8,000 inhabitants, the city suffered 262 executions. The officers stole cash from the city coffers and the soldiers rifled the pockets of those they had executed.

In **Tamines** (5,600 inhabitants) the German army left 383 dead and half the houses were set on fire.

The atrocities extended into Flanders, where in **Aarschot** 173 people, including the burgomaster, his brother and his son were shot, the ages of the victims ranging from one year to 90 years old.

On 4 September, one month after the invasion, the Flemish city of **Dendermonde** (Termonde) – where the inhabitants already knew what had happened in Visé and Aarschot, which makes it even more unlikely there would have been anyone foolhardy enough to fire on the invaders – six men were forced to dig their own graves before being shot and three more were bayonetted to death to avenge the death of a German officer killed by an artillery shell. The city was almost completely burned to the ground including the belfry with the medieval archives, after having been plundered. Several people were randomly shot dead.

Again and again the same scenario occurred: long before the arrival of the Germans the local authorities admonished the local civilian inhabitants to stay calm, refrain from any hostile acts towards the invaders, indeed to give them food and drink when so required and especially to get rid of firearms, when possible by throwing them in the rivers. Bills to that effect, some still to be seen in local museums, were posted everywhere. And in each place a small incident, for instance in Aarschot where a German officer was shot by one of his own men, triggered reprisals against non-existent *francs-tireurs* and the mass executions began at once and were sometimes protracted over several days. Sometimes court martials were hastily convened by officers, with predictable results, but usually such formalities were dispensed with. In a few cases soldiers seem to have resisted the orders to execute civilians they knew to be innocent, but this was rare indeed.

The case of **Louvain** (Leuven) merits special mention. Considered the Belgian Oxford, it houses one of the oldest universities in the western world dating from the Middle Ages and has always attracted students from far afield, including contingents from Asia, North and South America. As in most of Belgium, cultural influences from both the Germanic and the Latin worlds converge here. It was also an important market place and to this day famous for a world-renowned brewery. Its beautiful Gothic-style Town Hall is a testimony to its glorious history. German troops arrived, singing, on 19 August, after the Belgian army, which had had its headquarters there, evacuated and retreated to Antwerp. Here again, the aldermen of Louvain expressly warned the population not to protest against the Germans in any manner and in no case whatsoever to fire on them. The Germans made it known that anyone found in possession of a firearm would be executed forthwith, and took several hostages.

The population kept quiet. By 22 August, 15,000 German troops were quartered in the city.

On the evening of the 25th, the day the Belgian army sortied from Antwerp to the north-west, sirens could suddenly be heard, followed by shots. Exchange of fire, most probably between confused German soldiers started all over the city during the night of the 25th to the 26th. German troops entered homes, dragged the inhabitants out and in many cases simply shot them dead there and then after setting their houses on fire. Practically the whole city centre and the street leading from the railway station to the centre were burned down. The old Town Hall survived, but the 300,000 books of the university library did not, among them 1,000 handwritten medieval texts and 800 incunabula, books printed before 1500. A shower of paper debris fell on the city and its surroundings over the following days. The Gothic church of St Peter's was severely damaged, and its clock tower collapsed after having been deliberately set alight by German soldiers holding torches against the oak beams. Old Flemish paintings were saved by prudent individuals. By 29 August, almost all the population had fled, and a large part of the city, 11,800 houses lay in ashes, 248 civilians had been shot dead, and another 1,500, including one little girl, put on filthy boxcars returning to Germany after having brought in a supply of horses. At railway stations in Germany they were jeered and spat at, and locked in camps from which they were not released until 1915. A column of other inhabitants including several senior staff of the Catholic university of Louvain, was force-marched to Tervuren, close to Brussels, escorted by German Uhlan cavalry. University rector Monsignor Ladeuze, vice-rector van Cauwenberg , a well-known historian Alfred Cauchie and 80 other priests were all frogmarched for days. One among them, a young Jesuit priest, Eugène Duperieux was executed in front of the rest of the group, that included his twin brother, because a notebook had been found in his pocket in which he had compared the burning down of the Louvain library with the infamous destruction of the ancient library of Alexandria. Another group including Mgr Jules de Becker, rector of the American college of Louvain, was finally liberated at the insistence of members of the American embassy. One other group was finally liberated south of Brussels, after a very long march, because a Dutch journalist had stayed stubbornly by their side.

That the beautiful Louvain town hall was saved was a miracle, due to the fact that the Germans had established their headquarters there. Conversely, the university library seems to have been thought to harbour the centre of 'resistance' and was therefore deliberately put to the torch. The Duke of Arenberg, who held double Belgian and German nationality, owned a chateau at Heverlee outside Louvain and a number of people took refuge there.

Burning books is bad for a nation's image. The sack of Louvain horrified and hardened public opinion in France and Britain and, perhaps more importantly, also in neutral countries. Brand Withlock, the ambassador of the still neutral United States in Brussels, only 15 km away, as well as some other neutrals sent members of their staffs to verify what they had heard and send accurate reports to their governments. German officers were forbidding any effort to extinguish the fires and told American, Swedish and Mexican diplomats that the town would be burned down completely. Pyrotechnic devices seem to have been used. Reports were also filed by American and Dutch journalists. The sack of Louvain, together with the sinking of the Lusitania, may have done more than all the other outrages combined to turn world opinion against Germany.

After the Second World War, as a gesture of reconciliation, German Chancellor Adenauer was made a Doctor Honoris Causa of Louvain University.

Dinant also merits special mention: no fewer than 674 civilians, about 10 per cent of its population, lost their life in this peaceful, picturesque, mid-sized medieval city on the upper Meuse, close to the Ardennes region. An important trading centre in the Middle Ages, renowned for its situation on the steep banks of the river, it boasted a beautiful church with onion-domed steeple and an old fortified citadel on the top of the eastern bank of the Meuse. It is also the birthplace of Adolphe Sax, the inventor of the saxophone. A tradition of working copper dates from very old times and its quiet riverbanks have always attracted tourists. There were several hotels for holidaymakers. It was also the scene, on 23 August of one of the most savage scenes of destruction and mass execution of the war. The IIIrd Saxon Army reached Dinant via the eastern bank of the Meuse on 15 August. This time it was not the Belgian army's resistance that infuriated them but that of General Lanrezac's 5th French army, that had taken position on the western bank of the river to keep the important bridges from their enemies. Furious hand-to-hand fighting took place and a young French lieutenant, Charles de Gaulle of the French 33rd Infantry Regiment was severely wounded there.[5] Forced to withdraw under fire from French artillery, the Germans flowed back into downtown Dinant, still on the eastern bank where they had started. Renewed attacks followed and desperate fighting went on for several days. The citadel on top of the east bank was taken by the French, then lost again. More often than not German soldiers at night shot at each other in confusion, later to accuse, once again Belgian *francs-tireurs*.

On 23 August, a renewed German attack met with success because Lanrezac's army had been ordered to retreat following the battle of Charleroi, where the French had been forced to retreat and he risked being cut off. This time the Germans advanced along the river to the north, reached the suburb of Leffe where an ancient abbey is situated, and went on a killing spree looking for hidden French soldiers or armed civilians: 312 civilians were quickly shot or despatched with bayonets. At 1800 hrs Lieutenant Colonel Count von Kielmansegg, commanding the 100th Regiment of Grenadiers of the Imperial Guards, lined up about 100 civilians in four rows against the wall of a house belonging to local magistrate Tschoffen and ordered them to be executed. After the firing squads had done, survivors were given the coup de grâce with pistols. In a rare occurrence, a German took a picture of the 'Tschoffen wall' which we still have. On the back of the original picture one can read: *Erschossene Männer und Frauen in Dinant*, 'Executed men and women in Dinant'. The massacre went on the next day when 80 more people, including women with babes in arms, were executed. A 3-week-old baby, Mariette Fivet was not spared. The following days, the whole city centre was plundered and put to the torch, including the churches, hotels, thermal institute, schools, banks, town hall and so on.

In all, 750 public buildings and private dwellings were destroyed. In addition, more than 400 people were taken to Germany and detained in Kassel until November.

Apart from acting with such cruelty, German General von Hausen, the IIIrd Army Commander, had committed a tactical error. Instead of wasting two days massacring innocent civilians in Dinant his army would have been better employed pursuing the retreating French army of General Lanrezac, who in the event did so unmolested and in good order.

As well as the hundreds of instances of summary executions, there were other violations of the Hague Conventions of 1899 and 1907 on the Laws of War, to which Germany was a signatory; for example, in several places civilians were driven before them by German troops in the hope the Belgian army would not open fire, with often, predictable fatal results. (This practice would be repeated by the German army in 1940.) There is circumstantial evidence that a number of rapes occurred. However exact figures will probably remain unknown; indeed, attitudes were different to what they are today and young women at the time were unlikely to come forward to tell their stories, especially during the German occupation.

In practically all cities where massacres occurred, a substantial number of civilians including women and children, were driven under armed escort or pushed into the railway boxcars, some of which had served to transport horses and were soiled with dung, to be driven to camps in Germany. They were detained in squalid camps for months for no other reason than that someone had decided they were *francs-tireurs*.

Officers were not above plundering. Particularly at Louvain, where a rich bourgeoisie had developed around the university, booty in the shape of furniture, glassware, books and paintings was stolen and sent to Germany in motorcars, either to adorn the officers' houses or to be sold in antique markets.

Where regiments from protestant regions of Germany were involved, Catholic priests seem to have been particularly targeted. This ties in with the myth of *francs-tireurs*, as in the 1870 Franco-Prussian war French Catholic priests were said to have been prominent in the irregular troops fighting the protestant Prussians.

Some German soldiers showed compassion and deliberately aimed too high when ordered to shoot civilians, but this behaviour seems to have been the exception.

That senior staff were unaware of what was going on is given the lie by Ludendorff himself, who in a book written later says he saw the city of Wavre burn... Indeed, the alleged presence of *francs-tireurs* served as an excuse for some German generals to explain their slower than planned advance into Belgium in implementing the Schlieffen-Moltke plan, as can be read for example in the memoirs of General von Hausen.

One cannot rule out the likelihood that even before the invasion a premeditated policy of Shock and Awe (that concept would be invented by another army, a century later) was planned if Belgium resisted. The existence of some posters printed before the invasion in broken French and threatening terrible reprisals would point to that. When the German military, believing their own propaganda, persuaded themselves there were *francs-tireurs* it was an affront to their sense of superiority and strong belief in law and order. Rage at seeing Belgium resisting, and a failure to distinguish between regular troops and *francs-tireurs*, were followed by deliberate terrorization of the local population. The Germans had planned to leave only small occupation forces in place and did not want trouble on their communication lines. Belgian resistance forced them to divert troops that were needed elsewhere, a concrete example being troops already on trains in Louvain on their way to France that were made to detrain there when the Belgian army sortied from Antwerp.

That there was no organized civilian resistance in Belgium is an historical fact and the Germans twice had four years (1914–18 and 1940–44) to search through all the Belgian archives and documents to unearth evidence of any, which they signally failed to do. A furious farmer or two may have discharged a fowling piece at German soldiers after having seen his family massacred, his cattle slaughtered or his homestead burned to the ground, that is possible. That would make them *francs-tireurs*. But three-week-old Mariette Fivet, killed in her mother's arms in Dinant and 79-year-old Benedictus van de Meirsche, shot down at Dendermonde certainly were no such thing.[6]

Until recently the German flag was banned in Dinant in public places. In 2001 the burgomaster organized a ceremony of reconciliation where the German ambassador to Belgium publicly offered his apologies to the city and the German and Belgian flags were hoisted by two youngsters, one from each country.

2.3 Resistance of the Forts of Liège and Namur

The essence of the Schlieffen/Moltke plan is well known: to invade France in a large cartwheel movement whose axle would have been more or less situated at the Luxembourg/French border, thereby turning and enveloping the French army and taking Paris. Five strong German armies were to cross Belgium and Luxembourg and then turn south towards France. They were led respectively from north to south by Generals von Kluck, von Bülow, von Hausen, the Duke of Wurtenberg and the Kronprinz, heir to the German imperial throne. It was hoped the Belgian army would not resist but in case it did, a special corps, the army of the Meuse, was created under General von Emmich, and given a lot of artillery to take out the Belgian forts of Liège and Namur, capture the Meuse bridges and thus open the way to the larger German armies waiting behind to cross the Meuse and on to France. Von Emmich had 50,000 men, 166 guns and about 200 machine guns, thus by himself far outnumbering the Belgian garrison of Liège.

As is almost always the case plans, however elaborate and detailed, do not survive the first shots and certainly timetables are almost never adhered to. Far from 'lining up and presenting arms' as predicted by the German ambassador to Paris the Belgian army proved a harder nut to crack than expected. The Brialmont forts, obsolete though they might have been, opened withering and accurate fire when German troops were observed approaching Liège. King Albert had entrusted the *Position Fortifiée de*

Liège, that is its forts and the infantry troops guarding the intervals between them, namely the 4th Belgian army division, to General Leman, his former teacher at the Royal Military Academy. Though he had never commanded in the field, the moustachioed no-nonsense general carried out his mission and held the German juggernaut as long as he could with the means at his disposal. Between Liège and Namur, the Meuse valley forms a deep and abrupt partition, so forcing an invading army into a limited number of approaches to these cities or the other bridges over that river. From being hilly and covered in woods, the terrain suddenly sharply declines and changes to highly built-up industrial suburbs, where the dwellings of the factory workers of the Liège coal and steel industry have expanded in industrial suburbs along the river valley, not unlike those in central England. Here and there around Liège, *terrils*, high conical slagheaps, dot the landscape, obviously offering excellent observation posts.

For the Germans the siege of Liège was to be laid in three phases: first, a daring lunge at the bridges; second, the infantry attempting to fight its way through the intervals between the forts, thus isolating them; and third, pounding the forts into submission with their overwhelming artillery. Add to this a few Zeppelin raids on the civilian city centre for psychological effect, a historical first.

All around Liège, from 4 to 16 August, day and night, bitter fighting took place between the Belgian and German infantry, in small woods, in villages, even in cemeteries. They fought in both scorching heat and downpours of summer rain. When they could, the artillery of the forts gave their troops a helping hand – at night with their searchlights and sudden accurate salvoes they sometimes smashed a German column, an artillery battery, field kitchens, vital crossroads and so on. But it had not been possible to site all the Liège forts ideally, so some like Barchon and Pontisse left dead ground uncovered and when the observation posts supposed to remedy this were overrun, they became partially blinded.

Reconnaissance squads from some Belgian forts took requisitioned motorcars, on which they mounted light machine guns and wrought havoc with sudden hit-and-run attacks or ambushes on German cavalry columns. One called itself the Bande à Bonnot, after a Paris criminal gang who had recently attained fame by using fast cars to outrun the Paris police, who used bicycles. Some German columns lost their way in the mazes of the industrial suburbs and found themselves firing at other German columns equally confused. All these elements were no doubt factors in the *francs-tireurs* legend. Belgian infantry, who though inexperienced in fighting, knew the terrain, would lay well-sited ambushes, but quickly and wisely decamp when things became too hot.

One Belgian officer, Captain Kück, very popular in his regiment, was killed. Kück is definitely not a common family name in Belgium. He belonged to a German family that had immigrated to Belgium forty years earlier, had become naturalized and had made the army his career, only to be killed by a German bullet... In Herstal, one of the industrial suburbs of Liège,[7] the 89th Mecklenburg Regiment lost its colours to the Belgian 2nd Grenadiers, while German Prince von Arnim was killed and Leutnant Graf von Moltke, the general's grandson, was taken prisoner. On 6 August on the wooded hills of Sart Tilman, where part of the modern Liège University campus now is, a redoubt changed hands three times. Bayonets were widely used.

The German 9th Jäger Battalion now reached the northern outskirts of Liège and being mistaken for British troops was cheered and offered cigars and drinks. Against overwhelming odds, the eventual fall of the *Position Fortifiée de Liège* was inevitable, but one event might have precipitated it: a small group of German officers came up walking to the house in rue Sainte Foy in central Liège, where General Leman had his headquarters. They were first mistaken for British officers until at the very door, where a firefight broke out at point-blank range when they were recognized to be Germans. Belgian Commandant Marchand[8] was killed along with ten Germans. The rest fled or were wounded and taken. The leader of this daring raiding party trying to capture Leman, his maps and documents, seems to have been a Baron von Alvensleben, who, posing as a Danish businessman and using civilian clothes had hired a room in a nearby hotel the night before, changing into uniform to meet the rest of the party. A map with the itinerary was found on him. Leman may have been shaken by having almost been killed or captured and his staff, realizing he was too vulnerable, decided to shift his command post to the westernmost fort of Liège, Loncin, where he was taken by car. However maybe through lack of experience of command in the field, even in exercises, no provision was made for controlling the troops whilst the shift of command was completed as is usually done by an interim command post taking over temporarily. This caused confusion and instead of only the infantry on the east bank of the Meuse being withdrawn, as he had originally ordered, badly interpreted orders caused the whole of the 4th Army Division to move away westward, leaving the forts to their own devices.

However spirited the Belgian defence was, and even though on both sides the troops were inexperienced, after a few days German numbers began to tell. Apart from their overwhelming superiority in numbers and armament, another event was to help the Germans. At this point we see a German general officer enter the arena who would occupy its centre for the rest of the war. Ruthless, devoid of scruples, but highly efficient as he would prove to be, including in his treatment of Belgium during the occupation, Erich Ludendorff, who had earlier reconnoitred the area in mufti, had been attached to von Emmich's staff but given no command of his own. When the general commanding the 14th Brigade, one of the columns trying to approach Liège, was killed in action, he took over his command and drove his men on vigorously, leading them between the forts of Fléron and Pontisse, being the first to reach the bank of the Meuse at Jupille and then push on south along the bank to the old Chartreuse barracks. There the Ourthe River flows into the Meuse, not far from the important railway and road bridges of Liège. This was an achievement, because it led General Leman to perhaps prematurely retire the infantry occupying the intervals between the forts on the east bank, fearing to see them cut off and thus making it easier for the Germans to bring on their heavy artillery to pound the forts one after the other into submission. Meanwhile, the 14th German infantry Brigade quickly occupied downtown Liège, the railway station and the bridges, allowing the engineers to repair them.

For Liège it was thus only a question of time and as the forts were submitted to a continuous *Trommelfeuer*, a sound like the rolling of drums, increasing in deafening volume as more and heavier guns (the lesser ones keeping firing) were brought up, they fell one by one with disconcerting regularity: on 8 August, Fort de Barchon surrendered under heavy 210 mm fire, its garrison later being criticized for having been the first to do so. On 11 August, the first 420 mm shells, weighing 950 kg each[9] started falling on Fort d'Evegnée. It also gave up, followed on 13 August by Forts de Pontisse, d'Embourg and on 14 August, Fort de Chaudfontaine. Most had had practically all their gun turrets demolished and the underground galleries filled with acrid unbreathable smoke. Many had organized successful sorties and netted German prisoners. A German report spoke highly of the bravery of the commander of Fort de Pontisse, Commandant Speesen, and noted that Chaudfontaine had its magazine penetrated by a shell, causing one hundred KIAs. Forts de Liers and de Fléron surrendered on 14 August, the latter after fifty hours of uninterrupted shelling and after repelling an infantry attack.

The next day, 15 August, Forts de Boncelles and de Lantin surrendered and Fort de Loncin exploded, the Germans themselves being impressed by the catastrophic damage they had inflicted on it.

The last two Liège forts, Hollogne and Flémalle, surrendered on 16 August.

The siege of Namur,[10] though less well known, followed broadly the pattern of Liège, except that the Germans, mindful of the heavy infantry losses they incurred at Liège, took their time bringing up the heavy artillery, including this time batteries of Austro-Hungarian Skoda guns to reduce the forts of the *Position Fortifiée de Namur* to rubble one by one. On 22 August, 40,000 Germans and 300 guns of 150 mm, 210 mm and the super-heavy 420 mm reduced Fort de Marchovelette to rubble, but not before it had repulsed four bloody infantry attacks. The German guns were now joined by the Austro-Hungarian Skoda 305 mm heavy guns, that country only declaring war on Belgium a few days later on a mere pretext.

On 22 August, Fort de Maizeret was completely demolished.

On 23 August, the Belgian *10ème de Ligne* Infantry Regiment was decimated, one of its battalions losing two officers and 130 men out of 184.[11] General Michel, the CO of the *Position Fortifiée de Namur* had difficulties controlling his command after a lucky German shell destroyed the telephone exchange. Again, one by one the forts were reduced to rubble by massive uninterrupted artillery fire from all calibres. Fort de Cognelée surrendered and Fort de Marchovelette's magazine exploded when a 420 mm shell burst into its magazine. It was taken but like Loncin, never surrendered. It has been estimated that between them the forts of Namur received almost 27 tons of artillery ammunition of different calibres. The forts in northern France would later receive the same treatment.

On 23 August, the BEF fought its brilliant resistance at Mons, followed by a retreat. The British and French troops were in retreat in the south, the Belgian army to the north.

On 24 August, Fort de Malonne surrendered.

On 25 August, the last fort of Namur surrendered. The nine forts of Namur had held the Germans for three days and forced the enemy to expend a lot of artillery ammunition and take a number of losses, among them Prince Friedrich of Saxe-Meiningen, killed in action at Namur. Another aristocrat *Freiherr* (Baron) Manfred von Richthofen was serving in the cavalry and given reconnaissance tasks during the siege of Namur. He would later attain fame as the highest scoring ace of the war, dubbed the Red Baron because he had his Fokker Dr 1 painted that colour.

The 6th Belgian *Divison d'Armée* which like the 4th at Liège was tasked to occupy the intervals between the Namur forts ,was gradually pushed back and, cut off from the rest of the Belgian army it was withdrawn into France and taken by train to rejoin the bulk of the Belgian force at Antwerp via Rouen. The fighting of the French army in Belgium, along the upper course of the Meuse River and especially at Dinant, has been described earlier (section 2.2).

Belgium lost about 10,000 men between KIAs, WIAs, POWs and interned in the Netherlands. The City of Liège was given the Légion d'Honneur by France for its brave resistance. The role this resistance, indeed that of the Belgian army as a whole in August 1914, played in the Battle of the Marne and the eventual collapse of the Schlieffen/Moltke plan has been the object of endless discussion. It is probably fair to say it made the Germans lose precious time they could ill afford, but it would be exaggerated to conclude it was the determining factor.

It should also be noted that if the French army and the BEF, instead of fighting rearguard battles at Mons, at Charleroi and along the banks of the upper Meuse, had boldly entered Belgium and linked with the Belgians, which is what had been hoped, history might have been quite different. An encounter in central Belgium might have disrupted, indeed broken the German plans earlier, and avoided the industrial heartlands of Belgium as well as those of northern France, with its coalmines, factories and skilled labour, falling into German hands for the rest of the war.

It is also to be regretted that the French GHQ, which received accurate information from its Belgian counterparts on the real strength of the German troops advancing through Belgium, chose to disbelieve it, underestimating the numbers by half and thus not committing enough troops to its northern border while keeping too many reserves on the Alsace Lorraine front.

In 1970, the author, a young Chasseurs Ardennais officer in the Belgian army, serving in Germany under NATO command, was sent by his CO to fetch some documents with his jeep at a German barracks in Rhineland. Upon arrival, he read the name of the barracks: 'Lüttich Kaserne', the Liège barracks. The modern Bundeswehr was thus commemorating a German victory on one of its NATO allies, the taking of Liège in August 1914. Fair enough I thought, they won and several Belgian regimental colours have German defeats like Haelen written on them…

2.4 Haelen: The Battle of the Silver Helmets

Few non-Belgians will have heard of the Battle of Haelen (Halen in today's spelling) fought on 12 August 1914 and also known as the Battle of the Silver Helmets. It is an interesting battle though, from the military history point of view as much as for the evolution of tactics, i.e. the demise of the Napoleonic massed cavalry charge, utterly defeated by concealed breech-loading rifle fire and the fledgling machine gun. This happened before the BEF or the French defeated German cavalry with the same tactics, or Allied cavalry met the same fate a few days later. It was also the one battle in the Great War where the Belgian army, fighting completely on its own, soundly defeated a determined and important German attack without any help or artillery or logistic support from the British or French.

The context was as follows: the forts of Liège were still being besieged though the Germans had managed to cross the Meuse and flooded, following the Schlieffen plan, the slightly hilly plain between Liège and Antwerp, on their way to France. The Belgian army held a line roughly on the Gete River, which flows northwards and thus covered the approaches to Antwerp, at the time still considered as the future national redoubt by King Albert I, in command of the Belgian army. The Belgian Cavalry Division held the region of Hasselt and its surrounding farming villages, including the hitherto peaceful small town of Haelen. General von der Marwitz, commanding one of the two German cavalry corps, had crossed into Belgium at Gemmenich, at 0802 hrs on 2 August and by 1300 hrs was at the Visé bridge over the Meuse River. This he did not cross until 9 August and was ordered to reconnoitre 'in force' on 12 August the area between Liège, Brussels and Antwerp. His scouts reported the bridge at Haelen on the Gete was held by the Belgians and he sent more troops into the area to better identify the positions of the Belgian army. The area is fertile and there are lots of fruit trees in the region, luckily for the horses because, by an astonishing oversight of logistics, very little fodder was available for them, or food for the men. Water was also a problem in the August heat.

Surprisingly too, they failed to cut the prominent telephone lines, so the local burgomasters, train station masters and post office employees kept the Belgian HQ at Louvain precisely informed of their whereabouts.

The battlefield is about as extended as the one at Waterloo. Its highlight is the Ijzerwinning Farm, which was the focal point of repeated massed charges by the flower of the German cavalry, officered mostly by aristocrats as was also the case in the Belgian and other nations' cavalry corps, the infantry being considered less fashionable at the time. Among the German officers who lost their lives that day was a *Leutnant* von Blücher, and *Rittmeister* (Cavalry Captain) Von Kalmain, while the CO of *Dragonder Regiment 18* was Major Digeon de Monteton, no doubt a descendant of French Huguenots. *Rittmeister* von Bodecker was made a POW by the Belgians.

From both sides of the Farm, the Belgian defensive line extended roughly north to south. That line was effectively held by the Belgians during the whole day. De Witte also had a regiment of infantry, the *Carabiniers Cyclistes* and some horse artillery under his command.

General De Witte had the elite cavalry regiments of Lancers and Guides dismount and take positions with their carbines and their (few) machine guns behind ditches, hedges and wire fences. This went against his instincts as a cavalryman: horsemen fought on horseback, but he was apparently prevailed upon by a young officer later to become a general and advisor to King Leopold III: Captain Van Overstraeten.

By 0800 hrs, the Belgian cavalry dismounted and took up their defensive positions. The Stroobants family[12] who farmed at Ijzerwinning and had distributed large slices of bread to the Belgian soldiers had to be persuaded to leave because of the danger. A pregnant woman did so sobbing. At another farm, the farmer fled, not wanting to be taken for a *franc-tireur*, forgetting his dog. But 'Bieke' stayed with the troops, who looked after her and she survived the battle.

Cinquième Lanciers had one squadron detailed to protect the Belgian horse artillery in the rear, whilst another squadron stayed mounted and the rest was dispersed by platoons along the defensive line. One squadron of *Quatrième Lanciers* set up a road block with felled trees and carts on the road from Haelen. *Premier* and *Deuxième Guides* were similarly on the line, deployed with *Cyclistes* in support. Clever use was made of ditches and barbed wire fences. A small brewery was turned into a redoubt. All Belgian soldiers took up prone or kneeling firing positions or climbed on the sloped roofs of buildings from where they had a good field of fire.

Battle was joined at 1300 hrs when Belgian artillery opened fire, bringing about the first of the German cavalry charges.

Belgian horse artillery, deployed on a hill behind Ijzerwinning Farm and their German equivalent at the outskirts of Haelen village, to the east, gave covering fire and exchanged counterbattery fire throughout the day.

It must have been an overwhelming sight, the like of which we will never see again: the Belgian *Guides* wore amaranth red pantaloons with yellow side stripes, green tunics and black busbies. The Belgian *Cinquième Lanciers* (Fifth Lancers) Regiment had just been ceremonially presented with their colours a few days earlier, Belgian General De Witte addressing them as follows: 'Gentlemen, tomorrow we will fight. I hope we win. If not, I hope I can show you how a Belgian general dies. Long live the King!'

The *Lanciers* had blue grey trousers and dark blue tunics. They wore a leather tchapska helmet with a small square plate similar to that of the

German *Uhlanen*. The Belgian *Carabiniers Cyclistes* had bikes that could be folded up and carried if necessary. They were clad in dark grey-green and to this day the Belgian army units of that name wear a small bicycle wheel as a badge cap and *Haelen* is a battle honour on their regimental flags.

The Line Infantry, notably *4ème de Ligne* Regiment, who arrived in the afternoon wore dark blue uniform with red facings whilst Belgian artillery also wore blue uniforms.

The German Cavalry was even more impressively clad. All of old Prussia's military history was written on their colours or even helmets, like *Hohenfriedberg*, a battle won in 1745 by King Frederick II against the Austrians and Saxons, written on the helmets of the *Cuirassiers*, who rode such splendid horses. In fact, the doctrine of cavalry use dated back to regulations written by General Seydlitz, who commanded Frederick II's cavalry.

German *Jägers* (light infantry) skirmishers took the seventeenth-century stone bridge on the Gete, which had been incompletely blown up. Next the German *Dragonders*, *Uhlanen*, *Königin* (Queen of Prussia) *Cuirassiers*, *Totenkopf* (death's head) *Hussaren*,[13] their regimental standards flying, all splendidly adorned in nineteenth-century style uniforms, tight white cavalry trousers and polished black riding thighboots and shining *Picklehaube* helmets surmounted by a point (supposed to deflect sabre strikes), some even with shining breastplates, launched charge after charge beyond the bridge into a funnel-shaped field towards Ijzerwinning Farm, only to be met by the murderous musketry fire of the Belgians. Both sides took significant losses in men and, on the German side, horses. Belgian Captain Panquin, peering out of a roof window at the farm, was shot through the head.

The fighting between the infantry was also bitter. The two *Jäger* Battalions tried repeatedly to outflank the Belgian *Cyclistes* who were forward of the defensive line and some of those found themselves isolated in small groups in the open, firing away in all directions, some with pistols in Custer's Last Stand fashion.

Meanwhile, Belgian GHQ had ordered the 4th Infantry Brigade, stationed about 20 kilometres away, to reinforce De Witte and sent a motorcycle messenger to inform him. Dispersed over several villages, the units first had to be warned and given their orders and itineraries. Starting at about 1030 hrs, sweating and straining under the August sun in their thick woollen uniforms, they force marched to Haelen. Most men were called up reservists who had had little recent training in long hikes. The march was exhausting, shoes were too tight and water lacking. Some picked up unripe fruit in the orchards. The dogs pulling the wheel-mounted machine guns became exhausted and had to be left with local farmers, the soldiers pulling the weapons themselves.

Among them was Lieutenant V., who probably was to regret the heat of that day when spending the next four winters in the wet, cold misery of the trenches.

As the infantry battalions arrived in the early afternoon, they were fed piecemeal to the battlefield by De Witte, led by cavalry officers to where the German pressure was the heaviest. Thus, they were gradually spread out along the defensive line the cavalry men had held and started intense sniping at the charging Germans, who realized their enemy, far from slackening off, was being reinforced.

Gallantly but foolishly, several Belgian officers were killed by German fire because they remained standing behind their men who were lying down, instead of doing the same. The artillery of the 4th Brigade detached itself from the tail of the column and reinforced, amidst great clouds of dust, the Belgian artillery already in place.

The *Leibhusaren, Uhlanen, Cuirassiers, Dragonders* cavalry regiments, supported by the *Jägers* light infantry continued to make charge after charge against the Belgian defensive line, who forced the Germans into an ever reduced area where they could not deploy and had little recourse, with lances, swords or even carbines against their enemies firing from concealed positions – especially against such conspicuous and easy targets as horsemen in the open, wearing very visible uniforms. A hollow path between steep banks, hidden from view from the direction in which the horsemen attacked made several of them tumble in on top of each other and American diplomats visiting the battlefield a few days later saw the traces in the earth of the German horses' hooves as they made desperate attempts to climb back again on the other side. There was mayhem, turmoil, and the German cavalry, losing sight of each other whilst taking fire from positions they could not clearly see in the dry summer dust, were dazed and confused. Dead or wounded men and horses, lances and other weapons lay strewn about and riderless horses galloped around aimlessly. The noise must have been deafening. In some cases where the Germans had ridden beyond their positions the Belgians were even firing at their enemies from behind.

At 1430 hrs, Ijzerwinning farm was finally evacuated and was burned down by German artillery fire. Belgian infantry reinforcements had however started arriving in force by then and on the defensive line they relieved the exhausted Belgian dismounted cavalry and cyclists, who were close to collapse. This prevented the Germans from exploiting their advantage and breaking through. Colonel Rademakers, CO of 1st Battalion, *4ème de Ligne Regiment*, who had been the first of his unit to open fire on the enemy when arriving at the scene, had his horse shot from under him and was himself shot through both cheeks. A brilliant and popular officer, he survived but was later killed at Dixmude. Captains Van Vlierberghe and Wacquez were killed at his side by machine-gun fire.

At 1630 hrs, after the eighth charge and realizing he was taking losses with little gain, von der Marwitz called it a day and ordered a retreat to Hasselt, conceding an undisputable tactical victory to the Belgians, even if strategically Haelen did not alter the outcome of the campaign. But four elite German cavalry regiments of what was considered the best army of the world had been comprehensively beaten in a few hours by an inferior force using a good defensive position. The real significance of Haelen was not a Belgian strategic victory but the end of massed cavalry charges against concealed repeating fire. The Belgian army did not stop the German advance in Belgium, but showed at Haelen that defensive fire could stop a determined attack, especially a mounted assault.

For comparison, the British Light Brigade which famously charged during the Crimean War in comparable circumstances numbered about 600 men, whilst at Haelen the German cavalry charge was estimated to have been about 2,800.

In his famous book *Achtung Panzer!*, General Guderian dwells at length over Halen. The titles of the relevant chapters are, 'Lances against Machine Guns' and 'How did Positional Warfare Come about?'

According to Guderian, German losses were 24 officers and 468 other ranks killed in action, plus 843 horses, while 200 prisoners of war were taken by the Belgians. *Uhlanen Regiment* no. 9 was reduced to 28 unharmed troopers. About 400 horses were killed outright, the rest had to be put down. Hundreds of dead German horses were hastily buried by local farmers. Some Belgian sources put German losses at double that figure but it must have been (understandably) inflated by propaganda.

The Belgians lost 160 killed and 300 wounded in action. Belgian priests in robes with Red Cross armbands acted as stretcher bearers. There was good cooperation between the German and Belgian medical staff. One wounded German, *Unteroffizier* Schönberg of *Leibhusaren Regiment Nummer 1* was so well looked after by the nuns at Herk de Stad village that he later wrote to them from Russia, thanking them for saving his life.

One Arthur Brühe lost his horse in the charge. He was to come back in 1968 to lay a wreath, '*To the heroes on both sides*'. Like many he trooped back on foot to Haelen village, unit cohesion having been lost.

The hundreds of German horses lost at Haelen were difficult to replace and the battle significantly reduced the cavalry element of von Kluck's army – in effect its reconnaissance capability – just one week after the start of the war and during the coming weeks of Mons, Charleroi, the Marne and the Race to the Sea. The weakening of the German cavalry created a significant obstacle to the discovery of the BEF and to the German pursuit by cavalry of the Allies after the battles of Mons and Charleroi.

In spite of his relative failure, von der Marwitz was given important commands later in the war, whereas his victorious opponent General De Witte was made Baron De Witte de Haelen by King Albert, but was not given any noteworthy responsibilities for the rest of the war. Some criticism was levelled at him for not having sent his cavalry in pursuit of the retreating Germans, but it is doubtful this would have been possible.

Young diplomats at the US embassy in Brussels realized history was happening a few tens of miles from where they were sitting and set off for Haelen in their motorcar, adorned with prominent stars and stripes. They bought some captured German cavalry lances at Louvain from Belgian soldiers and could hear the guns of the Liège forts. They also heard and reported persistent rumours of innocent Belgian civilians being shot or otherwise abused by German troops, as early as August 12.[14]

During their later occupation of Belgium, the Germans erected a huge cross close to Ijzerwinning Farm, as a monument to their dead where the cavalry charges took place. It was inaugurated one year after the battle, German Governor General von Bissing attending. It is still standing, though the bodies previously buried there were moved in 1956 to other German military cemeteries in Belgium at Vladsloo and Langemark.

A local parish priest seeing all the shiny German metal helmets lying about among the dead men and horses, wrote a poem about the Silver Helmets, in a clear allusion to another battle in 1302, when the proud Flemish militias of Bruges, Ghent and Ypres had defeated a French cavalry army also charging headlong and had found many of the French knights' golden spurs on the battlefield after their victory.

As early as 1909 von Schlieffen had predicted that cavalry would be ousted from the battlefield by modern weaponry, yet in 1914 the German, French and British alike overestimated the effectiveness of operational reconnaissance by large bodies of cavalry while neglecting the possibilities offered by aviation, some types of plane already having a range of 400 km and capable of effective reconnaissance at infinitely less cost.

The British army had already abandoned the red tunic as combat gear as a result of the Boer war and adopted khaki. The French, German and Belgian army realized in the following months that colourful uniforms dating from the Napoleonic wars, meant to impress the enemy and enhance esprit de corps, had become a liability now that the rifle had replaced the musket and had become a precise weapon at greater distances. As a result, the colours of uniforms went dull, whilst artillery and especially the machine gun made land warfare go underground, into trenches and even tunnels. All this could have been noticed at Haelen and was by some, like future generals Van Overstraeten and Guderian.[15]

2.5 Antwerp

On August 18 a bitter battle took place at Sint-Margriet-Houtem close to Tienen (Tirlemont) between two brigades of the Belgian First Army Division and various German elements. including elite cavalry like *Uhlanen*. Belgian *2ème Régiment de Ligne* was half destroyed, losing 23 officers out of 40, and 1250 other ranks out of 2,100 between KIAs, WIAs, MIAs or POWs. Sint Margriet-Houtem was costly for the Belgians, forced to retreat under superior artillery fire and with aerial reconnaissance by Taube planes but it won their army precious time to retreat to Antwerp in good order. Future General Piron, who was to command the Belgian Brigade from Normandy to Germany in the Second World War, was a platoon commander in that regiment and saw his first action that day.

On the whole the Belgian infantry proved very effective in defensive combat and inflicted heavy losses while also taking heavy casualties. Several German generals were to praise the knack the Belgians had to retreat just in time not to be caught. The Germans were better at using machine guns, a new weapon at the time and with which they were provided in larger numbers.

The war had now reached central Belgium and Brussels was occupied on 20 August. On 14 September at Pont Brûlé/Verbrande Brug (Burned Bridge), *Caporal* Trésignies became a hero by volunteering to swim across the Brussels-Antwerp canal to close a bridge that had been abandoned open to the enemy, the closing mechanism being on the enemy side, which could thus open it at its discretion. Trésignies did not come back but fulfilled his mission, which he knew to be perilous in the extreme. He was mentioned in the Army Order of the Day.

As planned and to avoid being completely surrounded, a general retreat of the Belgian army and concentration on the Antwerp redoubt was now ordered and executed. The government and foreign diplomatic corps also retired to the second Belgian city (and its largest port), though some diplomats remained in Brussels.

The Belgian army was now reduced to about 100,000 men, between the field army that marched in exhausted and in need of reorganization, and the Antwerp garrison. Two German corps were ordered to lay siege to Antwerp, which meant that much less force available to be used against the British and French. The heavy siege guns were brought up and started to pound the Antwerp ring of forts. Some areas around Antwerp were deliberately inundated by the Belgians as a defensive tactic.

Antwerp was in 1914 one of the largest fortified cities in the world, with two concentric rings of forts and redoubts forming a circumference of about 95 km. The high water table had prevented the building of forts as strong as those of Liège and Namur, but the advantage was that moats could be dug and large areas flooded. For lack of funds only two large forts had been completed, Walem and Lier. Forts and redoubts had 150 mm, 120 mm, and 75 mm guns in steel turrets, the buildings being mostly brick. The Belgian army and garrison were now reinforced by 10,000 British troops from the Royal Naval Brigade and Royal Marines, led by no less than the 39-year-old First Lord of the Admiralty Winston Churchill. They had come overland from the Belgian North Sea ports, were mostly raw recruits and under-equipped. The Dutch government had stated that it would not allow warships of any country to sail up the Scheldt River, both banks of which it controlled. This made plans by the Royal Navy to reinforce the Antwerp redoubt with a large contingent unworkable.

The French let it be known they would have much preferred to see the Belgian army retreat to the south and link up with them, rather than hole itself up in Antwerp, with its back to the (neutral) Dutch border. The Germans sent peace feelers via the neutral embassies in Brussels. Three options were thus open to King Albert: first, a general surrender, Belgium having, according at least to the Germans done everything to save its honour and fulfil the obligations linked to its neutrality; second, to allow the Belgian army to be interned in the neutral Netherlands; or the last option, to break out west, across the Scheldt River into Flanders, there to link with French and British armies who were fighting the Germans at the Belgian/French border.

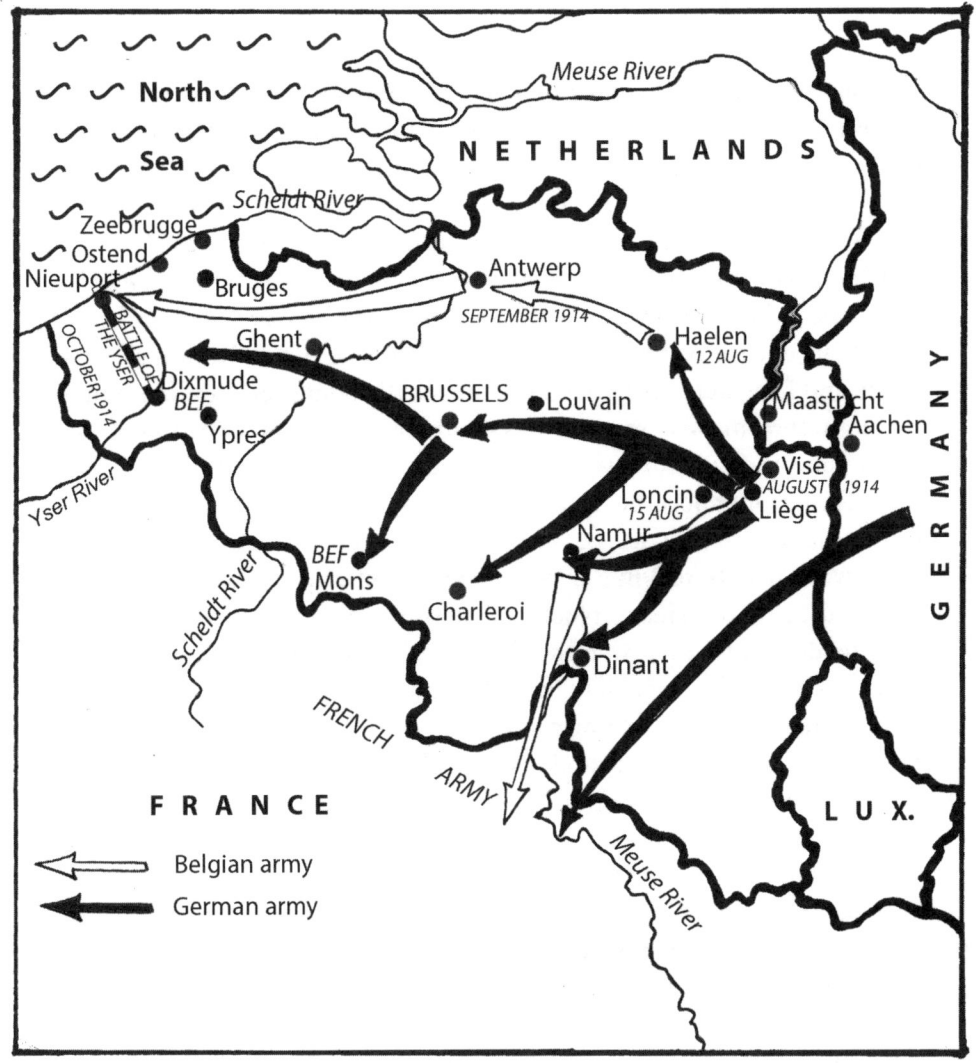

1. The campaign of 1914

In the meantime, two sorties out of Antwerp by the Belgians against the flanks of the German army on its way to France were executed: one on 24 August towards Mechelen (Malines) in the direction of Brussels and another set to coincide with the Battle of the Marne on 9 September towards Louvain, where atrocities against the local civilian population resulted.

Robert V. took part in these sorties with his unit.

King Albert is known to have hesitated, to have been deeply depressed during the siege of Antwerp. Seeing some of his close relatives like Crown Prince Rupprecht of Bavaria, married to his wife's sister, fighting his troops must not have helped. Or his first cousin Stéphanie, the widow of the late Crown Prince Rudolf of Austria-Hungary, who famously committed suicide at Mayerling, blaming him in a letter for not having allowed the German troops to cross Belgium unmolested. He never forgave the daughter of his uncle Leopold II and was never to have any contact with her again.[16]

After German zeppelins bombed Antwerp, King Albert sent his children to England, where they stayed with Lord Curzon who was a family friend.

By that time the Antwerp forts like Sint Katlijne Waver, Koningshooikt, Walem and Lier were receiving a 420 mm shell about every seven minutes. The noise they made coming in was compared to that of an express train. One by one the gun turrets of the Belgian forts were demolished; their guns of inferior calibre being useless anyway as the enemy infantry kept at a safe distance and let the heavy artillery do the job. Metres-thick vaults were penetrated like paper. Heavy steel cupolas were disjointed or hurled far away. Heavy blocks of masonry became loose and fell on the defenders. The air inside the forts became poisonous and everyone's nerves on edge. As at Loncin, catastrophic explosions took place when heavy shells penetrated fort magazines. Some of the survivors testified on television in the 1960s that under the continuous shellfire they felt their forts were moving like a ship in a storm. With Taube planes spotting and 'walking' the shells all over it from cupola to redoubt, Fort Sint Katelijne Waver sustained five hundred 420 mm and 305 mm shells and was reduced to rubble.[17] At Walem, sappers were heard digging to place a demolition mine. The Belgians exploded a countermine that destroyed the enemy tunnel and probably the diggers as well.

Albert at this point saw clearly that despite several assurances from the British and French that they would send his army reinforcements, none were in fact coming, apart from a very small number of inadequately trained and equipped Royal Marines. German pressure was mounting and by choosing to lock himself in the Antwerp national redoubt, he ran the risk of seeing his army crushed by the Germans, with little other choice than to allow it to be interned in the neutral and nearby Netherlands. After several days of agonizing, during which advice from Prime Minister de Broqueville and encouragement from Elisabeth seem to have aided his decision, the third option was chosen: a break-out across the river Scheldt, which at Antwerp could be crossed by using a tunnel and joining the French and British troops at the North Sea coast. Time was of the essence, since the Germans were already advancing towards the sea and the risk of being cut off in that direction mounted every passing hour. Apart from the troops, there were the wounded, plus ammunition and supplies, raw untrained recruits and so on, all needing to be evacuated.

Evacuation from Antwerp across the Scheldt was thus decided. The government, senior civil servants, foreign diplomatic corps, gold reserves and indispensable documents were sent by two Belgian merchant vessels down the Scheldt to Le Havre in France. The field army, partly using a pontoon bridge, partly the tunnel under the river, crossed into Flanders on the other bank and in three columns, covered by a cavalry screen to ward off German reconnaissance parties, started the long trek to the North Sea coast first to Ostend then to Nieuport, close to the French border. About halfway, at Melle outside Ghent a French naval contingent helped slow the pursuing Germans, the first time Belgians and French soldiers fought side by side under Belgian command.

Antwerp was told to hold out as long as possible, then surrender, which it did on 10 October. The Antwerp garrison however walked the few kilometres to the Dutch border to be interned, which was preferable to becoming prisoners of the invaders. The Germans accorded the garrison of the Walem Fort the honours of war when they filed out of their demolished fort, exhausted and several of them wounded.

The Antwerp Redoubt could have worked better and kept more German troops for longer from going to France, but two factors prevented that. First, the fact the Dutch who held both banks of the Scheldt River denied the Allies' naval reinforcements access to land troops – not unnaturally, as the Germans would have accused them of violating their neutrality by doing so. Second, because being forced to come overland the Allied troops were too slow to stop the Germans in Mons and Charleroi. Winston Churchill was later to write: 'The Belgian Army was left too long without succour. One week earlier the result would have been certain. A little later not even 200,000 men could have held it.' However, by lasting as long as it did, the *Position Fortifiée d'Anvers* (Antwerp) won the Allies precious time and probably saved Dunkirk, Calais and Boulogne.

2.6 The Battle of the Yser River

After the retreat from Antwerp and while his army was moving to the Belgian coast, King Albert was studying his options. Consistent with his attitude of not being an ally of France, at least not *de jure*, since no treaty to that effect bound the two nations, but a *de facto* ally since attacked as a neutral by an enemy of France, he wanted to avoid retiring his army into the territory of the

Republic, fearing with good reason it would make Belgium a vassal state of France, his army under total French control. More than a few times during the war the French and British would try to disperse the Belgian units among their own troops, an arrangement which Albert rejected (as the American General Pershing also adamantly refused to do later), as the Belgian army would have lost all cohesion and the King, its commander-in-chief, every control over it. If, however, the German military pressure on his by then hard pressed and depleted army became too strong, he would be forced to cross the frontier and preliminary feelers in writing to the French were made to that effect.

While the fighting retreat was on, bolstered by French and British troops and even an armoured train,[18] meetings were taking place with French General Pau[19] and British General Rawlinson in Ostend, on 10 October. On 12 October, the Germans took Ghent after a spirited rearguard action by the Belgian cavalry regiments of *Lanciers* and *Guides*, one company of which lost three officers and 50 per cent of its men. Reconnaissance parties were sent to the Yser and Yperlee rivers to see if a last defensive line in Belgium could be set up behind these obstacles. As fighting had never been envisaged in these parts, detailed maps were lacking. A meeting between the King and General Foch, put in charge by Generalissimo Joffre of a new French army in the north, seem to have clinched the decision to make a last stand on the Yser River. Rawlinson and his corps rejoined the BEF who took over Ypres and its surroundings, leaving the Belgians no choice but to fill the gap he left by doing so, and Foch who promised the exhausted 48,000 Belgians French reinforcements, this time kept his word.

On 13 October, King Albert also made a very stern proclamation to his troops: 'Soldiers, look to the future with confidence, fight with courage. In the positions where I will place you, look only forward and consider as a traitor to the Fatherland he who uses the word retreat without the formal order being given.' Staff officers were told to join the frontline.

The fact that the King stayed with the troops also did a lot to keep up the mens' spirits. The King (and Queen), up to a point were sharing the danger with them, not retiring to luxurious retreats in France and leaving them only with the generals to lead them.

There was little time for rest and reorganization, but ranks were filled with volunteers, while rankers who had shown leadership were made NCOs and new officers were assigned to companies that had lost their commanders.

In October 1914, Captain Robert V. was made CO of 1st Company, III Battalion, 4ème de Ligne Regiment, with which he would spend the rest of the war. It was said to have performed heroically at a bitter fight in Duffel and later at Schoorbakke, Pervyse (Pervijze) and Steenstraete (Steenstraat).

King Albert ordered his army, which had been fighting for two months by now, to deploy behind the Yser from Nieuport to Dixmude, this latter being under command of the French Admiral Ronarc'h with his 6,000 *Fusiliers Marins* (Marines), with 5,000 Belgian troops and artillery also under his orders. The six divisions of the Belgian army were deployed from north (Nieuport) to south (Dixmude): the 2nd Belgian Army Division, then the First, the 4th, the 5th and the 6th Divisions in the first line and the Cavalry, 3rd and 5th Army Divisions behind in reserve. This represented about 40 km of front. Originally each Division in line had bridgeheads on the east bank, but by 18 October these had been progressively pushed back by the Germans, the bridges over the Yser then being blown. Thus, the Bamburg Farm, east of Nieuport and the village of Keiem north of Dixmude, were eventually lost.

The King asked for and got naval support, this leading to the creation of the Dover Patrol, which at this stage included 4 light cruisers, 24 Tribal-class destroyers, 13 submarines and 3 shallow-draft river monitors originally built for Brazil and particularly suited for supplying gunfire inshore, since the North Sea is strewn with sandbanks along the Belgian coast. French light naval units also joined. They could be seen firing at the German positions and concentrations on demand. This provided a welcome morale booster to the Belgians, since the Germans had nothing comparable to oppose them, their heavy artillery being unable to deploy in the humid soil of the polders.

The Belgian Civic Guard was merged with the regular army.[20]

It should be noted that the Battle of the Yser was contemporary with, indeed part of, what British historians have called 'First Ypres' – that is the battle between British and French troops and the German army at the time of the latter's repeated efforts to break through to the Channel ports.

Under command of General Grossetti, the French 42nd Division arrived to reinforce the hard-pressed Belgians, later joined by two other French divisions, including Senegalese soldiers. The last stand on the Belgian front was supposed to hold for a few days; in fact, it held for a whole month. By 12/13 October it became clear the Germans were seeking to occupy the rest of Belgium and take the Channel ports, vital for the communications, reinforcements and supplies coming from Britain to France, the evacuation of wounded and so on. Fighting was bitter, often hand-to-hand. Just east of Nieuport, the large Bamburg farm was taken by the Germans and reinforced with a ring of machine guns. It was retaken at great cost by the Belgians, then lost again to the Germans, who penetrated as far as Ramskapelle on the west bank of the Yser River. It was vital to dislodge them from Ramskapelle,[21] because otherwise the whole Belgian line could be rolled up from the side and because losing it meant losing control of the sluices at De Ganzenpoot (literally, the 'goose's foot') locks at Nieuport, as will be explained later.

German assaults followed one after another, combat following combat, usually ending in bitter hand-to-hand fighting, bayonets being widely used. During night attacks the Germans sometimes only used cold steel. The dead-tired Belgians had to be propped up by their no less tired officers. They usually faced fresh troops recently arrived from Germany, sometimes students, whose promising lives were sacrificed. Attacks were followed by counter-attacks like ebb and flow. At night, only the orange flames of burning villages and isolated farmsteads illuminated the battlefield, reflected in the rising water. At dawn, piles of corpses could be discerned where there had been none the evening before. Wounded men from both sides sometimes drowned in shallow water, unable to save themselves. It was truly a vision from hell, but the line held and the way to Dunkirk and Calais was blocked. Belgian medium artillery now used French supplied shells, but these were not quite right and wore out the Belgian guns prematurely.

The city of Dixmude,[22] which lies mainly on the eastern bank of the little river Yser was burned to the ground, French marines and Belgian infantry being gradually pushed over. Admiral Ronarc'h found a chair in a ruin and, completely exposed in open ground close to where the bridge had stood before being blown, sat calmly surveying the situation. Using a 'dirty trick' not for the first or the last time,[23] the Germans pushed French POWs in front of them as human shields. In one instance the French just made a dash for it and swam over the river to safety. On another occasion, the French *Zouaves* were reported to have yelled at their compatriots to fire anyway, 'Tirez! Ce sont les Boches!'

On 21 October, the Germans attacked Dixmude by night but had to retreat, beaten, at dawn. One isolated platoon of sixty men with an officer took refuge in a café and surrendered to a corporal and two Belgian soldiers.

Major Count Henri d'Oultremont was holding the line on the Yser close to the Tervaete bridge with the 2nd Battalion of the 1st *Grenadiers* Regiment. A practising Catholic, he got into a quarrel with another officer, a well-known freemason.[24] At some point, the latter berated d'Oultremont and asked him if he was afraid, implying cowardice on the major's part. Reacting to the insult d'Oultremont led an attack, needlessly exposing himself to enemy fire and was promptly killed. A monument was erected on the Yser bank to his memory.

As can be seen on Map 2 (page 65), the 20 m wide Yser River is curved between Dixmude and the North Sea, and at the village of Tervaete there is a loop. All who know a bit about land tactics know you are at a disadvantage if you have to defend a loop, because you can be fired upon (and attacked) from three out of four directions, the more so in the flat valley of the Yser. Not unnaturally it was at Tervaete the Germans mounted their heaviest attacks and eventually overwhelmed the exhausted Belgians. A crisis developed, and here enters an old idea that several people were credited with having revived. It is a well-known fact victory has many fathers and defeat is always an orphan.[25] Flooding the terrain from which your enemy is attacking you is an old idea. It was used extensively by the Dutch when they were fighting for their independence against the Spanish in the sixteenth century and again around Nieuport, when the French invaded the Austrian Netherlands, as Belgium was known in 1793. Flooding the Yser valley is easier than any other parts of Belgium, because in fact all the land about 30 to 50 km inland from the current coastline is below sea level, at least at high tide. Over the centuries since the Middle Ages the land has been kept dry and tilled by the technique called poldering and the lands thus claimed are naturally called polders in Belgium, as they are in the Netherlands. A series of parallel ditches are dug, comb-like and these collect the groundwater (and rain), running into larger moats, themselves linked to rivers or canals that flow into the sea when the tide is going out. Of course, when the tide rises again floodgates have to keep the seawater out, otherwise the whole process would be pointless. After a few years of having only received (sweet) rainwater and burning a special weed that removes the salt, the land can be planted, or cows put out to graze.[26]

Nieuport was and still is an important point on the Belgian coast for controlling the water level beyond the coastline. Five canals or rivers, including the Yser, converge to a single canal and are controlled by a series of locks which, from a bird's eye view, look like a hand and its five fingers, or – and this is the name that stuck – the webbed foot of a goose. As mentioned above several people had the idea of reversing the flow to allow seawater in, so as to stop the German advance. The British, reconnoitring the area on horseback before the battle, inquired about it. Henry Geeraert,[27] head of the local polder administration was interviewed at length by the Belgian army engineers, especially Captain Thys, the son of a famous General.[28] It seems to have been Karel Cogge, who knew the region like the back of his hand, who gave the Belgian engineers the definitive help. After the fall of Lombartzijde, just east of Nieuport, the Germans were now a few tens of metres from the sluices. Clad in an ill-fitting Belgian uniform so as not to be shot as a *franc-tireur*, the former boatman went several nights running with the Belgian army engineers into no-man's-land, at hours determined by the tidal ebb and flow, to the place where he had hidden the heavy cranks in the undergrowth. He then opened or closed the sluices in such a way as to allow the seawater in and to keep it in when the tide fell again. Eventually the water level reached shoulder depth, making German attacks impossible. However, another problem had to be solved: when the line on the Yser River itself became untenable because the Germans had crossed it, Belgian GHQ decided to retire to a line a few kilometres behind, the chosen obstacle being the embankment of the Nieuport–Dixmude railway. This stretches in a straight line for only about 20 kilometres like the string of a bow, the bow being the Yser. However, there existed twenty-four bridges, tunnels and culverts under the embankment making small channels and water-draining ditches and these all had to be blocked by the Belgian engineers to prevent the 'Belgian' side of the new defensive line getting flooded as well. Surprisingly, the Germans do not seem to have realized what caused the flood, thinking perhaps it was their own shelling that had damaged the drainage system. If they had realized, they would undoubtedly have concentrated their attacks on the goose's foot, to control it to their advantage. Later the region behind the Belgian lines was flooded as well, as a precaution, and water allowed to flow in from France in canals, to bolster the Yser inundations.

By 21 October the flood level was high enough to seriously hamper the German assaults.

On 22 October Robert V.'s Regiment, 4ème de Ligne was told to hold Schoorbakke village and this they did despite serious losses, until forced back over the river the next day, blowing up the bridge in retreat. The CO, Colonel Rademakers, who had been wounded at Haelen in the cheek, was now shot through the knee. (He was killed in February 1915.) The Regiment defended Schoorbakke village, then counter-attacked in the Tervaete loop, with 2ème Carabiniers and 1er Grenadiers. With bugles sounding, a large bayonet charge was mounted, officers with swords unsheathed, the Belgians sometimes advancing with water up to their belts. The Bruges Regiment, 4ème de Ligne got to the German line and hand-to-hand fighting began.

By 24 October, a day of confusion, the retreat of the Belgians to the railway embankment was in full swing, the new line extending in a straight line from Nieuport to the *Boyau de la Mort* ('Trench of Death') a trench

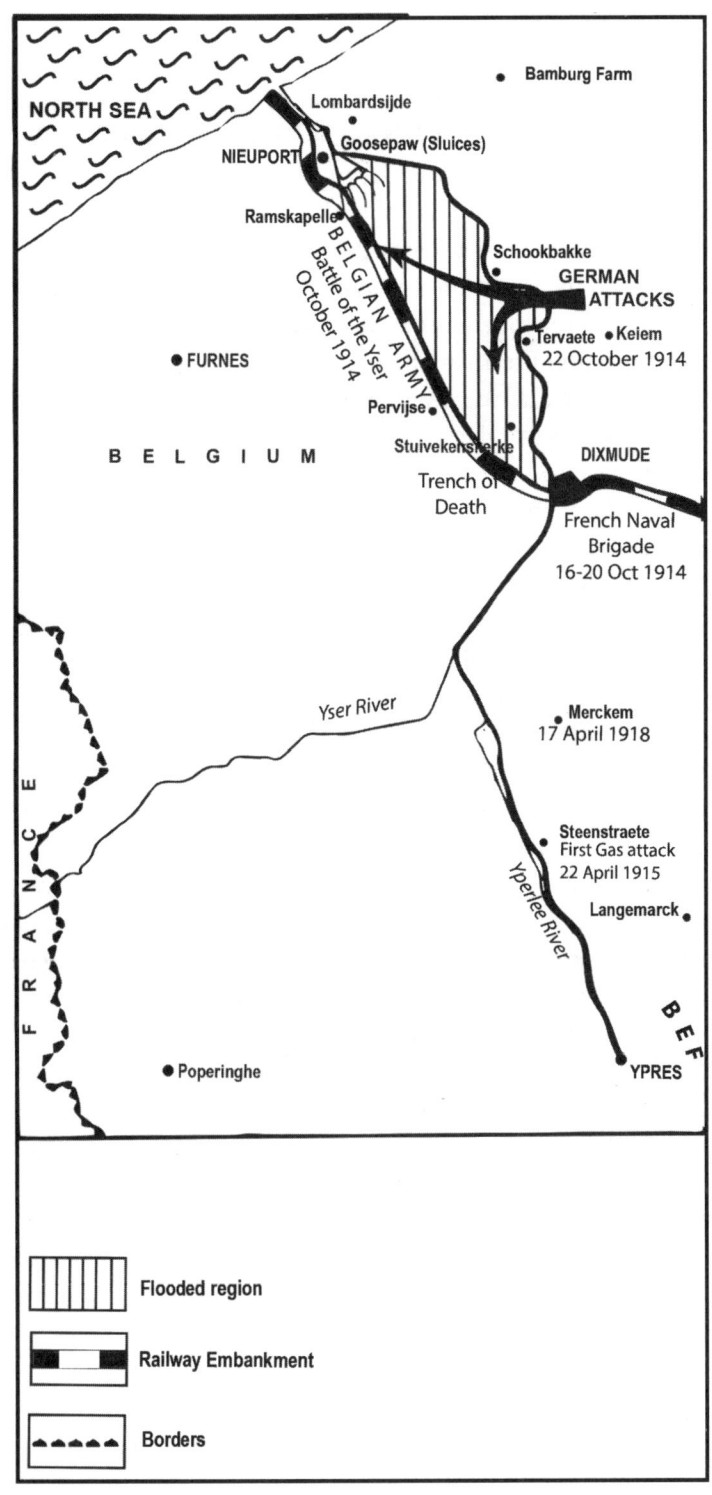

2. The Battle of the Yser

system on the bank of the Yser that has been preserved and can be visited today. It is situated just north of Dixmude.[29] It there rejoined the Yser River and the line continued to the boundary with the French army and the BEF. The railway embankment also had the advantage of being about half as long as the Yser River, making it easier to defend.

On 26 October the situation was almost desperate, but the Belgian army was told to hold on for four more days until the flooding took full effect.

By 30 October the Germans had reached the railway embankment, but their attacks petered out and by then the Belgians were firmly established on their new line. Several attacks were beaten back by the *Grenadiers, Carabiniers, 3ème, 5ème, 9ème, 10ème, 12ème, 13ème de Ligne* Regiments, in fact by almost the whole Belgian army, each Regiment eventually rotated to the front. Several monuments to their sacrifice are to be seen along the banks of the Yser River and the railway embankment.[30]

The Germans renewed their attacks where possible on 31 October, but the flooding had its effect and gradually their efforts lost momentum. After a last desperate try by the elite Prussian Guard on 15 November, the Germans gave up and no further serious attempt to break through the Belgian lines towards the Channel ports was attempted. The Belgian army, with the help of the British and French had won the Battle of the Yser and helped save the Channel ports. It had lost however, almost one third (14,000 men) of its strength in KIAs, WIAs, MIAs and POWs. Some sources indicate 11,000 KIAs and MIAs and 8,000 WIAs, several of which would later, however, rejoin their unit. It was one of the two heaviest losses the Belgian army suffered in this war, the other occasion being the final offensive in 1918. Together, the two battles account for half the total Belgian losses for the war. It is difficult to assess how many men the Germans lost against the Belgians, since they were simultaneously fighting three armies, but it can reasonably be estimated to be of at least the same order if not more. It was also a moral victory. As after Haelen the Belgians had shown they could beat the Germans.

On 2 November President Poincaré came to visit and congratulate King Albert and two days later so did King George V, who made Albert a Knight of the Garter.[31]

3

Stabilization: Mud and Misery, Dogs and Rats, Flies, Lice and Ice

When it became clear the Germans had given up hope of breaking through the Belgian lines to reach the Channel ports, a period of relative calm set in on the Belgian front between the sea and Dixmude. Stabilization did not mean there was no fighting – in fact fighting in the form of limited attacks, counter-attacks and raids of all sorts, as well as a few pitched battles we will describe would continue until November 1918, but massive attacks no longer took place.

By early November the Belgian army had fought practically without interruption for three months and was exhausted. The numbers (117,000 at the beginning of the campaign, apart from the forts' garrisons) had been about halved by losses, but new recruits arriving from Belgium through the Netherlands or from third countries (allied or neutral) brought the strength back to about the same level. A minute number were of course recruited in the region behind the lines and among the refugees in France and Britain a few young men also reached military age. A thorough reorganization was made, regiments and companies reset, and new officers and NCOs appointed on merit. Instruction centres for new recruits were opened in France, as were schools for officers and NCOs. New Mauser-type rifles[1] were procured in Britain and artillery in France. In November 1915, complete new uniforms were adopted, the old, colourful Napoleonic style, different for every regiment and far too visible, being discarded. The French Hadrian-style helmet was now used, but the khaki colour favoured by the British was introduced for all regiments, with only the collar patches in colour (red for infantry, blue for artillery etc.), with a numeral indicating the regiment on the shoulder straps. Rank insignia (stars and bars on the collar patches for the officers and stripes on the sleeves for NCOs) were also simplified. All this was meant to be less visible in the mud of Flanders.

Indeed, through circumstances, the Belgians now found themselves in their homeland, but in by far the more inhospitable and unhealthy part of the Western Front. Damp and freezing cold in the winter, hot and humid in the summer, and at sea level it was impossible to dig trenches. So sandbag protection had to be built up higher than the water level, but this stuck out like a sore thumb and immediately attracted the attentions of enemy artillery. Ruins of destroyed farms were known to host enemy observers from both sides and were of course shelled as a matter of routine. Dead bodies could not be buried and had to be left to rot when they could not be removed because of enemy fire. Evidently it was practically impossible (or useless) to dig latrines. The whole place quickly became a stinking unhealthy mess of mud, where rats feeding on cadavers grew to the size of small cats and sickness was rampant. Food and drinking water, even when you were surrounded by water, had to be carried up at great pains and danger to the carriers detailed. A massive and successful typhus vaccination campaign was undertaken and deemed successful, but lice, fleas, flies and mosquitoes were constant companions. Not surprisingly there were cases of tuberculosis. Dogs were brought in to kill the rats and contests were held between units for the highest number of rat tails collected.

Many books written at the time[2] describe the unspeakable circumstances of living day and night in the mud for most of the year, and in ice for two or three months. Of course heavy clothing, socks and boots were procured, but still many cases of trench foot occurred. In the British and French armies at this period of the war the ratio of those killed by enemy action to those who died from illness was 6:1; in the Belgian army it was 2:1. Soldiers were of course rotated and only stayed from one to a maximum of four days in the front-line trenches until relieved by another unit, usually during the night, and then they would go for rest, reorganization and training some 20 kilometres behind the lines. At changeover time, leaving and incoming officers and NCOs would pass on relevant information on the enemy lines and dispositions, advanced posts, ammunition stocks, food rations, rat traps, dogs and so on. If government property was missing it was conveniently blamed on the enemy and papers signed without fuss, so the bureaucrats would be satisfied. A quick handshake and wishes of good luck and that was it.

Training when not in line was of course now very different from what it had been before the war. At the lines there was always work to do, especially for the engineers: observation posts, trenches, redoubts or dugouts built or rebuilt when they had been shot up, concrete poured on the bottom to try to keep them dry, telephone lines extended, new communication trenches dug when necessary and possible. Camouflage was developed to an art. Tree stumps were replaced during the night with a hollow replica containing a periscope. At some places trap holes were dug into which a falling assailant would impale himself on a spike. Sometimes elaborate dugouts complete with kitchen and sleeping quarters were dug or rather built with concrete and inventive characters would bring in a piano or a gramophone, set telephone wires to the outposts when there was a quiet period and so give the soldiers on watch in the outer holes some distraction from the boredom, stress and cold they were feeling. Others read or painted or transformed empty shell cases into umbrella holders or spent cartridges into lighters with elaborate engraving. When they took them during raids, the Belgians noticed the hard-working Germans had built quite comfortable shelters for themselves.

In this dismal world there were brighter moments: at Christmas 1914 on the Belgian front as at the British front, firing stopped on both sides, Christmas carols were sung and oranges, cigarettes, loaves of thick German bread and other gifts were thrown across. Small Christmas trees could be seen on the parapets. There appears not to have been egress from the trenches or fraternization however, and all this was severely disapproved of by the hierarchy. It did not happen in the following years.

A German army chaplain hailed the Belgians and handed over to them a golden monstrance, which he had found intact in a ruined, shelled Flemish church. Packed in a sack, the precious object normally used to display a consecrated Host was let down with a rope to the waiting Belgians in a trench, both sides refraining from firing. At times too, truces were arranged with white flags to evacuate the wounded from no man's land.

The *piot* or 'Jass',[3] the nickname given the Belgian soldier equivalent to British Tommy or French *poilu*, learned to cope. He was not always impeccably turned out, but knew hygiene was important and tried to keep his body clean, to avoid places known to be exposed to snipers and to scrounge extra food by hook or by crook, whenever and wherever he could. *Tirez son plan*, literally 'make your own arrangements' is a typically Belgian expression meaning to get by, to sort yourself out. Some often would feel 'la kloppe' meaning nostalgia or depression, but a sense of humour was ever present, *teinture d'iode*, that is the iodine liberally applied to wounds, becoming 'teinture de piot' and cruel but accurate nicknames always found for unpopular or shirking NCOs. Whenever he could the *piot* would sleep or eat, a practice common to all armies throughout history. You never know when your next chance to do either will come…

Guards, patrols, and minor raids into enemy lines were of course organized, defensive works built or rebuilt when necessary. Artillery, mortar or small arms fire would sometimes start without any logic, last for days or just stop after a few minutes. Every night flares were fired by both sides to detect infiltrators or raiders. Usually the enemy was more heard than seen. Where the trenches were very close, some Belgians who had lived in Germany could even identify regional accents.

On 7 July 1915, Captain V. was commended for bravery and mentioned in the Army Order of the Day for 'having stoically remained at his post for several hours under heavy enemy shelling with a lieutenant and two men'. From April till November 1916 his Regiment, 4ème de Ligne was assigned a frontline sector of one and half kilometres of the railway embankment between Nieuport and Dixmude. In 1917, it was deployed between Steenstraete and Dixmude.

On 15 November 1915, Robert V. was made a Commandant (Senior Captain) and a Knight of the Order of the Crown. The Belgian Croix de Guerre was to follow next year. His notes state that he was a good officer, modest, respected and intelligent, with a great reputation for bravery and moral fortitude, if somewhat distant with his men. He kept notes on his men's family circumstances and tastes. In 1917, he was assigned for several months as an instructor to a Belgian training camp outside Caen in France.

Progressively, as more units were trained and became available the part of the front held by the Belgians was extended southwards and would eventually reach the northern outskirts of Ypres, where it linked with the British.

On both sides snipers were a constant threat and you quickly discovered which places to avoid. Some trenches were quiet for long periods but this sometimes suddenly changed when a different German unit took over on the other side. *Coups de main* or limited raids went on by both sides throughout the war. One such raid in June 1916 netted fourteen German POWs, their dugout being completely destroyed.

Some scouts or raiders built quite a reputation of brutal efficiency for themselves, like Lieutenant Dardenne or Lieutenant Kervyn de Merendree both from *4ème de Ligne*, Robert V.'s regiment. Kervyn was not a professional but had enlisted and was made an officer for the duration. He carried out multiple patrols, raids, and ambushes on enemy raids. On one raid on 13 September 1918 he brought back 50 German POWs and 8 machine guns, firing his light machine gun from the hip cowboy style while covering his men's retreat.

Lieutenant Garnier specialized in raids on isolated farms usually surrounded by flooded land, whilst Lieutenant Moray, a former ranker, raided a machine-gun nest he had located at the limit of the British sector.

Stabilization: Mud and Misery, Dogs and Rats, Flies, Lice and Ice 71

Having despatched the sentinel he uncapped a hand grenade, only to see it fall at his feet. Though wounded he managed to bring back the MG and a few POWs.

Late on a July 1918 evening, Lieutenants Kretz and Solot of *13ème de Ligne* set out with two privates for an infiltration raid. Reaching the enemy line, they seized a German by the throat and arms to take him back, but a second German showed up and started raising hell. Screaming the alarm, he jumped out of the trench into a shell hole and was dispatched with a pistol shot. All surprise was however lost by then and Solot gave the withdrawal order by blowing his whistle. A German machine gun opened fire, hitting him in the head. Strijbos, one of the soldiers, retraced his steps, lifted Solot on to his shoulders and ran to the Yser bank. They swam the river to the Belgian trenches and safety but Solot was to die later of his wounds.

War hardens but also reveals characters. Good lieutenants and captains were in fact more important than colonels or generals and their mortality rate far higher. Such was the respect Lieutenant Fred de Villiers de Waroux inspired that when he was killed with a bullet through the head and carried back all the men stood at attention and saluted him. Lieutenant Callemeyn, aged 20, of *10ème de Ligne*, wrote a moving letter to his parents whilst he lay dying. The infantry training school in southern Belgium now bears his name.

Medal parades were held or battle honours added to regimental flags, the King almost always distributing the honours himself.

All this, however, was not enough to keep up morale. Most soldiers had not had word from their families for months, indeed they had heard of the German atrocities but did not know what fate had befallen their families. Letters started arriving through the neutral Netherlands. The Germans also allowed letters posted through Germany and Switzerland, but one had to pay very high prices for the stamps. Others received letters and packages with canned food and chocolate, footballs, playing cards, extra clothing, even cameras from their *marraines de guerre* or 'war godmothers', ladies in allied countries or even the US who 'adopted' them through newspaper advertisements. Some clever individuals acquired several *marraines*, Americans being especially sought for their wealth. Houses were opened where soldiers of all ranks on leave could read or borrow books, write letters, play chess or draughts, play the piano or just relax and sleep. With the few exceptions of those coming from the small non-occupied part of the country, the Belgians were the only soldiers of the western front who for four years could not go on home leave, unlike the French or British, and this without knowing when it would all end.

Captain Robert V. received some letters from his father that had travelled through the Netherlands, England, Calais and finally to the Belgian front. His sisters also wrote. One mentioned she had met Berthe J., his future wife in downtown Bruges and that she had asked for news of him. In 1916, his sisters wrote that their father had died. A friend's letter said it had become extremely expensive to write because the Germans 'like the real scoundrels they are' were charging enormous amounts for postage stamps.

Leave could be taken in Paris or London, after extremely long train journeys. Some went to Lourdes, the train tickets to that destination being free of charge. Religious practice increased in the circumstances and padres played a more important role than in peacetime.

In December 1916, Robert V. took some leave on the Côte d'Azur and spent Christmas there. He walked on the Promenade des Anglais and wrote that he met lots of Belgians and Serbs (they were also prevented by occupation from taking home leave) and the local population was worried about developments on the Italian front. The return journey via Paris, Calais, Dunkirk and Furnes took 24 hours.

The medical chain that had been overwhelmed and found wanting in 1914 was completely overhauled. Doctor Depage, founder and president of the Belgian Red Cross and also founder of the nursing school where Edith Cavell was the matron, transformed a seaside hotel into the Hôpital de l'Océan, where he was helped by his wife Marie, a nurse who was to die on the Lusitania, by trained nurse Queen Elisabeth and by future Nobel Prize winner and cancer specialist Jules Bordet. About 24,000 wounded or sick would eventually be cared for in the former Grand Hôtel de l'Océan. Forward first-aid posts were established close to the frontline, where wounds were disinfected and dressed to avoid infection, especially peritonitis. Behind this a complete network of hospitals, some in barges on canals, was established while Belgian military hospitals were opened behind the lines in Belgium, France and Britain, including in Birmingham, Dunkirk and Paris. Celebrities from abroad like Marie Curie came to visit and study the methods. Madame Curie also offered some of the mobile X-ray units mounted on motorcars she had developed. The US Embassy donated an operating theatre. The Belgians had a higher recuperation rate of WIAs than the Allied armies and interns from several foreign armies came to study the methods.

Some colourful characters like Madame Tack lived behind the lines in non-occupied Belgium. She was the widow of a Belgian captain and they had lived there before the war. She adamantly refused to be evacuated from her cottage and only eventually relented in 1918 during the great German offensive. Riding her she-donkey Paula, she would do the rounds distributing sweets and cigarettes to the troops. Officers and men alike would stand to attention and give her the military salute. When soldiers from a recently arrived unit who didn't know her pinched Paula to carry their own impedimenta, her owner raised a big fuss that went to the top of the military hierarchy and the culprits were quickly made to bring Paula back. Each time she would meet troops from that regiment she would call them 'ezeldieven', donkey snatchers. She was introduced by King Albert to King George V and to President Poincaré of France when they visited.

Another was *Juffrouw* (Miss) Belpaire to whom Albert I once said she was doing very good work, trying to prevent depravity among the young Flemish soldiers. Very religious and *Vlaamsvoelend*, 'Flemish-feeling', she became one of the defining characters of the *Frontbeweging* movement, promoting Flemish culture and language, about which more later. Active and devoted ladies were not only Belgian, there were also two British women, Elsie Knocker and Mairi Chisholm, who ran their own first-aid post in Pervyse (Pervijze), just behind the Belgian lines. Surviving the heavy bombardments, sniper fire and gas attacks that killed so many they became very popular with the Belgian troops, VIPs started visiting and their pictures frequently appeared in the British press. Through donations they arranged for their cellar to be reinforced with concrete and had a steel door fitted, supplied by the London department store, Harrods. The women were both decorated by King Albert I with the Order of Leopold II.

Elsie Knocker had been orphaned at an early age. She married Leslie Duke Knocker in 1906, and they had a son, Kenneth Duke (later killed in RAF service in the Second World War). The marriage failed and she was divorced, but this being frowned upon at the time she said that her husband had died in Indonesia, leaving her a widow.

In January 1916, Elsie married again, to Baron Harold de 't Serclaes, a handsome pilot of the Belgian *Aéronautique militaire* and belonging to a very ancient family of Brussels nobility.

Knocker and Chisholm were engaged in multiple battlefield rescues, even carrying fallen men on their backs to their first-aid station. They sent a dog with a message over to the Germans, asking not to be fired upon when rescuing wounded in no-man's-land and received a positive answer, being asked not to use army helmets but other headgear in order to be identified. After they rescued a wounded German pilot in no-man's-land the women were each awarded the British Military Medal. Both were gassed during the German offensive in March 1918, taken to the Hôpital de l'Océan and after that had to return home. Elsie Knocker's marriage to Baron 't Serclaes broke down, when he found out about her previous marriage.

Another British nurse was Dorothie Fielding, daughter of the Count of Denbigh.

Discipline

There were twenty executions by firing squad, which included twelve soldiers, for various crimes, mainly desertion. Five civilians, including one woman and two German POWs were also shot. With the exception of 1914 volunteer Aloïs Walput, on 3 June 1918, these executions all took place in 1914 and 1915. After that there were none, except when Artillery Sergeant Emiel Verfaille was beheaded on 26 March 1918 by means of a French guillotine and an executioner 'borrowed' from France, in Furnes, Belgium. One civilian executed for spying was actually cleared of this charge posthumously after the war.

Less serious offences like drunken brawls, insubordination, disrespect to officers or NCOs, thefts or vandalism of course happened when soldiers were on leave. Watering holes prospered and developed reputations. A house rarely without customers was called the *Veertien Billekes*, the fourteen (pretty little) thighs, because seven ladies of the night worked there. As can be imagined, venereal diseases were not unknown.

At the beginning of the war desertions were rare as many did not wish to go to occupied Belgium. In spite of the death penalty they never stopped however and rose in 1916 (1,200), 1917 (5,600) and 1918. Interestingly, water, the best defensive asset the Belgian army had, helped deserters, since in winter it became ice and could be walked over.

A few days after he came back from leave at the Côte d'Azur, Robert V. had a great shock: four men of his company had deserted by walking over the ice, leaving their arms and equipment behind. Commandant V. was given a dressing down by his CO and this incident was to hamper his career as we shall see.

Steenstraete

German officer and chemist Fritz Haber[4] worked for years on the development of various poison gases. Belgian military intelligence had

had warnings that the Germans were having gas masks manufactured in Ghent and a POW was found in the possession of one. A few days before the attack materialized German POWs, including an officer, warned the Belgians of a pending gas attack. On 22 April 1915, the first such attack in history was made at Steenstraete.[5] The greenish-yellow clouds coming over from the German lines were first thought to be caused by a fire, but then quickly identified as poison gas. It fully hit a French Algerian division whose soldiers either died or ran. On their southern flank the Canadians set up a perpendicular defence hook to their own front to contain the breach and the Belgian *Grenadiers* did the same on their northern side. Chlorine was quickly identified by several Belgian officers and soldiers with knowledge of chemistry or medicine and a provisional defence developed in the form of rags or handkerchief soaked with water or – even better, because it contains ammonia – urine, held before one's mouth and nose. The 5 km wide breach opened by the Germans was thus effectively contained and reconquered in part by the Belgians with the loss of thirty officers and several thousand men, the enemy failing to immediately exploit their advantage. But gas masks soon became an integral part of the already miserable life at the front. One young officer was said to have later died in torment after having urinated in a puddle containing mustard gas.

The Somme and Passchendaele

During the Battle of the Somme all the Belgian army was put on the line to attack in support of the British should a breakthrough be achieved. During Third Ypres or Passchendaele, part of the Belgian artillery was placed at the British army's disposal. Unfortunately, severe unprecedented rain combined with the heavy artillery bombardment turned the Flemish lowland perhaps unwisely chosen for the attack into a sea of mud, the more so because the artillery bombardments preceding the attacks had destroyed the drainage system. The village of Passchendaele itself, finally taken after so much blood had been spilled by British and Commonwealth troops, was lost again to the Germans in 1918 (it would only be retaken by the Belgians during the final offensive of the war).

In December 1917, after the Russian defection, the Belgian army adopted a strictly defensive posture, with a defence in depth of about 20 km. The idea on the whole front was to hold out until the Americans arrived in force to tip the balance.

In March 1918 at Reigersvliet, a strong German attack coming from the Houthulst Forest towards Poperinghe menaced the British rear and supplies.

It was successfully resisted by three Belgian divisions, who managed to stop the enemy and take 800 POWs. The *Carabiniers, Chasseurs à Cheval* and *Lanciers* could add another battle honour for *Reigersvliet* to their regimental colours.

On 17 April 1918, the Germans attacked the Belgian front in the Merckem-Langemark sector. Eight Belgian battalions mainly from *Neuvième de Ligne* defeated 23 German battalions and took 20 German officers and 759 other ranks prisoner.

3.1 In Flanders Skies: Of Camels and Pups, SPADS and Fokkers

In Flanders fields the poppies grew. Above, in Flanders skies, the roundels flew. (With due respect to John McCrae's 'In Flanders Fields'.)

Blue, white and red Royal Flying Corps or Royal Naval Air Service roundels, red, white and blue French roundels and another combination of the same three colours when the United States joined the fray, all faced the black crosses of the Germans. In the far north of the Western Front black, yellow and red cockades, the three colours of the Belgian flag could also be seen, over the desolate landscapes of Nieuport, Dixmude and Ypres, sometimes flying far inland over country where the pilots of those planes could not go on leave, as far as Bruges, Ghent and Brussels.

Belgium was an early starter in military aviation – a company of balloons (*Compagnie d'Aérostiers*) already existed in the nineteenth century. In the early 1900s, several affluent Belgians in Antwerp and Ghent bought themselves knocked down kits of French Farman or Blériot machines, which they built in their backyards and tried out, sometimes at great risk. One of them was Jan Olieslagers, of whom we will hear more. They were encouraged by the future King Albert, who took a keen interest in all things mechanical and particularly in flying. Twice he flew himself in balloons, to his uncle's (King Leopold II) great wrath, who after a reprimand the first time, confined the heir to the throne to quarters as punishment for insubordination the second time. Albert tried in vain to interest sceptical Belgian generals in the future of aviation in warfare. In 1910, the *Compagnie des Aviateurs* was created at Brasschaat, outside Antwerp.[6] The same year the Tsar (King) of Bulgaria was taken for a balloon ride in Brasschaat. The first licences were given to military pilots. One machine was sent by sea to the Belgian Congo, where it soon crashed.

In 1912 the first official air unit in the Belgian armed forces was established and trials held at Brasschaat with Lewis guns strapped to Farmans, shooting at white sheets spread over the ground. There were mixed results.

By 1914, thirty-seven Belgian officers and NCOs had pilots' licences. Among them was the future ace, Jan Olieslagers. When war broke out he volunteered with his hand-built Blériot planes, together with a group of other pilots.

Two squadrons existed by then, one outside Liège and the other outside Namur. From 3 August 1914, they executed several reconnaissance missions to cover the German advance in Belgium. On 11 August, the French donated eight Farmans and two Blériots. Pilots initially went unarmed and would sometimes even salute their opposite numbers as they met them. Gradually they began to take pistols, rifles, grenades or pointed, 12 cm-long steel darts called *fléchettes*, which could inflict serious wounds when dropped in numbers from height on to men, horses or even horse artillery. It was said a German general on horseback met his (undignified) end this way.

One German Taube was forced to land outside Brussels and its dismayed pilot taken prisoner. On the other hand, Edmond Thieffry, a volunteer just out of law school, was also captured in 1914 but escaped and rode to neutral Holland on a stolen motorcycle. He rejoined the army, became an artillery balloon observer then transferred to aviation. His first victory was scored on 15 March 1917, his second two days later. He made 'ace', that is holder of at least five victories, on 3 July, shooting down a pair of German Navy Albatross D IIIs over Dixmude. In another fight, alone against nine enemy aircraft, he managed to down three, making him the first Belgian to destroy ten enemy planes. On 24 January 1917, Thieffry flew his Nieuport 17 all the way to Brussels and dropped Belgian flags and messages over his former public school, the Jesuit Collège Saint Michel (still in existence) and over his fiancée's home. His unit, *5ème Escadrille* had converted to SPADs and Thieffry went on to shoot down four more German planes, until brought down himself and seriously wounded in February 1918. Taken to a German military hospital in Ghent he survived and became a POW. His comrades thought he had died, until told this was not the case via the International Red Cross. This time the Germans kept a better watch on him, though he did make four attempts at escaping and was caught each time, the last time within miles of the Swiss border. After the war he picked up his lawyer's career again but the desire to fly was still strong. In 1925, he flew to the Belgian Congo in a Handley Page, a first that took fifty-one days to complete, and there founded the local airline as well as what would become SABENA, the now defunct Belgian national carrier. He was to lose his life in an air crash caused by a violent tropical storm in Tanganyika on 11 April 1929; one of the three-men crew in the Avimeta CM 92 survived the crash. Aged just thirty-six, Thiéffry left a wife and five children. He was an officer in the Order of Leopold.

The first photo reconnaissance mission was flown on 23 September 1914 and the first bombing mission against a German supply train in Belgium on 21 December 1914.

Late in 1914, as the front shifted and then stabilized, the Belgian military air force had lost most of its planes in spite of French additions. It was reequipped with more modern machines and reorganized under the command of Fernand Jacquet, who was the first Belgian to win an air victory on 17 April 1915; in a Farman with Lieutenant Vindevogel he shot down an Aviatik by killing its pilot with a Lewis gun. Jacquet was also the first Belgian ace. As well as Belgian medals he received the British DFC.

On a clear day in 1915, *Adjudant* Robaert defiantly did aerobatics for about an hour above a German base in Flanders, while being shot at. Unfortunately, that fine but somewhat reckless pilot was lost the following year when he crashed into the sea.

First combats with Nieuport Bébés, piloted by Jan Olieslagers, were fought over the Yser in early 1915. In January 1916, the first true fighter units, Escadrilles 1 and 5 were established at Les Moëres behind the Belgian front. First Squadron emblems, used to this day, appeared – the Thistle, the fiery red Comet, the paper horse (Cocotte) red or white, and the Penguin. They are still to be seen today on modern jets of the Belgian Air Component.

In 1916, Belgian military aviation was reorganized and reequipped, also being provided with a Farman 'Kodak', whose mission is obvious. A permanent base was established at Les Moëres, not far from Poperinghe and a rear depot for maintenance at Calais, where Belgian Schrek FBA flying boats were also based.

The fledgling Belgian air force had several handicaps: like the rest of the army it was cut off from its national industrial base, by then in occupied Belgium and had to rely on supplies from France and Britain, which naturally gave priority to their own needs. Until 1918, when reequipped with Sopwith Camels, the Belgians were given second-rate planes, the skill and motivation of the pilots having to make up for the inadequacy of their machines. Inferior planes, superior pilots, the Belgians would proudly say. Moreover, Belgian planes had to fly against the prevailing winds, which come from the sea and blow inland. German planes damaged in combat were helped by the wind to fly back to their own lines and sometimes crash land there, while the contrary was true for the Belgians. Along the North Sea coast weather can be very bad, as is well known. It has been calculated that only about a third of the many days the war lasted offered weather good enough to fly, at least with the planes available then.

The French dominated the aircraft industry at that time and the new, nimble Nieuport was all the rage. Armed with a single Lewis gun it looks like a child's toy compared to a modern F-35, Rafale or Eurofighter, but the Allies' finest pilots became aces in Nieuports 11, 17 and 23, designed by Edouard de Niéport (who called himself Nieuport, though there was no obvious link to the Belgian town of that name). Alongside their French, British, Italian and American colleagues, Belgian pilots quickly became proficient in shooting down Aviatiks and Taubes, which were rapidly replaced by more modern German machines. One such pilot was André De Meulemeester, who hailed from Bruges. He volunteered when war broke out and was posted to the 1st Escadrille. He claimed his first victory on 1 February 1917, but it was not confirmed. The Belgian 'points and victories' system was tighter than that of the Allies – only enemy planes effectively having been seen by an officer to crash after being fired at were accepted, not those forced to land or obviously severely damaged, though shared victories were allowed for. The overall Belgian tally for the war probably would have been higher if using less restrictive criteria. De Meulemeester's first official victory is dated 30 April 1917, shared with a British Sopwith Scout. The second came on 12 June 1917, together with Georges Kervyn de Lettenhove, also from Bruges. The next two were in July and August, De Meulemeester being wounded in the latter combat. His sixth victory in a Nieuport was in November, again flying with Georges Kervyn. De Meulemeester later flew Hanriot machines and his final official score was eleven official victories; in fact it might have been far more, as many as twenty-eight. More often than not he would tuck his mascot, a little dog called Stabilo, in his flying jacket. On 11 July 1918, he crashed and broke a few teeth but survived the war, joined the Belgian occupation forces in Germany and then went on to run the family brewery business in Bruges, where he died in 1973, aged seventy-nine.

During the terrible Battle of Passchendaele, the Belgian pilots supported the British offensive and De Meulemeester and Thieffry each shot down four German planes, as did two other Belgian pilots.

On 10 September 1917, French ace of aces Georges Guynemer (50 victories)[7] landed his SPAD XIII with engine trouble at the Belgian field of Les Moëres, just behind the Belgian front. The next day he was shot down and killed over Poelcapelle just behind the German lines. His body was never recovered, the ground having been heavily shelled by British artillery.

The Germans let it be known he had been killed. The pictures taken at Les Moëres were the last ones of Guynemer.

Jan Olieslagers, the 'Devil from Antwerp', was another prominent Belgian ace, at the age of nineteen already a motorcycle champion. In 1909 he bought a Blériot and taught himself to fly, beating several world records. Joining the then newly formed *Aéronautique militaire belge*, he became on 12 September 1915 the first Belgian to claim an aerial victory, having shot down an Aviatik in a Nieuport 10. Later he flew Nieuports 10 and 11 and Hanriots. With this last plane he made ace, with a fifth and then a sixth victory, but it is highly probable his actual tally was far more since he flew no fewer than 193 patrols and took part in 52 air combats, this only in the year 1916, with comparable numbers of flights and fights in the two following years. His Nieuport 23 was adorned with a red comet with flaming tail, the emblem of 5th Escadrille, which still features as the emblem of a Belgian Air Component F-16 squadron.

On 15 October 1918, eight Belgian planes were attacked by fifteen Fokkers but managed to drive them off and make base safely.

The Belgian ace of aces was Willy Coppens, born in Brussels in 1892, who was drafted into the elite Grenadier Regiment in 1914 and volunteered for the Belgian Flying School in France the next year. He first flew BE2Gs and later Sopwith 1 ½ Strutters and saw his first aerial combat over the Belgian coast in July 1915. He eventually scored 37 air victories, mainly on Drachen artillery observation balloons. Some might think a large captive balloon which could be seen for miles was easy prey, a sitting duck. However, those launching them would recognize their vulnerability and ring them with anti-aircraft artillery; more often than not German fighter planes were also on hand to protect them. Shooting them down was not so easy either, in spite or maybe because of their large bulk: there was a shortage of special incendiary 11 mm bullets and rockets developed for the purpose and the blimps were resistant to ordinary machine-gun bursts. All this made attacking them particularly dangerous and pilots risking it had to be careful and were lucky to survive long. Coppens became an expert, sending scores of Drachen and other balloons plummeting down, usually in flames. On one occasion, the wheels of his Hanriot even touched and rolled briefly over the top of the balloon he was attacking. He often attacked at dawn, coming out of the rising sun. Since he had had his plane painted sky blue, the Germans dubbed him *der blaue Teufel*, 'the Blue Devil'. The Germans decided to trick him by preparing a balloon full of explosive, hoping the Blue Devil would blow himself up. This backfired (literally) as the contraption exploded prematurely, causing many casualties among the expectant Germans.

On 18 February 1918 he flew to Brussels, circling five times over his parents' home, seeing his father at the window and letting many of the capital's residents see the Belgian cockades on the underside of his Hanriot. By then he had slated up ten victories and was still only an NCO. So he bought an officer's uniform on which he pinned a second lieutenant's stars himself. The bureaucracy relented and confirmed his new rank. On one occasion he shot two Drachens in a row, only to be attacked by mistake by two British RE8s. The pilots later sent their apologies. Such mistakes were not rare, for example in October 1918, RNAS planes forced a Belgian plane to land, the pilot luckily unharmed; Gustave De Mevius was shot down by British pilots; and on 8 March 1918, Charles de Montigny rushed to the rescue of a British two-seater attacked by two German planes who fled, but as a reward for his trouble, the British in turn fired at him! Such incidents were later referred to as 'blue on blue'. But on other occasions Allies and Belgians cooperated, as on 13 November 1917 when Belgian John de Roest, flying a Sopwith 1 ½ Strutter was attacked by an Albatros and saved by an RNAS pilot who shot down the German. On 15 September 1918, Captain Dony was attacked by four Fokkers, but rescued by British Sopwith Camels.

Between 24 June and 22 July 1918, Coppens shot down five Drachen and on 31 July King Albert gave him the medals of Officer of the Order of the Crown and of Knight of the Order of Leopold.

By that autumn, he had scored 35 balloons and two planes, but on 14 October his luck finally ran out. Attacking a balloon again over Torhout, between Bruges and the front, he was severely wounded by an explosive AA bullet. He lost a lot of blood and the control of his plane, but the machine gun he was using continued to fire and shot down the balloon more or less by itself. He managed to fly back to the Allied lines, but had his left leg amputated at the Hôpital de l'Océan in La Panne by Dr Depage. For him the war was over, and he was made Chevalier (Knight) Coppens de Houthulst by the King. Apart from the Belgian Croix de Guerre and Order of Leopold he also held the French Legion d'Honneur, the British MC and DSO and Polish, Portuguese and Italian medals. Coppens' tally of balloons was the highest, Allied or German. After the war he kept in close contact with the *Aéronautique militaire*, holding consulting positions, but fell out with the hierarchy when it was decided just before the Second World War to order Italian CR 42 biplanes, which Coppens thought were hopelessly obsolete (a point of view many shared). There are reports he had become a disgruntled old man by the end of his life, making a nuisance of himself at hotels he stayed in. He lived with Olieslagers' daughter and wrote the latter's biography as well as that of Fulco Ruffo di Calabria, the great Italian ace whose daughter became Queen of the Belgians at the end of the twentieth century having married Prince Albert, later King Albert II.

Albert's grandfather, King Albert I, had not lost his interest and appetite for flying. In fact, he saw it as a welcome distraction from the dreary existence he was living at the Villa Maskens, year after year with no end date in sight. So he often visited the Belgian squadrons which by 1918 had grown to five, distributed medals there and took to the air himself several times during the war. This time no superior officer could confine him to quarters as punishment, but the government in exile at Sainte Adresse was not happy with the risk, remonstrated with him and pointed out not without reason the potentially catastrophic consequences for the country or even the Allied cause if he was shot down and taken prisoner, his eldest son, the future Leopold III being a mere adolescent. The courtiers and top brass were dismayed too, but held their peace. On 18 March 1917, he flew a Farman escorted by four Nieuport 17s over the front and they were shot at by German AA. More flights followed on Belgian Sopwith 1 ½ Strutters, with an RN Handley Page, an RFC Bristol Fighter, that flight ending up in a dogfight over Ostend which earned King Albert a DFC. Several more flights were made over or beyond the front line and one went so far the church steeples and famous belfry of Bruges could be seen. Albert did not pilot himself but made use of two-seaters like the SPAD XI and was escorted by single-seat fighters. On one such flight on Armistice Day, Queen Elisabeth flew alongside in another plane and on the way back she asked her pilot, Lieutenant Crombez to loop the loop, which he did three times. That such adventures were not without risk is demonstrated by the fact that after the war, flying in southern Belgium, King Albert inadvertently switched off the power from his back seat, forcing the pilot to land (smoothly) in a field. To my knowledge King Albert was the only C-in-C to fly in combat zones, at least in this conflict. King Albert and Queen Elisabeth also flew from Calais to Dover on Belgian FBA flying boats, being welcomed in England by Admiral Keyes and then flying on to attend King George V and Queen Mary's silver wedding jubilee.

During the First World War, Belgian pilots scored 125 aerial victories on both planes and balloons. As explained, this figure is probably lower than it would have been in another airforce, Allied or German. The top scorers were: Coppens (37), De Meulemeester (11), Thieffry (10),

Jacquet (7) and Olieslagers (6). A total of 72 Belgian pilots were killed in action and 56 planes lost through enemy action. This is in proportion with the other air forces on both sides. During the course of the war, a Belgian flying school was established at Étampes in France and another at Hendon.

On 22 November 1918, a large aerial victory parade was flown over Brussels, with most of the available Belgian planes and several Allied machines.

The main types of plane used by the Belgians were:

- Farmans and Blériots at the beginning of the war;
- all types of Nieuport, but mainly the Nieuport 11;
- 15 SPADs XI and 35 SPADs XIII;
- 80 Hanriot HD 1. For some reason these machines resembling the Nieuport in size and shape but with a strong dihedral on the upper wing, were shunned by the French pilots but appreciated by the Belgians and Italians. Olieslagers, De Meulemeester and Coppens made good use of them;
- conversely, the French Ponnier was found to be utterly unstable and soon relegated to ground training;
- 6 Sopwith Pups, 38 Sopwith 1 ½ Strutters and 44 Sopwith Camels;
- a number of Breguet XIVs which were mainly used after the war;
- a large German Friedrichshafen G III bomber, one of a pair which were captured after forced landings, repaired and 'turn coated'.

Belgium also took charge of a large number of Fokker D VIIs, which were either captured during the reconquest of Belgium or handed over under the terms of the 11 November 1918 armistice, in which they were especially mentioned. Dutchman Anthony Fokker, who had manufactured them, commented it was a good but expensive advertisement for his products. They flew on under Belgian cockades well into the 1920s.

During the war, bombing raids were flown by German Gotha bombers based in Ghent against several British cities, including London. One bomb aimed at Victoria station fell on the Royal Hospital in Chelsea, killing several people. The raids made Britain improve its defences and for the first but not the last time, some Londoners took refuge in the Underground stations.

Some of the planes the Germans used were left behind when they evacuated Belgium in 1918 and can be seen today in the Brussels military museum.[8]

3.2 Off Flanders Coast: Bruges, Zeebrugge and the U-Boats

When the Germans realized they were not going to break through the Belgian and Entente lines barring their way to the Channel Ports, they also concluded the war was going to last longer than they had planned, but the bonus was they now controlled about 100 kilometres of North Sea coast. The Royal Navy held and would continue to hold overall strategic superiority and control over the seas, but the ports on the Belgian coast could be put to good use for smaller surface craft that could raid the coast of south-west England and harass the traffic between say, Dover and Calais, especially at night. Even more important, their now fledgling submarine arm could also be based on that coast, avoiding the long and fuel-hungry sailings from the ports in the German Bight and around Scotland. The British and French navies did everything in their power to stop the U-boats making their way down the Channel to wreak havoc there or in the Atlantic. The Dover Patrol under command of Admiral Keyes eventually developed into a fleet of hundreds of cruisers, monitors, destroyers, armed trawlers and even submarines. Substantive French naval forces were also based in Calais, Dunkirk and Boulogne. Successive layers of antisubmarine nets were installed with mines attached, staggered lengthwise and at different depths. However, the U-boat traffic from the Flanders coast into the Channel and back never completely stopped, though it gradually decreased. Also, the later-built, larger German submarines eventually had a greater range and could reach the Atlantic by circumnavigating to the north of the British Isles, then either enter the Irish sea or the open Atlantic, rather than run the gauntlet in the Channel.

All through the war fighting took place off the Belgian coast between the Dover Patrol and French Dunkirk-based forces on the one hand, whose main task was to try to prevent German submarines from reaching the vital Dover–Calais crossings and the Channel, against Zeebrugge-based German light naval units. The German naval command had buoys and other navigation aids displaced at irregular intervals and the dredging of shipping lanes between the Flemish banks was stopped altogether.

Since it was obviously within the power of the British and French to land forces on that coast, as demonstrated by the Gallipoli landings, the coast of Flanders was heavily fortified by the occupiers with gun emplacements, hundreds of machine-gun nests in the dunes and heavy anti-aircraft defences around Bruges, Ostend and Zeebrugge. These were manned in large part by the *Kaiserliche Marinekorps*, the German equivalent of the

Royal Marines, under the command of Admiral von Schröder. One always reads the Western front went all the way from the Swiss border to the North Sea, but it would be more accurate to say from the Swiss–French border to the Belgian–Dutch border.

Though it was not such a plum as the French Atlantic ports of Saint Nazaire, Lorient and La Rochelle that they would find themselves controlling in June 1940, the Flemish coastal ports were a great strategic asset for the German submarine arm in 1914 and they were not slow putting them to use. Nieuport, of course, could not be used as it was on the frontline and neither could the mammoth port of Antwerp, because its outlet to the sea, the Scheldt estuary, crossed into the Netherlands' territory and the Dutch government at the outset of war had declared it would strictly enforce its neutrality by never allowing warships of any belligerent nation into it. It is ironic the British had insisted, when Belgian independence was negotiated in the 1830s, that both the northern and the southern banks of the Scheldt estuary should be Dutch territory, because they feared Antwerp as a military harbour could one day be a threat to England if the French were to occupy Belgium. Little did they know this would turn out to be totally against their interest some decades later…

Zeebrugge, a totally artificial port, basically a mole entering the sandy North Sea, had been built in 1907 at the whim of the ever-busy Leopold II, who had in mind that shipping had to cross Dutch territory to reach or leave the two other Belgian merchant seaports, Antwerp and Ghent. Zeebrugge, on the open North Sea coast did not have that disadvantage and was built, by the way, to the great dismay, still lingering today, of Antwerp shipping interests. It was not meant as a naval port, Belgium having no real navy at the time, but the *Kaiserliche Marine*, in late 1914, sent small dismantled submarines by railway from Germany to Antwerp, where they were reassembled and sent by inland waterways to Zeebrugge. In 1915, *Kapitänleutnant* Fürbringer sailed the first U-boat directly by sea, from Germany along the Dutch coast to Zeebrugge, soon to be followed by many others which would be based there, together with small surface vessels and seaplanes (mainly of the Hansa Brandenburg type) and Zeppelins until the end of the war. As many as 200 seaplanes and Zeppelins were eventually stationed in the Bruges area, while two large batteries, the Tirpitz battery in Ostend, with four 280 mm guns, and the even larger König Wilhelm II battery with 305 mm guns at Knokke, at the Dutch border, controlled the approaches and the Scheldt estuary.[9] Knokke, where many hotels had been built for tourists before the war, was used by the German Army and Navy for rest and recreation.

Ostend and Zeebrugge are on the coast itself. Both are linked to the beautiful medieval port of Bruges, 15 kilometres inland, by relatively straight canals. Thus the Germans could avoid having to repair and overhaul their submarines at the coast where they were vulnerable to attack from the sea, but could do this miles inland at the same time as the rest and recreation needed by the crews, without being annoyed by long-range inaccurate naval fire, that would be countered by their shore batteries. Against aerial bombardments several 150 mm anti-aircraft batteries were deployed around Bruges. As from 1915, large concrete pens were built that could hold up to 18 submarines and 25 torpedo boats, which were still around (I saw them) in the early 1960s, in the harbour of the old Flemish city, complete with workshops, fuel depots, torpedo, electrical and engine workshops, while more shelters existed in Zeebrugge and Ostend. Bruges, always a tourist attraction, had many hotels and these were requisitioned to serve as officers' messes and other ranks' accommodation.

The Kaiser and his brother, Admiral Prince Heinrich of Prussia, Inspector of the German Fleet, visited the Bruges naval officers' mess more than once. Unbeknownst to the British, the Kaiser had been visiting Bruges just before the attack and had spent the night at a chateau outside the city. There is plenty of literature in English on the attack on Zeebrugge by Admiral Sir Roger Keyes, on 23 April 1918 and it is of little use to recount it in detail here.

Berthe J. was woken up during the night by the tremendous din of artillery of different calibres, this time coming from the north not the south-west as usual.

Panicking German soldiers ran through the streets of Bruges yelling that the British had landed on the coast. Next morning, manacled German NCOs and enlisted men were led under armed escort to the Bruges jail, under the gleeful gaze of the locals, for having abandoned their posts. Their eventual fate is unknown, but Germany executed hundreds of deserters in both world wars. German officers were seen giving the military salute to British soldiers made prisoners and taken through Bruges to embark for POW camps in Germany. Kaiser Wilhelm II pinned the *Pour le Mérite* medal on Admiral von Schröder's chest a few days later, during a parade held on the square in front of the medieval town hall of Bruges.

Bruges was of course crawling with spies and when Captain Fürbringer was taken prisoner in 1918 by the Royal Navy after a destroyer rammed his UB110, his captors surprised him by knowing which of his fellow captains had been on what cruise and on what boat, the nicknames the captains used when addressing each other and other details. They asked him how old the newspapers were he had on board, to find out when he had left Bruges, information he refused to give. They also asked him if it had been Captain Amberger who had sunk a hospital ship in the Irish Sea. In fact, according to Fürbringer's memoirs,[10] Captain Schwieger, the same who sank the RMS *Lusitania*, tried to torpedo a hospital ship in the Irish Sea because he clearly saw it was packed with armed British soldiers. Fürbringer also writes that RN ratings from the destroyer hurled large chunks of coal at the heads of some of his crew while they were in the water after having had their boat sunk under them, killing several, but that later he and the survivors were picked up and treated decently by the Royal Navy. Fürbringer says that by the end of the war life had become utterly miserable, the U-boat crews having to endure day-long depth-charge bombings in the shallow waters of the North Sea. They were decimated by decoy Q-ships and even Allied submarines lying in wait for them, sometimes towed, submerged, behind innocent-looking fishing trawlers.

Captain Schwieger of *Lusitania* fame, who did not survive the war, and Captain Max Valentiner, who was included in an Allied list of war criminals accused of machine-gunning survivors in the water, were based in Bruges at least during part of the war.

As is well known the sinking of the RMS *Lusitania* in May 1915 was an important factor in bringing the United States into the war. Among the prominent victims was a Belgian, Marie Depage, née Picard. She was a trained nurse, worked at the Hôpital de l'Océan and was married to its director Dr Depage. She was travelling back from a successful fundraising tour through several American cities. She survived the initial torpedoing and was seen swimming. However, she seems to have become entangled in some wires, was dragged under and drowned. Back at La Panne her husband was devastated and never fully recovered from the blow. In his private memoirs,[11] King Albert remarked how ferocious the war had become and that the Germans now stopped at nothing, which might hopefully be a sign of their despair. Marie Depage's remains were brought back from Ireland and buried provisionally in the dunes close to La Panne.

Fürbringer's memoirs are especially interesting because very few U-boat captains survived the First World War, which explains the relative dearth of literature on the subject. The German submarine force was, during both conflicts, the object of passionate and understandable hatred. That they were brave, however, is beyond dispute, because they suffered such a high rate of losses: about 80 per cent failed to return in both conflicts, one of the highest attrition rates of any armed force for any nation in modern wartime.[12]

At the end of the war, when news of the state of affairs back home reached Bruges and its surrounding area, the German soldiers and sailors there mutinied against their officers, some of whom were roughed up and the admiral mobbed.

As these lines were written (summer of 2017), the practically intact German First World War submarine UB 29 was discovered on the sea bottom not far from Ostend, the exact location being kept secret. The remains of the crew are probably still inside.

4

King Albert, his Bavarian Queen, a Post Office and a Saintly Address

Albert of Saxe-Coburg-Gotha, later to reign as Albert I, was born in Brussels on 8 April 1875, the son of Leopold II's younger brother and Marie of Hohenzollern-Sigmaringen of the Catholic branch of that famous German family. Queen Victoria had arranged the marriage. At first Albert was not destined to be king, but his first cousin, son of Leopold II, and then his own elder brother, both unexpectedly died young, which made him heir to the throne. A shy boy, prone to reading and introspection, young Albert developed an interest in mechanics and would enjoy dismantling old clocks to find out how they worked. He delighted in memorizing train schedules. Later, as we have seen he had escapades in balloons and planes to the great displeasure of his uncle the King. Like all Belgian princes and kings before and after him he received a solid military education and aged seventeen went to the Brussels Royal Military Academy, where he met several of his future advisers.

He joined the *Carabiniers* and later the elite *Grenadiers* Regiments, being sworn in as a second lieutenant in 1892.

Albert first met his wife Elisabeth, Duchess in (not of) Bavaria, at the funeral in Paris of her aunt, the Duchess of Alençon. German born, the late duchess was the sister of another Elisabeth, the famous Sissi, Empress of Austria and godmother of the future Elisabeth of Belgium. Sophie, Sissi's sister had been engaged to mad King Ludwig of Bavaria but later married a French aristocrat of the Bourbon-Orléans branch of royal pretenders and lived in Paris. She died tragically on 4 May 1897 in the fire of a Paris charity sale, *le Bazar de la Charité*, where several other prominent members of Paris high society lost their lives. Sophie's son would later marry one of Albert's sisters.

Elisabeth, the future Queen of the Belgians was the daughter of a colourful member of the Wittelsbach family, which has forever been linked with the history of Bavaria. Karl-Theodor, Duke in Bavaria worked as an ophthalmologist as a hobby and usually did not charge the patients he operated on for cataracts. Elisabeth's mother was a Portuguese princess and she would name her daughter Marie-José after her. Elisabeth was born on 25 July 1876 and grew up at the Possenhofen family estate. Her father trained her as a nurse. Her two sisters married Crown Prince Rupprecht of Bavaria and Count Törring, a German nobleman.

After some months, the shy Albert asked Elisabeth if she thought she would be able to withstand the (rainy) Belgian climate. The answer was positive, and they married on 1 October 1900 in Munich. Ruppert of Bavaria, later to command an army corps in Belgium, attended the wedding. The newlyweds travelled to Germany, France, Britain and Italy together in the years just before the war and rapidly became a popular couple, whose impeccable family life contrasted with the scandalous behaviour of Leopold II. Three children blessed their household: Leopold, Charles and Marie José, who would later become the last Queen of Italy. Elisabeth would play her violin every evening to the family.

On 23 December 1909, a rainy day shortly after Leopold II's death, Albert took the oath of office. He was the first king of the Belgians to do so in both languages, French and Dutch. He would always be more receptive than the average political establishment to both the Flemish aspirations and those of the socialists. In his oath, Albert promised to uphold the integrity of Belgian territory: five years later this is exactly what he found himself doing.

Before he was crowned, Albert visited the US and Canada as well as the Congo, which had become a Belgian colony in 1908, using a bicycle for some stretches of this last trip. In the Congo he insisted on reforms in line with the wishes of the Belgian public, which was keen to prove to international opinion that the colony could be well administered after the many abuses committed there before 1908, when it had been Leopold II's personal fiefdom. Unfortunately world opinion did not appreciate the difference between the regimes and some, especially Britain, would use somewhat hypocritically the lingering bad image from the past to oppose Belgian wishes for colonial expansion after the war, when these clashed with British interests.[1]

Albert's speech before the Belgian Parliament on 4 August 1914, the day of the German invasion gave him enormous prestige. In line with Article 68 of the Belgian Constitution, which says that the king commands the armies of land and sea, he took personal command of the armed forces and would keep it until 1918. He was the only head of state to stay permanently with his troops throughout the war. Albert proved to be an energetic leader insisting on tough training, sacking underperforming officers but inspiring great devotion and loyalty among his troops, who felt he shielded them from unnecessary losses. When he thought it was warranted he confirmed death sentences for deserters or spies, or violent criminals, as in the case of a man of military age who had murdered an old woman to rob her. Albert reasoned that it would be unfair to soldiers risking their lives at the front to see a murderer spend the rest of the war in the safety of a cell.

Albert could be prone to pessimism and depression and more than once Elisabeth helped him surmount days of doubt and self-questioning. Apart from seeing his country invaded and devastated, later completely plundered, his relatives cruelly divided in a deadly war no one could foresee the end of, he suffered from seeing what he felt was the self-destruction of Europe. He felt a great loss when the poet Emile Verhaeren died in a railway accident in France, having had his leg severed when falling off the platform. He was also profoundly saddened when nurse Marie Picard, wife of Dr Depage, lost her life in the *Lusitania*. Marie's and Verhaeren's bodies were provisionally buried in the dunes in non-occupied Belgium. In his private notes Albert wrote of the *Lusitania* affair: 'This war has become ever more ferocious. The Germans now no longer hesitate to use all possible, even extreme means.'

In April 1918, King Albert sent heartfelt congratulations to Admiral Keyes for the Zeebrugge and Ostend raids, saying, 'It is the most daring action of the whole war and proves what splendid traditions prevail in the Royal Navy.' It should be noted here that Albert always recognized the tremendous sacrifices British and Commonwealth sailors and soldiers suffered all through the war to liberate his country, something he never forgot even when seriously at odds with some British politicians.

After the Battle of the Yser, the Belgian army found itself aligned with 9 divisions holding about 40 kilometres of front, from the North Sea at Nieuport, patrolled by British monitors and destroyers whose guns would occasionally give a helping hand, to just north of Ypres where the British sector started, the boundary between the two armies varying over the years.

The Royal Family were occupying three seaside holiday villas behind the lines, one of which, the Villa Maskens, belonged to a Belgian diplomat. They were simple dwellings devoid of luxury, with open fireplaces in the living and dining rooms but no heating in the sleeping quarters. The winter of 1917 was particularly harsh, the sea freezing over on the La Panne beach. Only 9 kilometres from the front, the site was exposed to enemy artillery and air raids. Albert flew into a rage when a French journalist foolishly published their exact location. A German air attack seems in fact to have been planned but was stopped at the urging of a member of the Austrian imperial family, the future Empress Zita of Bourbon Parme, wife of Archduke Karl, the new heir to the throne, and sister-in-law of Queen Elisabeth. At the villas, Albert would work, keep in contact with the local population and the army, which he often visited (including the air bases), and when he wanted to relax he would take horse rides on the beach with a single equerry in attendance. The villas were destroyed by Allied bombings in the Second World War, when they were a part of the Atlantic Wall.

Elisabeth, for whom all this must have been heartbreaking, since most of her close relatives were on the enemy side, definitively chose the side of her adopted country and never wavered.[2]

Being a trained nurse, she would go regularly to the Hôpital de l'Océan to change bandages. She was also heavily involved in training nurses and in the care of about 300 orphans, who were given shelter in large buildings she had organized. She also set up a symphony orchestra and a theatre for the troops and generally spent time on various initiatives to enhance the welfare of the Belgian soldiers, cut off from their families. In 1915 in occupied Belgium, 1,143 baby girls were christened Elisabeth.

Prince Leopold, the heir to the throne, first went to Eton and later received a military training and was enlisted in the *12ème de Ligne* Regiment that had fought valiantly to defend Liège. His brother Charles joined the Royal Naval College at Osborne in 1917, then served aboard HMS *Renown*. Both were to succeed their father, one as king, the other as regent after the Second World War. Princess Marie José was sent to a boarding school in Italy.

For the royal family to stay put, despite the very real danger involved, on the small part of Belgian territory that was never occupied by the invaders had an obvious political significance. The King remained in Belgium at the head of his army and not in exile, relying on a host who, however benign, had not necessarily the same aims and priorities and would have had the means to force his own wishes upon his guest.

At La Panne, Albert and Elisabeth had numerous visitors, including King George V in 1915, the French President, Poincaré, Sir Douglas Haig, Admirals Bacon and Keyes, Prince Alexander of Teck (Queen Mary's brother), French Admiral Ronarc'h of Dixmude fame, Field Marshal Smuts with whom the King spoke Dutch, French Generals Joffre, Nivelle, Lyautey and Foch, American General Pershing, and Pierre and Marie Curie also visited the Hôpital de l'Océan to study Dr Depage's methods. Other scientists included Albert Einstein, later to become a firm friend and regular visitor to Belgium. Neutral diplomats posted in Brussels came via the neutral Netherlands or Britain, like American Brand Withlock, the

Spanish Marquis of Villa Lobar and Dutchman van Vollenhoven, who all played prominent roles helping relieve the misery in occupied Belgium. Burgomaster Adolphe Max, before he was deported also came, as did Cardinal Mercier and other prominent Belgians like the industrialist Emile Francqui and financier Léon Lambert. Other visitors were Lord Curzon and of course Belgian politicians and diplomats from Le Havre, like Broqueville, Hymans, Vandervelde, Beyens et cetera. One day at La Panne, a Belgian soldier standing on guard did not know Lord Curzon and locked him in a basement while he went to inform his superiors. Equally ignorant of whom they were addressing, two young French officers on leave invited Queen Elisabeth to have tea with them. She politely declined.

The King Albert's Book

As we will discuss in more depth later, Brave Little Belgium and the *Roi Chevalier*, its 'Knightly King', heroically resisting the overwhelming German juggernaut and its untold brutalities with a small but valiant army, were too good an opportunity for the French and British propaganda machines to miss. To his amused surprise, Albert saw himself in the press in autumn 1914 compared to King Leonidas of the Spartans, to a modern Charlemagne, to King Saint Louis of France and his court likened to Camelot. He himself considered he had just done his duty, the duty the Belgian people had entrusted his (German) family to fulfil in 1831 and mistrusted those who wanted to use his popularity for their own ends.

By Christmas 1914, there was hardly a drawing room in Britain where *King Albert's Book* could not be seen on the table. Probably one of the most interesting propaganda tools (and bibliographical curiosities) in history, it was launched by the London *Daily Telegraph* and sold for the benefit of that newspaper's Belgian Fund.

Artists, composers, scientists, generals, admirals and politicians from several countries contributed texts, poems, and drawings. Some sent a few lines, others whole pages. All paid tribute to Albert, his country and his army. The last line of the Introduction by Hall Caine, the coordinator, read as follows: 'Belgians, in the person of your heroic young Sovereign we salute you. The statesmanship, the learning, the wisdom, the genius of the world lay their tribute at your feet.'

Good taste was not always present, the flourishing style of some contributions bordering on the downright ridiculous. Among the contributors: Kipling, Baden Powell, General Booth who founded the Salvation Army, Admirals Fisher and Jellicoe, the Earls Kitchener and

Curzon, the Lords Gladstone and Hardinge, Asquith, Balfour, Bonar Law, Sir Edward Grey and Churchill, John Redmond, who encouraged Irishmen to join the British army, pointing out the Belgian atrocities and suffragette Emmeline Pankhurst. Also John Galsworthy and Baroness Orczy, Belgian writers Verhaeren and Maeterlinck, composers Debussy and Paderewski, Anatole France, Henri Bergson, Pierre Loti, Romain Rolland, Edmond Rostand and Sarah Bernhardt, all stars of the French literary scene, painter Claude Monet, writer Blasco Ibañez, explorer Fridtjof Nansen and Andrew Carnegie. Ironically, several contributors had been very critical of Albert's predecessor's actions in the Congo. Two merit special mention: French politician Ribot and especially Lloyd George, who were to do everything in their power to thwart Belgian hopes and aspirations at Versailles, in particular Lloyd George who displayed a strong anti-Belgian prejudice, in spite of writing in 1914: 'This unfortunate country is now overwhelmed by the barbarian flood; but when the sanguinary deluge subsides Belgium will emerge a great and glorious land which every lover of liberty will honour, and every tyrant henceforth shun.'

The Real Albert

It is important to realize that for King Albert[3] Belgium was and remained a neutral country, involuntarily thrust by the German invasion into a situation where it must fight to maintain its independence. It was not a belligerent ally of the Entente Powers, France and Britain (as well as Tsarist Russia and Italy), whose war aims it did not share. Even after 1914, Albert always insisted on this separate status as 'Associated Power' which the US and others eventually also adopted. At the beginning of the war only Serbia shared this status, though Albert always refused to be too closely associated with this Balkan country. He had been horrified by the massacre of the Obrenovic royal family.[4]

Albert knew that Belgian neutrality was a necessity to keep the balance in Europe. The country had obviously to show solidarity with the Entente guarantors who had come to defend its neutrality, but without being locked in any formal alliance with them, which could only mean becoming a vassal state. Thus Albert only accepted a concerted common action to resist German invasion and guarantee the future independence of Belgium.

The war aims of the Entente are well known: for Britain it was mainly thwarting German naval expansion and preventing that power from dominating the Continent. France had a very strong desire to re-annexe Alsace and Lorraine, lost in 1871. This was of no interest to Belgium which,

Albert thought, should strive only for the restoration of its independence, compensation for the destruction it had suffered and the safeguarding of its colony. The government in exile also wanted to put an end to the forced neutrality imposed by the Treaty of 1839, and as we shall see hoped for territorial annexations, which Albert for his part never really approved of.

Albert was always in favour of a negotiated peace; he did not want Germany to be crushed because he (rightly) foresaw it would renege on any hard, imposed peace settlement and would seek revenge when it had rebuilt its forces. In 1918, as well as finding the conditions imposed on Germany too harsh, he would deplore the dismantling of the Austro-Hungarian empire, which led to a permanent imbalance in central Europe and the creation of weak countries, at odds with each other and ruled by dictatorial regimes.

The King, unsurprisingly a monarchist rather than a republican, especially in his time and with his background, mistrusted most politicians especially French ones, finding them devious, incompetent, chatterboxes. He trusted the British more than the French because they had more interest in Belgium's independence and had a vested interest in defending the Channel ports, coinciding with Belgian interests; whereas he was never convinced that France would not turn his country into a vassal state and in the present situation the French were mainly interested in protecting Paris. He developed sincere and lasting friendships with Lord Curzon and Admiral Keyes, but suspected some other British politicians cynically didn't mind seeing the continentals exhaust each other in this long and bloody war. The dislike Lloyd George seemed always to have felt for all things Belgian seems to have been reciprocated by Albert (whom he had described as nasty and silly). The King noted the Welsh politician appeared to be proud of the Bolshevik revolution, ignoring the fact that the fall of Russia (and Romania) liberated 100 German divisions!

Albert was not innocent of a slight anti-Semitic prejudice which was not unusual at the time, as can be read in his comments after the visit of Baron Lambert, a prominent Belgian Jewish financier ('a real Jew!'), although Elisabeth and he would later closely befriend Albert Einstein, and Elisabeth saved the lives of a number of Jews during the second German occupation. One of Albert's trusted divisional army commanders was General Bernheim, later to become President of the Belgian Jewish Consistoire.

From August 1914 till September 1918, King Albert exercised the high command of the army by virtue of Article 68 of the Belgian Constitution. This unique arrangement that had the historical rationale we have seen, allowed him to make important military and even political decisions, without needing government's approval. However, it was thought by some Belgian politicians in the government in exile to clash with another important part of the Constitution, namely Article 64, that states no act of the King is valid without being countersigned by a member of the government responsible to Parliament. Disagreements on this point did happen, but were to take a far more dramatic turn in the Second World War, eventually contributing to Leopold III's abdication in 1950.

Albert always commanded his army and kept it as a unified force, never accepting a subordinate position such as when the French wanted to distribute his units along the French front. Nevertheless, he always cooperated loyally with the Allies and more than once Belgian artillery batteries were detached and put under the control of the neighbouring BEF when German pushes made this necessary.

Albert realized the Germans had the means to destroy the Belgian army if they decided to do so. In order to give his efforts (which we will look at in the next chapter) more of a chance to obtain a negotiated peace, he refrained from recalling too often the atrocities the Germans had committed in his country in August and September 1914, which of course does not mean he had not felt enormous distress at their having taken place.

First and foremost, Albert did not believe in the *offensives à outrance*, 'mass offensives' which were in line with military thinking at the time, especially in France. The development of effective defensive tactics, mainly the trench, the machine gun and the artillery barrage, had made these tactics obsolete and very costly indeed. The catastrophic losses on both sides at Verdun, in the Chemin des Dames offensive which nearly caused the collapse of the French army through mutiny, the massive British losses in the Somme and Passchendaele offensives, for practically no gain, seem to have proved him right. Under his command the Belgian army fought valiantly at Liège and Haelen, even heroically at the Battle of the Yser to defend the Channel Ports, vital to the Allies. For four long years it kept an active watch on the same Yser with bouts of violent action and only engaged again in the final offensive in October 1918, where it took heavy losses. Belgian public opinion was then, and is now, grateful that he never allowed his small army to be involved in what he saw as useless slaughter. The Belgian army suffered, in proportion, seven times less in the way of losses than the French or British armies, thanks to Albert. As we shall see this caused bitterness in London and Paris and did not help Belgian diplomacy at the Versailles Treaty negotiations. But can a general be censored for having tried to spare his soldiers' blood and for refusing costly sacrifices he rightly considered to be useless?

Albert's concerns were not limited to the lives of his soldiers, and when he heard that British bombing raids in May and June 1918 had caused civilian casualties in Zeebrugge, Bruges, Ostend, Torhout and Kortrijk, which might have been avoided, he was prompted to write a protest letter to King George V – it was not well received.

A Saintly Address and a Post Office

When the fall of Antwerp was imminent, the Belgian government asked permission from France to set up a government in exile on French territory. On 13 October 1914, two Belgian merchant vessels arrived at Le Havre from Antwerp bringing nine of the ten members of the Belgian government. The French Minister of Marine had come down from Paris to welcome them. Only Prime Minister Charles de Broqueville was not on board, having stayed in Dunkirk. The Belgian ministers and their staff were taken to Sainte-Adresse, a seaside suburb of Le Havre where in peacetime hotels and holiday villas had long catered to holidaymakers. It was to become the effective capital of Belgium for four years.

The 1914 government had only members of the Catholic party, but in 1916 this was extended, taking in three members of the liberal opposition including Paul Hymans, as well as the socialist Émile Vandervelde, creating a 'Sacred Union' and the first tripartite coalition in the history of the kingdom. Two ministers died in Sainte-Adresse during the war. There were also several hundred Belgian civil servants and a garrison of 4,000 Belgian soldiers.

The Prime Minister[5] Charles de Broqueville – also Minister of War – resided only episodically in Sainte-Adresse, preferring to stay near the border, close to the army and the King. Sainte-Adresse was leased to the Belgian government for the duration of hostilities and had at its disposal a post office using Belgian postage stamps, as well as a car repair centre, a hospital and a school. There was also a Belgian weapons factory close by, which accidentally exploded on 11 December 1915, killing a hundred people.

Quarrels between Albert and his government

There were many incidents between the King and Broqueville, who eventually resigned in May 1918 and was replaced by the more malleable Cooreman. Broqueville, more of a Francophile than Albert, was closer to French ideas about the war and its aims and favoured annexing territories around Belgium after the eventual victory.

Other points of contention between the King and his government included Albert's complete opposition to letting the politicians interfere in the conduct of military operations, the degree of integration of the Belgian army in the Allied armies, and the peace feelers with Germany which Albert allowed or even made.

The Sainte Adresse Declaration

On 14 February 1916, France, Britain and Russia gave the Belgian government in Sainte-Adresse a solemn guarantee that Belgium would be restored to its former independence and integrity and would be compensated for damages incurred. This last is not without importance because, as we shall see, if Belgium was indeed restored at Versailles it got far less compensation than it had hoped for or thought warranted.

One could comment however, that in fact it was the Allies' total victory over Germany that secured Belgium's restoration and, even if less than expected, probably more compensation than would have been the case with the negotiated peace Albert had striven for.

4.1 Peace Feelers

As early as the end of August 1914, when fighting was going on after the fall of Liège, Germany sent peace feelers to Belgium via the neutral Netherlands, accompanied (tactlessly, like the offers made before the war) by offers of territorial compensations in northern France, that country at the time already fighting alongside Belgium.

Belgium did not join the 1915 London Pact, whereby the Entente Powers bound themselves not to sign a separate peace with Germany. This was later joined by Italy, but as we know, disrespected by Soviet Russia. Belgium, or at least King Albert, always maintained that as a neutral country suffering aggression it had a special status, even, according to some legal interpretations, not deemed technically at war[6] but free to pursue its own diplomatic course and if possible seek peace. As seen earlier, Albert in no way considered his country bound by the Entente war aims or interests, and definitively did not think Belgian soldiers should die in order for Istanbul/Constantinople to become Russian, or for the oil in the Middle East to be guaranteed to Britain. On the contrary, throughout the war he sought or encouraged contacts to explore possibilities of a negotiated peace settlement that would restore his country's independence and conserve its African colony. There were several of these contacts but essentially they yielded no result.

Stockholm and other Informal Contacts

As we have seen in spite of the last-minute conference organized in Brussels just before war broke out, the Socialist International fell apart when the war began in 1914. The German socialist members of parliament voted on the war credits. The Belgian socialists were co-opted into the Belgian government whose principle and *raison d'être* was *union sacrée*, a truce between parties, as long as the German invader occupied the country, Belgians of all political tendencies should set aside differences and cooperate to restore the country. However, the Bureau of the Socialist International led by Belgian Camille Huysmans, decided to relocate in neutral Stockholm in April 1917. Huysmans, who would later be prime minister and speaker of the Belgian House of Representatives, tried to mediate between socialists from the belligerent countries. He was discreetly encouraged by King Albert. With the Russian Revolution as a background, Huysmans and some other socialists began actively to advocate a peace conference in neutral Sweden. By May 1917, it had become clear that the British and French governments as well as the Belgian government in exile would oppose such a conference. Bilateral and multilateral negotiations took place but the governments of the Allied countries refused to issue passports to those who wanted to travel to Stockholm. In the end, the planned conference never took place. Huysmans was severely criticized for his actions, considered treasonable by some in Belgium and France. The criticism continued unabated after the war. There is a principle in Belgian political life that is (almost) always respected: one never 'uncovers the Crown', that is reveals what the King has told or asked you and what you have told him in private talks – to preserve his impartial status. Thus Huysmans never made public that Albert had encouraged him. When criticism became so heavy as to become unbearable, the King wrote releasing him from his pledge of discretion. Such was Albert's prestige, this immediately brought an end to the accusations against Huysmans.

All through the war there were other informal contacts between the belligerents, as when Jan Christiaan Smuts, the former Boer General turned British Field Marshal, went to Switzerland at Lloyd George's prompting to meet Austrian delegates in 1917, or when Colonel House, Woodrow Wilson's adviser, also made the rounds. Meeting King Albert in April 1916, House proposed that the Belgian Congo and Portuguese Angola and Mozambique be sold to Germany in return for Belgium's restoration. This robbing of Paul to pay Peter was obviously very unlikely to garner support from the Belgian monarch, not to say of dubious morality.

The neutral diplomats posted in Brussels, like the American and Spanish envoys Brand Withlock and de Villa Lobar had several contacts via the Netherlands, passed messages to Britain through the British Minister in The Hague, travelled to France and saw King Albert in La Panne. The Holy See, including the active Cardinal Pacelli,[7] who as papal nuncio in Munich knew Germany very well, also tried to mediate, though both sides seem to have mistrusted the Vatican and especially the Pontiff Benedictus XV.

Switzerland and the Netherlands also tried to help, passing messages between the two sides and exchanging heavily wounded or maimed prisoners via their neutral territories. Freemasons of the allied and neutral countries met in Paris in April 1917. But all these efforts were of little avail.

Three peace feelers involved Belgium more directly, which we shall examine now.

Törring-Waxweiler

In mid-1915, Count Hans zu Törring Jettenbach, a member of the Bavarian parliament and married to Sophie of Bavaria, a sister of Albert's wife, wrote a letter to his sister-in-law Queen Elisabeth asking for a talk about a 'family affair'. The letter was brought to La Panne by Elisabeth and Sophie's aunt, a Portuguese princess. The Belgian royal couple accepted contact but ruled out personal meetings. King Albert kept the Belgian government in exile in the dark because they would have opposed such talks – they considered Belgium had to keep fighting until final victory, while Albert thought it in the country's interest to seek a compromise. The King therefore considered it appropriate to at least consider German peace proposals, even though he realized he could not make peace alone. It has been said that in failing to inform the government he took some liberty with the Belgian Constitution, as political acts should be covered by responsible ministers. Only Albert's trusted military adviser, Major Galet, was made privy to the situation.

Albert sent Professor Emile Waxweiler, Director of the Solvay Institute of Sociology of the Brussels University, and his personal friend and advisor, to represent him. Törring acted in agreement with the German government.

Törring and Waxweiler, who spoke fluent German since his family was of German origin, met several times in secret in a hotel in Zurich between November 1915 and February 1916, the Belgian travelling back to report and even bring a letter from Albert to his German brother-in-law. Since the German proposals included ceding Belgian territory, the King reminded Törring his oath of office expressly forbade this.

The German proposals eventually proved unacceptable to Albert, who wanted no less than the restoration of the pre-1914 situation, without the compulsory neutrality imposed by the 1839 treaties but with reparations for the damage his country had suffered. Berlin, on the other hand, not only promised French and even Dutch territory to Belgium, but asked for control of the port of Antwerp and the coast, of the forts of Liège and Namur, of the Belgian railways and, icing on the cake, the precise right of passage that had been denied in 1914. They also wanted Belgium to join a German customs union. All this, clearly inspired by the military, was of course unacceptable and would have turned Belgium into a vassal state of Germany. No progress being made, the Zurich conversations eventually petered out. Waxweiler was to die soon after, run over by a London bus, but interestingly all the others in the know, including Törring, kept their peace and these contacts only became known to the surprise of many after all the protagonists had died in the 1960s.

Lancken-Briand

Baron von der Lancken was a former German army officer turned diplomat and was attached to the staff of the military governor of Belgium, von Bissing in 1916 and 1917. While in Brussels he met the French-born Countess Pauline de Mérode, née de la Rochefoucault and asked her if the contacts she kept in her home country could lead to peace conversations. The Kaiser, Hindenburg and Ludendorff were contacted and agreed to discuss the evacuation of Belgium and even of Alsace-Lorraine. King Albert was kept informed. A meeting was arranged in Switzerland between von der Lancken and French former prime minister Aristide Briand. Von der Lancken duly travelled to Switzerland but Briand never showed up. Apparently, and this was not the only time it happened, the talks were scuppered by French President Poincaré and the foreign minister Alexandre Ribot, hard liners both, and probably also by Briand's arch political enemy Clémenceau. In fact Ludendorff had postponed the Austrian/German offensive against Italy in Caporetto to wait for the outcome of the talks. Von der Lancken was to write after the war that he was sure a solution could have been found and that because of the stubbornness of some French politicians, millions more had to die. And in Belgium, the administrative separation of Flanders and Wallonia and, far worse, the deportations and systematic plundering of the country were still to come.

Bourbon-Parma

In 1886, France having been a republic again for only about ten years, the daughter of a prince of the Orléans family of pretenders to the throne became engaged to the heir of the Portuguese monarchy. The father of the future queen got carried away and foolishly gave a grand reception that was so lavish and successful in its attendance as to worry the republicans in Paris, who passed a law exiling all members of any family that had reigned in France. This applied also to the Bourbon family, who had reigned over France until the Revolution and whose Bourbon-Parma branch had been chased from the throne by Italian reunification in 1859. While one of their brothers served in the Austrian army,[8] Sixte and Xavier de Bourbon-Parma, two other sons of the deposed Duke of Parma, who had nineteen children by two wives, found themselves barred from serving in the French army so volunteered to join the Belgian army, where they became artillery officers. As it happened, their sister Zita was the wife of Archduke Karl of Habsburg, the new heir to the throne of Austria-Hungary after the assassination of Franz Ferdinand at Sarajevo. When the old emperor Franz Josef died in Vienna, the new emperor realized the war would inevitably bring catastrophe to the double monarchy and established contacts with his brothers-in-law. Sixte and Xavier were granted leave of absence from their regiment, though Albert had some misgivings about seeing officers of his army engaging in parallel diplomacy. Sixte went first to Paris and heard from the Allies their minimum requirement to discuss peace: Alsace-Lorraine restored to France, Belgium as well the Belgian Congo guaranteed, and Trentino to go to Italy. This is not the only time Italy's aspirations were to complicate matters, as other parallel negotiations were held directly between Austria and Italy in Switzerland. Sixte and Xavier went to see their brother-in-law, who also sent Sixte several handwritten letters in which he responded positively, but then his foreign minister Czernin, who was more German-inclined, in an unprecedented gaffe made the negotiations public, in rather aggressive terms for the French. At this President Poincaré, Prime Minister Clémenceau and Foreign Minister Ribot who were hardliners, published one of Emperor Karl's letters, in spite of having given their solemn word to Sixte that they wouldn't. All this caused extreme wrath to the powers in Berlin, whom Emperor Karl[9] had kept only partly informed and he had to come to the German GHQ in Spa to explain himself – some have said apologize to his ally, Wilhelm II. Hindenburg and Ludendorff decided to place Austria-Hungary under strict control. Albert and Elisabeth were also furious at what the French had done. In fact the negotiations suffered a quiet death because the French and British wanted to involve the Italians, to whom a lot had been promised in order to convince them to enter the war. This created a complicating factor since the territories the Allies had promised Rome belonged to Austria-Hungary.

The main conclusion to draw from the perhaps very unfortunate lack of success of all these peace feelers is that the possession by Germany (which could have been avoided had the French advanced more resolutely in 1914 to help the Belgian army and had the British seriously reinforced Antwerp) of most of the Belgian territory close to the Channel ports, its canals and railroads and other resources, of the Belgian and northern French coalfields and the iron ore mines of Lorraine, made a compromise peace wherein Germany would cede those possessions quite unlikely, not to say impossible, especially after the hardliner Ludendorff took over. Germany was known to want to recover its overseas colonies very badly but it was a forlorn hope they would agree to evacuate Belgium unconditionally in exchange, as was envisaged by the Allies.

Although Belgium was offered restoration and some degree of reparation by Germany, this also entailed a degree of vassalage. Under these conditions Belgium could not accept a separate peace, which the Allies would probably have made impossible anyway, although there might have been a chance the momentum so created would have opened possibilities of a general peace. We shall never know.

Another aspect is that the longer the war dragged on, the more the human and material losses became catastrophic, the less inclined both sides were to renounce what each had set themselves as a goal: in fact, total victory over the other side. To accept compromise or even a separate peace with a willing Austria-Hungary meant in fact accepting all these losses had been at least partly in vain. This played into the hands of the hardliners on both sides: Ludendorff, Clémenceau and Lloyd George. This was well illustrated when Lord Landsdowne, minister without portfolio but certainly not without influence, who in the past had kept Albert and Elisabeth informed of discussions going on about their country's future, published a famous article in the *Daily Telegraph* on 29 November 1917, in which he quite properly asked for the war aims to be defined and questioned the desirability of the annihilation of Germany as a great power. This, as Albert privately noted, caused the press baron Lord Northcliffe and his warmongering newspapers to have an absolute fit. In spite of the fact that the separate peace between Soviet Russia and Germany had considerably augmented the number of troops Germany could send to the Western Front, neither Lloyd-George nor Clémenceau ever seemed really interested in peace proposals, rather waiting, at great risk, for the Americans to tip the balance and deliver

104 Belgium in the Great War

the 'knock-out blow'.[10] The fact that Austria and Hungary were Catholic countries, while Clémenceau was a notorious freemason and Lloyd George had Baptist roots but had lost his religious faith when a young man, may also have played a role.

4.2 The *Frontbeweging*, the Flemish Movement at the Belgian Front

War has been described as long periods of boredom and waiting interspersed with intense terror and action. The long boredom was certainly there at the Yser front, held by the Belgian army after stabilization – that is between November 1914 and the last summer of the war in 1918. Most Belgian soldiers tried to keep themselves busy as we have seen, but for the Flemings among them having lots of time on their hands was particularly propitious for reflecting on who they were and what they were doing there. Most officers were French speakers from Wallonia and Brussels or French-speaking Flemings, the latter usually bilingual. Those who only spoke French rarely bothered to learn Dutch, even when encouraged to do so by the hierarchy. Only a few Flemish intellectuals had gone through the reserve officers training (some were later organized in Dutch). A number of the educated Flemish were NCOs or were even in the ranks. Others were teachers, priests, monks or seminarians, who usually acted as stretcher bearers or male nurses. Since the level of education was lower in mainly rural Flanders than in the (then) more developed industrial and urbanized Wallonia, a larger proportion of Flemings were serving in infantry units, while the proportion was inverted in the engineers, artillery and so on. With the advent of trench warfare the distinction between cavalry and infantry had disappeared in practice and *Lanciers*, *Guides* and *Chasseurs à Cheval* were now fighting dismounted.

A lot has been written about the respective proportions of Flemish and Walloon soldiers in infantry and the other arms, of the losses incurred and so forth. A few facts are thus in order here – as so often, political expediency has spawned myths. The proportion of Flemish soldiers in the infantry units was indeed higher than that of Walloons (about 60 per cent versus 37 per cent, the balance being difficult to classify) but it was not overwhelmingly so (not 80 per cent Flemish infantrymen as has been written by some). And according to some, 90 per cent of the Belgian soldiers killed in action were Flemish and many had died because they could not understand the orders given them in French! Serious Belgian (including Flemish) historians have taken a closer look at all this and worked on official army archives

Above left: Leopold of Saxe-Coburg-Gotha, first King of the Belgians. A minor German prince, he had married Charlotte, Princess of Wales. After she died he became King of the Belgians and shrewdly managed to place his relatives in practically every court in Europe, including his nephew Albert, Victoria's husband. (Author's collection)

Above right: Leopold II, second King of the Belgians. His reputation is very bad in the Anglo-Saxon world. There certainly were severe abuses when the Congo was his personal fiefdom though not quasi-genocide as some have claimed. Eventually Belgium annexed the Congo as a colony and most abuse stopped. Contrary to what many still believe, the Belgian Congo was not administered in a worse manner than the neighbouring colonies. (Author's collection)

Brave Little Belgium: the sketch in *Punch* that helped to sway British opinion in favour of Belgium.

Lancer Fonck, the first Belgian casualty of the Great War. The monument stands at the spot where he was shot by German reconnaissance cavalry a few hours after the invasion began. (Author's collection)

Belgian soldiers in their 1914 uniform. Dogs of the now extinct Belgian mastiff breed were used to pull the machine guns. (War Heritage Institute, Brussels)

The strategic Visé bridge over the Meuse River was blown up by the Belgian army before the Germans arrived. The invaders built a pontoon bridge that came under heavy fire from the forts of Liège. They then forded the river close to the Dutch border. (Author's collection)

Above: The historic centre of Louvain (Leuven), which was completely devastated by the Germans in August 1914. (War Heritage Institute, Brussels)

Below: Plan of Fort de Loncin, typical of a Brialmont-type fort. The main gate is at the bottom. The magazine explosion took place about where the left *coupole* (turret) of 12 cm stood. The garrison's last stand was fought at the top point, Saillant II. *Fossé* means 'ditch'. (From *Loncin* by Colonel Naessens)

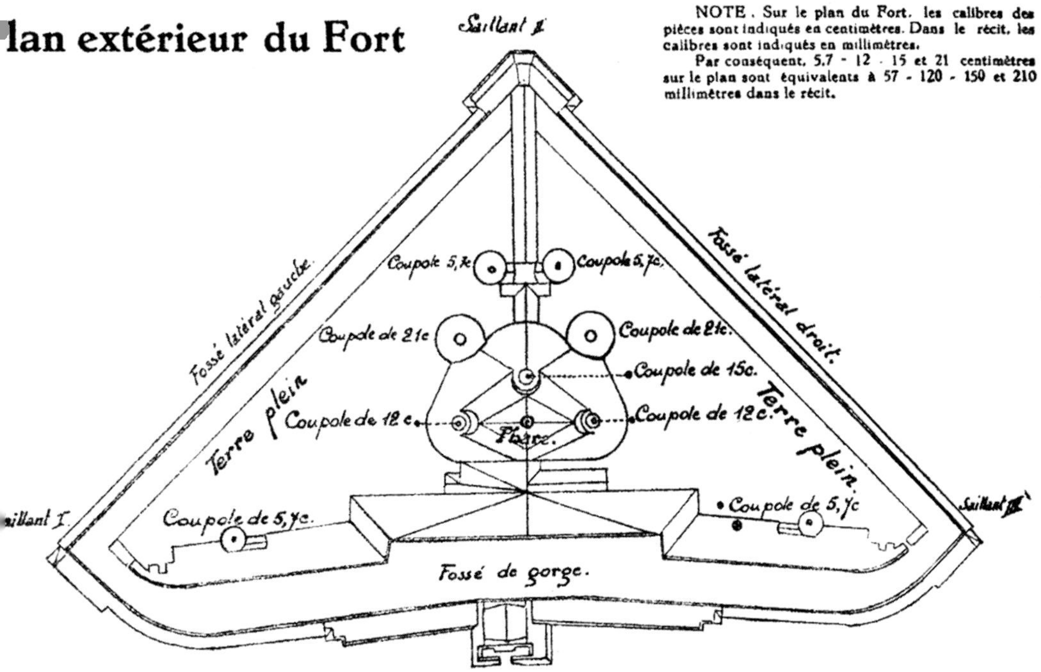

General Leman, in his Napoleonic-style uniform He had taught King Albert at the Belgian military academy and was given command of the vital Liège fortifications. Captured unconscious after Fort de Loncin exploded he was freed by the Germans later in the war. (Author's collection)

Left: The mammoth 420 mm German naval Krupp gun adapted to demolish the Belgian forts from a safe distance. Its shells were almost a metre long. (Musée Fort de Loncin)

Below: One of the gun turrets of the Brialmont forts pre-war. (Musée Fort de Loncin)

Effects of the 420 mm shells on one of Loncin's turrets. The round hole is the gun's breach. (Author's collection)

Above: Haelen: Belgian Lancers hold a barricade against an attack by Mecklenburg Dragoons.

Below: Haelen: the German cavalry charges. Yzerwinning Farm is on the left.

King Albert of the Belgians holds a medal parade. All still wear the old style Belgian uniform. (War Heritage Institute, Brussels)

Above: Two of the beautiful German helmets that are to be seen in large number at the Haelen Museum. (Silver Helmets Musem, Haelen)

Left: Haelen: the monument the Germans erected close to Yzerwinning Farm. (Author's collection)

The 'Goose's foot' at Nieuport (Nieuwpoort). (Author's collection)

Above: Contemporary drawing of hand-to-hand fighting during the Battle of the Yser. (War Heritage Institute Brussels)

Right: Aerial view of the 'Goose's foot' in Nieuport where the drainage canals converge that were used to flood the 'German' bank of the Yser River. (War Heritage Institute, Brussels)

Above: The Kaiserliche (Imperial) Marinekorps was responsible for defending the coast, from the front to the Dutch border. (Kriegsalbum des Marinekorps – Author's collection)

Below: The Kaiser visits his troops at the front in Flanders. (Kriegsalbum des Marinekorps)

Stabilization. Endless watching over the desolate, inundated front. (War Heritage Institute, Brussels)

The 'Trench of Death' on the bank of the Yser River has been preserved; it is close to Dixmude (Diksmuide).

Above: Madam Tack and her donkey Paula would bring sweets to the soldiers. (War Heritage Institute, Brussels)

Right: Albert I, King of the Belgians, in the new khaki uniform introduced in 1915, with the French Hadrian helmet. Refusing to engage his men in offensives he did not believe in, the King became very popular. (Author's collection)

Left: Bavarian-born Queen Elisabeth's loyalty to her husband's country never wavered, though most of her close relatives were on the other side. Encouraging her husband, like him she became very popular through multiple social and artistic activities. (Author's collection)

Below: The Sainte Adresse government in exile in France. Prime Minister de Broqueville is third from the right. (War Heritage Institute, Brussels)

Belgian Henri Farman 20, early in the war. (Daniel Brackx collection via Didier Waelkens)

Famous balloon buster André de Meulemeester with his Hanriot Dupont biplane. (Daniel Brackx)

Spad XI two-seater of the type King Albert sometimes flew across the lines, to the great dismay of his government. (Daniel Brackx)

The Belgian Congolese *Force publique* during the campaign in German East Africa. (War Heritage Institute, Brussels)

The 'auto-cannons' and their colourful CO. Blocked in Russia by the Soviet revolution they came home via Siberia and the USA. (War Heritage Institute, Brussels)

The 'auto-cannons'. Note one of the soldiers relaxing on the top armoured plates. (War Heritage Institute, Brussels)

Cardinal Mercier. His pastoral letter denying the Belgians owed any loyalty or obedience to the occupiers had a considerable impact. (Author's collection)

Above left: Brussels Burgomaster (*Maire*) Adolphe Max. Protesting too loudly the heavy taxes his city was made to pay, he was exiled to Germany for the rest of the war. Many other Belgians went the same way. (Author's collection)

Above right: Gabrielle Petit was executed as a spy by the Germans at the same spot as Edith Cavell. She was 23 years old. (Author's collection)

Below: The Tir national shooting range in Brussels where many executions took place. Edith Cavell was probably made to stand where the white plaque is sited. (Author's collection)

The Belgian army at the battle of Merksem (Merxem). The soldier top right is holding a French Chauchat light machine gun, which was an inferior weapon prone to jamming. The Americans also used it. (War Heritage Institute, Brussels)

Before evacuating Belgium the Germans systematically plundered or destroyed the Belgian industrial infrastructure. (War Heritage Institute, Brussels)

The final offensive. Belgian soldiers find themselves out of the muddy, devastated front line. (War Heritage Institute, Brussels)

Right: Among his many honours, King Albert was made Colonel-in-Chief of the Inniskilling Dragoon Guards. This portrait hangs at the entrance of the Belgian ambassador's residence in London. (Author's collection)

Below: Belgian troops occupying Aachen, Germany, Charlemagne's capital. The Dom (Cathedral) can be seen in the background. (War Heritage Institute, Brussels)

The large cemetery at Poelkapelle. Most of the 1,722 Belgian soldiers buried there were killed in the final offensive of September 1918. There are also 81 Italian POWs the Germans had used as forced labour. (Author's collection)

The Ijzertoren (Yser tower) monument in Dixmude (Diksmuide) is the symbol of Flemish aspirations for more cultural and political autonomy. Built after the Great War it was blown up by persons unknown and rebuilt stronger and taller. (Author's collection)

The monument to the dead at Warsage village, where the Germans executed a number of civilians in August 1914. Such monuments are to be found in every village and city in Belgium. (Author's collection)

Stocks of shells found in the fields by farmers and waiting to be destroyed. Every year between 250 and 300 tons are made harmless. (Author's collection)

documenting the cases of KIAs, their unit, place of birth, circumstances of demise and so on[11] and have reported facts, not hearsay. First, the population of Flanders was (and still is) larger than that of Wallonia. Next, the German invasion having come from the east there had been no time to mobilize many of the young Walloons, whereas the hostilities had moved gradually back into Flanders allowing more time to organize a complete call-up. Also, fewer Flemings than Walloons having the benefit of basic education there was a tendency to assign them to the infantry, where basic training was simpler for rankers than the engineers or artillery units, where greater skills were needed. Thus, in a typical infantry regiment (*9ème de Ligne*) 55 per cent were found by the Flemish historian F. Stevens to be Flemish, 10 per cent from Brussels and 35 per cent Walloon. This could be extrapolated to all infantry and made for higher losses (according to sources between 3 and 9 per cent more, compared to the general population of the language groups in Belgium) among those Flemish who were at the front itself most of the time, as opposed to members of other units that were either behind the lines, like artillery, or only occasionally engaged like the engineers.

What about the persistent myth that some Flemish soldiers were killed or even executed because they could not understand the orders given by the officers? This has been disproved by contemporary historians.[12] In fact everybody who has served in a seriously organized army (and remember the Belgian army certainly gave a good account of itself in the Great War) knows this does not hold water: a unit would not be placed facing the enemy if the officers had not previously trained their soldiers and knew for sure that basic instructions like orders to advance, to open or cease fire, take cover, retreat and so on, would be clearly understood by their men. Doing otherwise would have been a recipe for disaster and most orders could be relayed/translated by bilingual NCOs anyway, possibly in the version of patois (like Bruges Dutch, for example) the soldiers of that particular unit understood best if they mostly came from the same region or city, as was often the case. In all armies NCOs play an intermediary role between officers and enlisted men. Naturally, there are good and bad NCOs and that there were some who bullied Flemish soldiers and mocked their clumsiness is quite likely. That some were foolish enough to have called out loud on parade, after orders had been given in French by officers: 'Et pour les Flamands, la même chose!' ('The same goes for the Flemish!') – a stupid joke indeed, but highly probable. But the myths, especially this one about incomprehension of orders, seem to have been invented *after the war* by extreme Flemish nationalists, possibly August Borms.[13] As for executions, a myth that sometimes crops up in the press or literature in Flanders to this day, no one has ever been able to convincingly point out names or cases, places of occurrence of the 'crime', why the King did not grant stay of execution, or date of actual execution. There were indeed executions for desertion or for serious offences like rape and murder as we have seen, but not for 'not having understood their orders or actions taken or failure to take them for that cause'.

Among the Flemish intellectuals reflecting on the Fleming cause and rights were: Second Lieutenant Joris Van Severen, who was to play an important political role in the 1930s,[14] only to be executed summarily by French soldiers in May 1940; Doctor Frans Daels, a gynecologist who seems to have been one of the first to devise gas masks and had been a volunteer; Ernest Claes, who became a prolific novelist but was at that time a bureaucrat at Sainte Adresse; another writer, Filip De Pillecijn (who was later to meet Goebbels); Adiel Debeuckelaere, an NCO for whom his companions revived the long disappeared title of *Ruwaert*, or 'Regent of Flanders' (for the absent and enemy kings of France in the Middle Ages); and especially Father Cyriel Verschaeve, whose parish was in the non-occupied part of Belgium, and who wrote articles against the immoral behaviour (visiting prostitutes, drinking etc.) of many young Flemish men after having been called up. Verschaeve's Christian and Flemish nationalist feelings inspired the slogan *Alles voor Vlaanderen, Vlaanderen voor Kristus*, 'Everything for Flanders, Flanders for Christ', in abbreviation AVV-VVK, which can still be seen in Flanders on books, newspapers, flags and monuments to this day. His opinions led him to outright collaboration during the Second World War, a death sentence in absentia, and he ended his life in exile in Austria. Another priest, Father Joe English, was, despite his name of Irish extraction and introduced the Celtic Cross as one of the emblems of Flemish nationalism, in homage to his origins – another people undergoing oppression, as he saw it. It should be noted that the Catholic Church, especially the lower clergy, played an important role in the Flemish Movement as a whole. Another notable was Mrs Belpaire, living in the non-occupied part of the country, who was highly respected by King Albert amongst others, and also ranted against immorality behind the front.

When Wilson's Fourteen Points were published, some did not fail to take note of the point about self-determination.[15] And the Pope's efforts to bring about peace were of course supported by the overwhelmingly Catholic Flemings.

Some Flemings from a rural background only became aware of their 'Flemishness' at the front whilst in contact with Flemish intellectuals. *Vlaamsvoelenden* or 'Flemish-feeling persons'[16] started having meetings to further their cause, to read poems or other works of literature. Reading rooms with Dutch language books and other publications were opened (King Albert contributed money to buy Dutch books), where paper to write letters could also be found, lectures could be heard, songs sung and plays staged, Christmas parties with gifts organized, educational courses given and so on. Some of these activities were innocent enough, but others were more aggressive in tone. The slogan *Hier ons bloed, wanneer ons recht?* 'Here is our blood, when will we enjoy our rights?' was often heard at more politically orientated meetings.

When King Albert visited a unit, *1e Jagers te Paard*, where a large part of the soldiers were Flemish, to pin a medal on its colours, he made it a point to address the parade in Dutch. Albert I was the first Belgian monarch to be bilingual.

On 11 July 1917, the anniversary date of the Battle of the Golden Spurs in 1302,[17] a group of Flemish activists at the front wrote him an open letter stating their grievances, which were mainly regarding legislation about the use of languages that in fact already existed, but had not been implemented when war broke out, about access to higher education in the Dutch language after the war and largely political autonomy for Flanders, where the Dutch language would be used for official business like the courts and administrative affairs. The fact that headstones in military cemeteries for Flemish soldiers who had fallen were inscribed in French also caused understandable resentment.

The existence of Belgium was not questioned and at the beginning of the war all of Flanders certainly stood behind King Albert, who had recalled the courage of the Flemish militias at the battle of the Golden Spurs in 1302, as well as an equivalent Walloon prowess, in his famous speech in Parliament the day Belgium was invaded. Many Flemings, including some with strong feelings about Flemish rights, volunteered when the country was invaded and most Flemings realized it would be very dangerous to pin their hopes for cultural and political autonomy and redress of wrongs on the Germans, when the outcome of the war was far from clear. But the expression of these grievances was going too far for some in the military hierarchy, especially the secret services and censors who kept a very vigilant eye on such activities. Some activists, especially those who had drafted the letter to the King, were threatened with demotion or court martial. The King himself, without answering the letter directly, let it be known he felt sympathy for the aspirations expressed. He tasked his private secretary Jules Ingenbleek to examine the question of unilingual units (in fact Flemish regiments, alongside French-speaking ones). Ingenbleek reported favourably on this and it was pointed out that other armies (though on the other side) like the Austro-Hungarian had done so, creating Czech and Polish-speaking units alongside the already separate Austrian and Hungarian armies. The Belgian army top brass, however, would have none of this and the King could not risk the major disruption that might be caused by such a profound reorganization of the army in wartime. He also realized it would severely antagonize the officer corps, a risk he was not willing to take. So things more or less remained the way they were.

Stating these grievances, which would all be realized/redressed in later times, seems acceptable today but it was not so regarded by some at the time. Arch Belgian nationalist and newspaper tycoon Fernand Neuray violently attacked what he saw as separatism and inevitably, though unfairly, lumped the *Frontbeweging* in with the German *Flamenpolitik* (policy of dividing the Belgians, about which more later) – in fact with collaboration and treason. Cardinal Mercier also had little time for the Flemish aspirations and did not hide it, while the army padres, though some like the King were not entirely hostile, discouraged political activities as long as the war lasted and recommended patience until peacetime.

One important Belgian politician, the member of parliament for Antwerp, Frans Van Cauwelaert was a very prominent 'Flemish feeler' before the war, but he took great care to stay well away from anything the Germans did or promised. A refugee in the Netherlands, he came over to the front when his brother, who was in the army, was wounded, and visited the King and the government at Sainte Adresse. During the Second World War he was to take refuge in London and chair the group of Belgian members of parliament there.

The war dragged on and in 1917 and 1918 the number of desertions increased. Some of these were probably in part motivated by despair at not knowing how much longer the misery would last, others were at least partly politically motivated and were known Flemish activists. A new name was coined for them, the *overlopers*, 'those who ran to the other side', or 'turncoats'. One second lieutenant was among them, the only officer. To their surprise they were usually not welcomed home, indeed some were even boycotted by their own families. One of them, whom even his father refused to see, fled to the Netherlands after the war, where he taught French for a living... Some took part in uniform in demonstrations in occupied Belgium. In fact the leaders of the *Frontbeweging* themselves took steps to stem the desertions, realizing the *overlopers*/collaborators risked bringing the whole

Flemish Movement into disrepute. Very few approved of Borms' actions in occupied Flanders, as we shall see later. Mrs Belpaire and Van Cauwelaert both stated very clearly that it was not from the (hated) Germans they would or should accept a Flemish university.

Part of the Flemish movement at the front was thus irreproachable, but excesses happened. One of the *overlopers* wrote an open letter to the Flemish soldiers he had left behind, telling them they should stop fighting for the French and the English, these last 'the murderers of the Irish and the Boers'. In fact several times, especially after the Easter Rising, parallels were drawn between the Flemish and Irish causes. A pamphlet insulted General Bernheim, the CO of the 1st Army Division calling him a German Jew. Bernheim was Jewish and would later chair the Belgian Jewish Consistoire. Considering what happened in the 1930s and 40s this was obviously quite sinister. Some Flemish soldiers got worked up after going to a play and after a few drinks a small riot developed, where officers who had also attended the play were roughed up. A few times there were fisticuffs between Flemish and Walloon recruits in Belgian army training camps in France.

When Adiel Debeuckelaere was taken prisoner in September 1918 the Germans soon found out he was the *Ruwaert* and his actions became outright treasonable: he went so far as to promise to intervene to facilitate the surrender of the Belgian army if the Germans managed to encircle it during their offensive in the summer of 1918 (though the Germans didn't really trust him). When they lost the initiative he became less vocal.

The Germans of course exploited all this by sending pamphlets in hollowed out artillery shells, dropping them from planes, or even by little boats on the flooded areas, and by erecting big boards promising they would not open fire at this place, at that time, to make it easier for *overlopers* to come over (the boards were usually shot to shreds), but only to a certain point as Ludendorff himself did not think the thing was worth much effort except at very end of the war, when he clung to every straw to stave off disaster. In fact the Germans were well aware of the *Frontbeweging* but did not make the mistake of overrating its importance and were conscious of its limitations, such as the very relative trust the Flemish soldiers put in German promises – on the whole they were faithful to King Albert. The massive deportations to Germany which did not spare some of their relatives did not help, of course. So the *Frontbeweging* 'died a silent death' in the general euphoria of November 1918 and the Flemish Movement would only come back in the late 1920s and 30s in a different guise, as a political party, the Vlaams Nationaal Verbond (VNV) the Flemish National Union.

4.3 Belgians Abroad, or Where Agatha Christie Found her Inspiration

Refugees

From the beginning of August 1914, cohorts of civilians were thrown on to the roads. At least one and a half million people fled the fighting. Panic-driven by the persistent (and true) reports of the atrocious behaviour of German troops in the Belgian territory they had invaded, they fled to neighbouring countries, largely the Netherlands, the easiest place to reach by land, or to France, which could also be reached overland and to Britain. When things calmed down, large numbers of these refugees, mainly the citizens of Antwerp which is not far from the Netherlands or those from Liège who had taken refuge in nearby Maastricht and environs, walked back in the weeks following the stabilization. The Dutch government, understandably not wanting to be saddled with an enormous number of refugees it would have to care for, encouraged them to go home, guaranteeing nothing untoward would happen to them. That was later to put The Hague in a very uncomfortable position when the Germans started to deport Belgian civilians, in some cases the same ones the Dutch had convinced to go home.

It should be noted that the Dutch government, whose neutrality in matters of arms sales to Germany (notably Dutchman Anthony Fokker's infamous wares) was less than impeccable, did on the whole deal very fairly with the Belgian civilian refugees who chose to remain for the duration, allowing young Belgians who had crossed illegally into its territory to join the Belgian army to do so discreetly, whilst the interned Belgian soldiers, mainly a part of the Antwerp garrison who crossed in 1914 when the rest moved to the Yser, were treated as well as possible in the difficult circumstances.

In contrast, with the exception of those stranded in the part of France that was occupied by the Germans, few Belgian refugees went home from France and even fewer from Britain, because this would have meant crossing the lines of the opposing armies, an obvious impossibility. Some who could afford it travelled through neutral Switzerland or the Netherlands, but the majority stayed put for the duration. So in France, gradually, cities, hospitals, army training centres, schools, and the like sprang up, administered by the government in exile in Sainte Adresse.

Many women worked as nurses in the Belgian hospitals in France, such as the Hôpital Albert 1er in Paris. Men not drafted into the army took jobs in French or dedicated Belgian ammunition factories, worked as civilians in Belgian army training camps, in rehabilitation centres for the wounded in Sainte Adresse and so on. Others took refuge with relatives and some, it should be said, pursued less useful but sometimes quite lucrative activities… In France there were reports of women who, though married to French soldiers, eloped with Belgian refugees.

In Britain, one often hears that Agatha Christie's famous sleuth, Hercules Poirot, was inspired by her meeting with a Belgian detective who had taken refuge in Britain. Apparently he impressed her by his powers of deduction. Other Belgians also used their little grey cells as well as their muscles to contribute to the war effort.

As in France, maybe even more so, there was definitely a great deal of sympathy among the British population for the Belgian refugees. Refugee committees sprang up in many towns in the UK. After it was realized the war would last longer than originally expected, by the end of 1914 the shell shortage scandal coincided with the awareness that many Belgian refugees were skilled workers and the British government, while keen to safeguard the British workers' interests and prevent what would later be called social dumping (i.e. preventing them from working for lower wages than their British counterparts), sought to put that idle workforce to good use. By the end of March 1915, many thousands of Belgians were working in munitions factories all over Britain – Vickers alone employed 3,000.

A new village was even built of prefabricated huts outside Britley between Durham and Newcastle, appropriately named Elisabethville (with an S), next to a projectile factory at Britley itself, where most of the able-bodied non-drafted Belgians went to work every weekday. Eventually 6,000 Belgians would live there. It was complete with a church, a school manned by unfit soldiers for the boys and nuns for the girls, a food store, a dining hall, a hospital/maternity ward, a jail and a cemetery where thirteen Belgian military were laid to rest. Several 'Britley babies' were born. There was a lot of gardening. It was declared a sovereign Belgian enclave and for a time Belgian Gendarmes were tasked to uphold the (Belgian military and British civil) law. The lack of tact of the Belgian policemen led to a riot over the wearing of uniform at work (uncomfortable near the hot furnaces) and in pubs (unlawful) and they were replaced by English bobbies. When the war was over, Elisabethville quickly emptied, with a few exceptions due to local marriages and today little is left of it.[18]

In November 1918, between 500,000 and 600,000 refugees still lived outside the borders.

5

Out of Africa and around the World

5.1 The African Campaign

What was later called the Scramble for Africa occurred during the second half of the nineteenth century, and involved the carving up of north and Black Africa among the European powers. Even the United States, a former colony itself, presided closely over the creation of Liberia where former slaves came from North America and in fact colonized the territory and its inhabitants, to the US's profit. Washington had a strong influence in the capital, Monrovia. The rest of the continent was divided among Britain, France, Belgium, Portugal, Germany, Italy and Spain (in about that order of size), the only exception being Abyssinia, now Ethiopia, which kept its independence after fighting off an Italian invasion in 1882.

The many conferences that brought about the partition of Africa regrettably took no account of local ethnic divisions, which meant that peoples speaking the same language and who felt kinship with each other became separated. Some were split among several colonial rulers, like the Bakongo, who live along the Atlantic Ocean on both sides of the Equator,[1] who found themselves ruled by French, Belgian and Portuguese masters (this even in two different territories, Cabinda and Angola, separated by the Belgian Congo). Or the Makonde people who lived on both banks of the Rovuma River separating German East Africa from Mozambique.

One of these conferences was in Berlin in 1885, hosted by Bismarck and one article of its Final Act stipulated the perpetual neutrality of the basin of the Congo River, that is, what after 1908 became the Belgian Congo and its contiguous British, German and Portuguese territories.

Germany, two of whose colonies, German East Africa (Deutsch Ost Afrika – DOA) and Kamerun (German Cameroon), shared a border with the Belgian colony, had ambitions on the Belgian Congo and so had Britain. As late as 1914 there were negotiations between London and Berlin about dividing the Belgian and Portuguese colonies in Africa between them. And all through the campaign the British were wary of Belgian ambitions over the German colony neighbouring theirs.

In 1891, the Etat Indépendant du Congo (EIC),[2] in fact Leopold II's controversial private domain, recruited Zanzibar mercenaries, who were progressively replaced by native Congolese recruits with a cadre of Belgian officers and NCOs. Each indigenous chief had to furnish a yearly contingent of recruits to serve five years, plus two years in the reserve force. Training establishments like an NCO school for Africans were opened. The *Force publique* is invariably shown by Hollywood attacking innocent villagers and massacring them because, it is implied, they had failed to deliver their assigned quota of ivory and wild (vine) rubber. There might have been such cases of abuse, just as in the British and French colonies and in the American-administered Philippines. But history based on documentary evidence rather than on propaganda has established that the *Force publique* was used mainly to repress the flourishing slave trade run by Zanzibaris and Sudanese, with the complicity of local potentates, who were devastating vast zones of the east and north Congo basin to transport young, fit Congolese to the Horn of Africa and the Middle East, effectively depopulating whole regions. Heroic deeds are recounted, as when two Belgian officers held captive by a slaver king refused to swim across a river to safety because a third officer had been left behind, ill at the slaver's village – they stayed, though a Belgian officer and his unit were in position on the other bank to cover their escape. All three prisoners were massacred the next day.

The *Force publique* campaigned against Arab slavers in 1892–5 and the Mahdists 1893–1910. There were mutinies in 1877, 1895 (a major one in Luluabourg) and 1900. When the Congo became a Belgian colony in 1908, the *Force publique* came with it. It was in fact a mixture of army and police. Numbering about 17,000 men, it was in 1914 the strongest armed force in central Africa, far more than the British or German colonial forces in the neighbouring territories. They were spread out over the immense territory of the Belgian colony, whose extreme points stretched as far as Lisbon from Prague and Brussels from Sicily. They were divided into companies of 600 men, each subdivided into platoons, each in charge of a sector, where they kept (colonial) law and order. It should be noted that the law was a mixture of Belgian law and *Droit coutumier*, the local customs and traditions which you could quote in court when land was disputed or in family affairs.

The *Force publique* was trained more for administrative surveillance and police duties, tax collection and repression of smuggling, poaching and native rebellions (as was also the case in the neighbouring British and German colonies), than for military warfare against a well organized, well-armed foe. Recruits came from all regions of the Congo and care was taken that never more than a quarter of a given unit was composed of members of the local tribe. They were not always the *crème de la crème* as local chieftains who had to provide a fixed contingent often found this a convenient way to get rid of troublemakers or petty criminals. Discipline was – had to be – harsh and included corporal punishment, namely the *chicotte*, a Portuguese word for the lash, of which however a maximum of twenty could be given (on the buttocks) on parade. To communicate, *lingala*, the language of one of the prevailing tribes was used along with French, which some of the native soldiers did not master well. Gradually the number of African NCOs increased.

In 1914, several hundred Belgian officers arrived from the Yser and more African soldiers were recruited, thus creating a large force that combined the Belgians' knowledge of modern weaponry, mainly machine guns and artillery, with the Africans' experience of bush warfare. The weapons were at first a mixture of Belgian-made Mauser 7.65 mm rifles, old ex-Belgian army Albini 11 mm rifles, French Gras rifles, 60 American Colt machine guns and the same number of French Hotchkiss MGs. There were also 47 mm Nordenfelt guns and French Saint Chamond 70 mm guns that could be dismantled, as well as some mortars. Gradually the armaments became more standardized, but the fact that the Belgian arms industry, mainly in the Liège region, was in occupied Belgium forced the government to turn to its allies, principally France, for new supplies. Though lacking tactical training (they would learn the hard way), the *Force publique* became a good fighting force and its contribution to the East African Campaign, unfortunately under-reported when not ignored altogether by British historians, was in fact a determining one, because Britain did not want to commit too large a part of its forces in Africa as opposed to France and Flanders.

On 4 August 1914, the Belgian colonial authorities were informed by telegraph that a state of war existed between Belgium and Germany. At first it was hoped in Goma, the capital of the Belgian Congo (Léopoldville, now called Kinshasa, became the capital in 1923), that in accordance with the Act of Berlin, no hostile action would be taken in the Congo Basin. In fact Schnee, the governor of German East Africa (Deutsch Ost Afrika, DOA) favoured this stance but the military commander, with whom he would frequently clash, the soon to become famous Lieutenant Colonel von Lettow-Vorbeck had other views and saw it as his duty to immobilize as many enemy troops and resources as possible in Africa to prevent them from joining the decisive Western Front – in fact, smart reasoning. Lettow-Vorbeck had fought in the Boxer rebellion in China, had observed the Boer War, and fought again in the (savage) repression of the Herero revolt in Süd West Afrika (now Namibia). He was to become very popular with the *askaris*, the native troops raised in DOA. He thus started mobilizing and expanding the colony's well-trained forces, the *Schutztruppen*, who had a good and numerous cadre of German officers and NCOs, at a higher proportion than in the Belgian and British European colonial troops. A retired German general, Kurt Wahle, happened to be visiting relatives locally and put himself at Lettow-Vorbeck's disposal, though he technically outranked him. On hearing all this the Belgian CO of the *Force Publique*, General Tombeur also mobilized, and on 15 August 1914, two German warships on Lake Tanganyika where they held naval supremacy at the time, the SMS *Hedwig von Wissmann* and the SMS *Kingani*, caused the Belgian steamer *Alexandre Delcommune* to become stranded.

In Europe also, the Belgian monarch and government for various reasons would have preferred not to see the war in Europe spread to Africa and made representations to that effect in London and Paris, citing the 'civilising mission of the Europeans in Africa'. However France and Britain had other views and wanted to attack Germany wherever possible. Britain had supremacy of the seas, which made it a virtual impossibility for Germany to supply her colonies (attempts were however made, as we shall see) and France wanted to enlarge her empire, especially with a part of the French Congo colony it had been forced to cede a few years earlier by virtue of a compromise involving Morocco. But it seems to have been the Germans who fired the first shots, while attacking the British colony of East Africa (now Kenya) on the slopes of Mount Kilimanjaro, as well as attacking the Belgian Congo across Lake Tanganyika which was part of the common border. This last made sense tactically since they had, at least at that stage, naval superiority on the large lake and strategically, for the reasons explained before: tie in as many as possible of the Allied troops away from the European theatre.

Belgian troops helped the French conquer German Togoland (now just Togo, a neighbour of Ghana) as early as August 1914 and in German Kamerun two *Force publique* companies consisting of 10 Belgian officers and 570 Belgian Congolese troops entered the capital Yaunde in January 1916. French, British and Belgian flags were hoisted over the capital, now known as Yaounde in Cameroon (next to Nigeria). Riverboats used in this campaign were aptly renamed *Haelen*, *Liège* and *Luxembourg*. The Belgians left on 18 February 1916.

No Belgian troops took part in the conquest of German Süd West Afrika, which was carried out mainly by South African troops, who did not leave until the 1990s.

It was decided, too, that unlike France and Britain, Belgium would not send any colonial troops to fight in Europe.[3]

The Belgians were dismayed to hear about the botched landing at Tanga, in German East Africa, where the Germans captured large quantities of arms and ammunitions from the British Indian Army.

Copper is a very important commodity in wartime for manufacturing ammunition and its production in the Congo was increased threefold between 1914 and 1917. The Belgian Congolese authorities were aware of the threat to the important copper mines in the Katanga region in the south east of the colony. In 1915, the Germans attempted to raid the Kilo Moto gold mines in the North East of the colony.

The first serious Belgo-German clashes in Central Africa occurred when Belgian contingents were sent from Katanga in September 1914, to relieve a British garrison under siege in northern Nyasaland (now Malawi).

In northern Rhodesia, British troops found themselves besieged in Abercorn, in what is today Zambia, and were relieved by a Belgian column led by Colonel Olsen, chief of staff of the commander of the *Force publique*. Belgian troops remained there until November 1915 after having repelled a fresh German assault.

As we have seen, the weapons used by the *Force publique* were of many different kinds, which did not simplify the supply of ammunition. This on top of the necessity to carry drinking water and food in a land mostly devoid of roads and railways could not have made the logisticians' task easy! Thousands of porters walked hundreds of kilometres and a Belgian officer calculated that if a porter was 12 days from a depot he required 10 kilos of the load he carried to take his own food for the way back, meaning he worked for 25 days to carry just 3 useful kilos – say one light artillery shell or a single box of rifle ammunition for the fighting troops. Many porters recruited in the hot and humid climate of the western Congo and unaccustomed to the dry cold air of the region they were taken to, fell ill or deserted. Some Congolese porters were 'lent' to the British, where they joined colleagues from Zanzibar and the Seychelles Islands. Mule trains and carts were also used where possible and the logistic 'tail' with mobile hospitals, engineer and signal units stretched back thousands of kilometres, over the mountains separating the great African Lakes from the Congo River, to whatever railways existed at the time in the Belgian Congo and then to either South Africa or Mombasa in Kenya. A new railway linking the Congo River basin with Lake Tanganyika was built.

A steel gunboat, the *Paul Renkin*, named after a Belgian minister for the colonies, was built in Paris, then dismantled and taken with great pains to

Lake Tanganyika to cover the Royal Navy's setting up of HMS *Toutou* and HMS *Mimi*, two motorboats sent from England to South Africa, which were hauled to and floated on a river, manhandled and hauled again by steam-powered locomobiles and finally re-floated on the lake.[4] There SMS *Hedwig von Wissmann* struck her colours to them and became HMS *Fifi*. The Belgian ship *Netta* took part in the naval battle. Plans to bring a French submarine to the lake were eventually ditched but four Short 827 floatplanes were bought in Britain and transported by Belgian steamer, along with spare parts, fuel and ammunition, to Matadi on the Atlantic coast of the Belgian Congo. From there the crates went by rail to Léopoldville, then by boat on the Congo River to Stanleyville (today called Kisangani), by railway again around rapids, then river and train again to arrive finally on the banks of Lake Tanganyika, having travelled 2,850 km from the Atlantic coast, roughly the distance from London to Istanbul. Reassembled, the amphibious planes raided the German shore of the great lake (which is roughly 650 km long and 8 km across) and after several unsuccessful raids and mishaps that included forced landings on the water, finally sank SMS *Graf von Götzen*[5] and another ship under construction in Kigoma harbour, on the DOA shore on 17 July 1915. One pilot died of exhaustion but the others were sent back to Europe to fly patrols out of Calais with Schrek FBA flying boats. Seaplanes bought in both France and Britain and brought dismantled, were also used for reconnaissance and bombing of German lake transports.

To conquer Deutsch Ost Afrika (now Tanzania, and Zanzibar, a British possession, was later annexed to it), the largest, richest and most populous German colony, the British mobilized about 42,000 men, mainly British, South Africans, Nigerians, Ghanaians and Kenyans, Indians, but also men from the British West Indies (the Caribbean). The first British commander was sacked and General, later Field Marshal, Jan Christiaan Smuts, who had given the British a lot of headaches with his guerrilla tactics during the Boer War, was appointed in his place. Later in the war he too was replaced, by his compatriot Van Deventer, both men Afrikaners of Dutch descent. East Africa eventually became the most important non-European theatre of the war.

The railway across DOA, from Dar es Salaam on the Indian Ocean to Kigoma on Lake Tanganyika was of obvious strategic importance. Tabora, the second most important city in the German colony stood about two thirds of the way up its 1,250 km length. Von Lettow-Vorbeck had at that time 3,000 Germans and 11,000 Africans under his command.

The actual Belgian intervention consisted of two different successive phases: the first from March till September 1916 conquered Ruanda and Urundi, and stopped when Tabora was taken.

The second offensive lasted longer and ended with the fall of Mahengé or rather with the surrender of the German troops in November 1918.

Seeing on the map where Mahengé is, not very far from the Mozambique border, it is fair to say the Belgians conquered about half the German colony by themselves, though this is not always recognized by British historians, who tend to focus on their country's or rather on their Empire's participation.

By January 1916, two brigades of fifteen infantry battalions and three artillery batteries were ready, under the overall command of Colonel Tombeur, a north column under Colonel Olsen and a south column under Colonel Molitor. The first offensive began in March 1916. In coordination with British troops coming south from Lake Victoria, they methodically invaded the two westernmost parts of DOA, the ancient kingdoms of Ruanda and Urundi. On 6 May they entered Kigali, now the capital of modern Rwanda. In this difficult terrain, devoid of roads and railways, they depended on porters or oxcarts.

Von Lettow-Vorbeck had given General Wahle, a good logistician, an independent command in the region while he himself resisted then escaped the first of innumerable attempts by Smuts to encircle him in the Kilimanjaro region and later further south. The Belgians and British were helped by the interception of German radio communications. Usumbura, the capital of Urundi, was occupied on 6 June 1916 by the South Brigade but a strong German counter-attack on the Belgian columns resulted in savage hand-to-hand fighting. The Belgians pushed on and reached the Tanganyika–Dar es Salaam railway, which they could only put to limited use due to lack of rolling stock.

At Usoke, one Belgian platoon that had outrun the Germans then found itself surrounded. Both sides were reinforced and a fierce fight ensued.[6]

On 18 September 1916, after a determined defence and counter-attacks in which 105 mm guns were used, Tabora, the second largest city in the German colony, with 40,000 inhabitants fell to the two Belgian converging columns and a British column. The *Force publique* made its quarters in the *boma*, the German-built garrison fort. Interned there were 9 Belgians, 100 British, 3 French and 47 Italians, who were all freed; all were civilians and 35 were missionaries. Tombeur received a congratulatory telegram from King Albert.

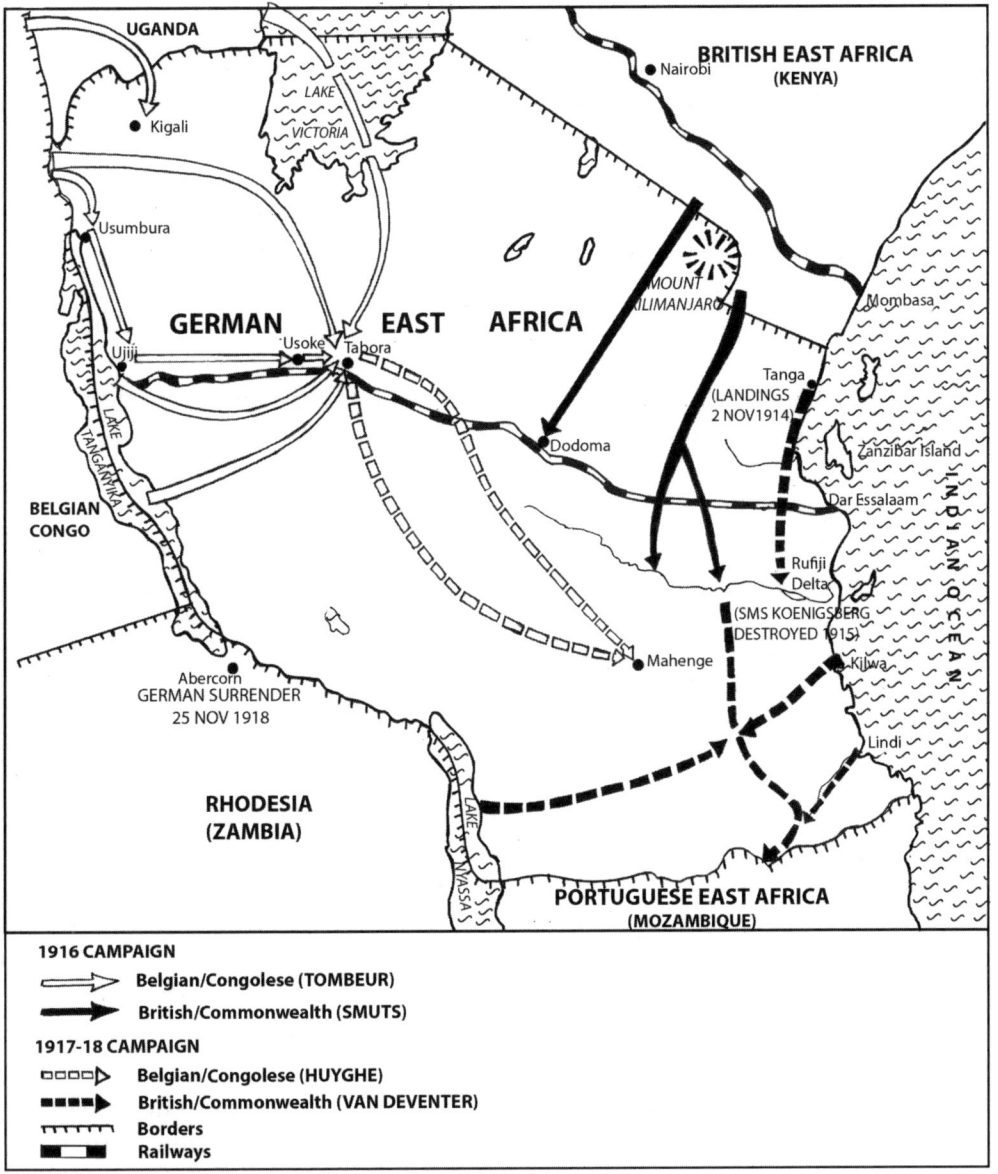

3. The East African campaign

After Tabora fell, most of the Belgian officers, including Tombeur himself and many NCOs started for Europe, prompted by Smuts whose masters in London distrusted Belgian expansionist views on the shores of Lake Victoria, not without reason it should be said. But re-embarkation was stopped when it was learned in November 1917 that von Lettow-Vorbeck, now a major general, had invaded Portuguese Mozambique, capturing large quantities of arms and ammunition there and that two German columns were threatening Rhodesia and the part of DOA that had been conquered and occupied by the Belgians. The British, who didn't want the Belgians too much and too long around in the German colony, delayed their decision as to how to react, which was regrettable because it gave the Germans precious time. A new Belgian battle corps was organized and placed under command of Colonel Huyghé. Meetings took place in Dar es Salaam between the British and Belgian commanding officers. These Belgo-British meetings and cooperations were not always exempt from mutual recriminations or clash of personalities. Another long trek/pursuit followed over the rugged hills, fighting sometimes evolving into trench warfare, the Germans however always managing to fight their way out of ambushes and escape encirclement. In July, heavy fighting resulted in Major Rouling, a Belgian regimental CO being severely wounded, as well as German *Hauptmann* (Captain) Godovius. There were 300 KIAs and 17 German POWs, as well as a German field hospital captured. Another German column under command of *Hauptmann* Tafel ran out of food and was forced to surrender. By then the Belgian/Congolese force had trekked through and conquered 350 kilometres and Smuts sent Huyghé a congratulatory telegram. Malaria was rampant and morale oscillated in accordance with success or failure. On 9 October 1917 Mahenge fell, while in the meantime Huyghé had been replaced by Colonel, later General Olsen. The *Force publique* at that time controlled about two thirds of the territory of DOA. Mahenge was taken over by the British and two Belgian Congolese battalions were transported to Dar es Salaam and on to Kilwa on the Kenyan coast.

Contrary to what some British authors have written, the Belgian campaign was thus not limited to the conquest of Ruanda and Urundi or even only the taking of Tabora.

Von Lettow-Vorbeck and his men fought a long but remarkable war, living off the land or captured arms and supplies, manufacturing uniforms from home-grown and spun cotton dyed with bark extracts, and manufacturing quinine to fight malaria. There were no accurate maps. Swampy terrain alternated with small desert areas and shrubby, steep hills over which artillery and supplies had to be hauled. Columns would split up to gather more food than a single column could. Surprisingly this force may have been one of the first 'integrated' ones in history, as white German rankers could be found fighting along the African *askaris*. From Germany, several attempts were made to resupply them by blockade-breaking ships and even a Zeppelin, this last failing after its crew was made to believe when already over Sudan that von Lettow-Vorbeck had surrendered. Smuts, though considered a guerrilla expert because of his Boer past, in fact never managed to corner von Lettow-Vorbeck, who brilliantly succeeded in diverting an important part of the Allied war effort away from the Western Front.

In July 1915, the raiding cruiser SMS *Königsberg* was cornered in the Rufiji delta and blown up after a great effort by three RN monitors that had previously been shelling the Germans from off the Flemish coast in support of the Belgian army.[7] But the resourceful Germans salvaged her 105 mm naval guns and built wheels for them, and the 720-man naval crews joined von Lettow-Vorbeck's force as part of the artillery. Two of those guns were eventually taken by the Belgian/Congolese.

It was not until 13 November 1918, after being informed by the British of the Armistice in Europe, that the undefeated von Lettow-Vorbeck ceremonially surrendered at Fife in Northern Rhodesia (now Zambia) to the British and Belgians, not far from Abercorn where the first Belgian-German fighting had taken place.

On the whole, the East African Campaign was a 'clean' war: POWs and captured civilians were treated chivalrously, the wounded of both sides looked after, white flags of truce and Red Cross emblems respected. When during an attack a British machine gun opened fire from a hilltop at a German first aid post, it was enough for an angry yelling German doctor to come out in the open waving a Red Cross flag for the assault to cease. Things were not the same on the Western Front...

The enemies sometimes communicated with each other by leaving messages nailed to trees, or with wounded soldiers left behind for the enemy to care for, and it was from a British source that von Lettow-Vorbeck heard he had been awarded a very distinguished medal and promoted by the Kaiser. When the Germans finally surrendered, they were worried the Belgians would exact vengeance for what had happened in Belgium in August 1914. However their fears proved unfounded and German civilians captured at Kigoma, Tabora or Bismarckburg found they had less to fear from the Batetela, Bakongo and Baluba soldiers[8] of the *Force publique* than the inhabitants of Visé, Louvain, Aarschot and Dinant had in August 1914 from the 'civilized' Westfalians, Silesians and East Prussian soldiers. Instead, the German officers were treated to a banquet by their Belgian counterparts with white tablecloths and at which wine, which they had not seen for years, was served. The German *askaris* (native soldiers) were disbanded and sent home and so were the Germans who returned to the Fatherland via neutral Rotterdam.

Belgian forces had done well in East Africa. This campaign and the Belgian contribution is today largely forgotten but at the time it was appreciated by the Allies. At Versailles, Belgium received mandates from the League of Nations to administer Ruanda-Urundi, the regions it had conquered. The two mandate territories were administered together but separately from the Belgian Congo, though contiguous to it and both became independent in 1962, two years after the Congo, under the names Rwanda and Burundi. Their history has been eventful and bloody, especially during the 1994 Rwanda genocide. The British took the lion's share of the German colonial empire in Africa.

General Tombeur was made Baron Tombeur de Tabora, which had an ironic side to it as 'tombeur' means 'he who makes (a city) fall'. Huyghé was knighted. Until the 1980s some Congolese veterans were still drawing pensions. Cemeteries of Belgian and Congolese soldiers still exist in Tanzania.

The number of Belgian officers and NCOs came to 719, commanding 11,700 Congolese soldiers and 260,000 carriers, these numbers of course varying during the campaign. Casualties were 58 Belgians and 1,895 Congolese KIA, 69 Belgians and 1,203 Congolese WIA. Loss of life through disease and exhaustion was very heavy indeed among the porters, totalling 7,124. Belgian/Congolese losses amounted to over 10,000 men and there was also, of course, enormous financial cost. For four years about a million British, Belgian, African and Asian soldiers and carriers had been held in check by a far smaller number of Germans and their *askaris*. In this von Lettow-Vorbeck, his 2,700 Germans, 12,000 *askaris* (roughly the same number as the Belgian Congolese troops only) and 45,000 porters had certainly been successful as these Allied troops and the materiel the latter used or expended was kept from other fronts.[9]

The indisputable courage of their Congolese soldiers caused admiration and sympathy from the Belgian officers, triggering new interest in their lives after the war and prompting them to look after the families of those killed. Something hitherto unknown in Africa had happened: black men (on both sides) had been ordered to fire at and kill white men. This was to have long-term consequences for attitudes in Africa. In the Belgian Congo many families found their lives irremediably disrupted by the long (sometimes final) absence of soldiers or carriers.

Because of the colonies the belligerent countries possessed in Africa and Asia, what had started as a European war became a world war, changing the face of the globe for ever.

5.2 The 'Auto-Cannons' from Russia to New York and Bordeaux

In August 1914, some affluent Belgian officers had armoured plate and Hotchkiss machine guns bolted on to their private luxury cars – often Belgian-made Minervas, now an extinct brand – and started 'hunting' for German patrols. Some like the 'Bonnot Gang' of Belgian soldiers operating from the Liège forts, seem to have been quite successful at harassing isolated German patrols and shot up a few, especially cavalry, with little or no loss to themselves.

However, when the front stabilized on the Yser in mud and water these contraptions, in fact creative novelties, became useless in the terrain the Belgian army was now having to negotiate. On the other hand the Belgian HQ recognized, as did Britain at the same time, that these fast vehicles could be useful for reconnaissance and infantry support missions, so a few purpose-built, 4-ton armoured cars had been constructed by Minerva, armed either with a light gun or a machine gun, anticipating the day when the German lines were eventually pierced and they would be able to roam behind the enemy lines. This of course did not materialize until 1918 and in the meantime the 'auto-cannons' and their crews stood idle. Enter the Belgian military attaché in Paris and the Russian military attaché to the Belgian government who thought that on the far more mobile eastern front, where their respective countries were fighting a common enemy, armoured cars could be making themselves useful. King Albert and the top brass gave their approval and in September 1915, 400 auto-cannons (the name had now come to mean the soldiers themselves) embarked at Brest, in France for Archangel. Under their CO, Major Collon, an eccentric character replaced in 1916 by Major Semet, they had with them 15 armoured cars, 25 motorcycles, 34 lorries, some of which were mobile workshops, and 130 bicycles. Among the personnel, all volunteers, were aristocrats, artists and a Belgian communist, Julien Lahaut, who was later to distinguish himself by shouting 'Vive la République!' in Parliament at the very moment in 1950 when King Baudouin was about to take his oath. He was to pay dearly for this, as persons unknown shot him dead at his home a few days later.

The auto-cannons were taken a thousand kilometres from Archangel to Petrograd (St Petersburg) and inspected at Tsarskoye Selo Palace on 6 December 1915, by Tsar Nicolas II, in temperatures of minus 30° C, unheard of in Belgium. All wore Belgian uniforms with added Russian rank insignia, since otherwise the Russians would not have been able to tell officers from other ranks. Some thirty Russians were also attached to them. They then were quickly engaged in combat in Galicia against Austro-Hungarian troops, fighting there till the end of 1915. Fifteen of them were killed in action. In 1916 and 1917 they took part in the Broussilov offensive, where they gave supporting fire and some German infantry surrendered to their armoured cars, probably a first in history. They were also engaged in the final Russian efforts made by the provisional government of Kerensky. In heavy fighting there were a further 11 killed in action, 4 dead from other causes and 40 wounded, with one vehicle lost. After the Bolshevik Revolution of October 1917 things became complicated for the auto-cannons. Civil war raged, the ways to the ports held by Tsarist forces were blocked by communists and there was obviously no way back through central Europe dominated by Germany and its allies. The only way out was east. The Minerva armoured cars and other motor vehicles were sabotaged or disabled and in exchange for a stock of vodka they had captured in Kiev and a written pledge not to fight against them, the Belgians secured from the communists permission to entrain for Siberia.

The trip took them to Moscow, Yekaterinburg, Irkutsk, Omsk and the terminus of the Trans-Siberian railway. Four Belgian soldiers deserted to go and fight with the White Russians. They did not return home until the 1920s. On the Russian Pacific the auto-cannons embarked on an American freighter, the SS *Wray Castle* that took them across the Pacific to San Francisco. The city mayor wanted to organize a fitting reception for the 'heroic' Belgians and felt a Belgian band should open their parade. Since the auto-cannons had no band except a bugle and a drum, but did have a stock of Belgian uniforms, forty burly American bandsmen wriggled into the slightly too small khaki uniforms and blasted away through the streets of San Francisco, followed in step by the Belgian colour party and the rest of the troops...

East by train the party went again, via Sacramento, Salt Lake City, Cheyenne, Omaha, Des Moines, Chicago, Detroit, Buffalo and finally New York. Each city outdid itself to give the Belgians a rapturous welcome. This was not completely devoid of a hidden agenda, as the US had just entered the war after a long hesitation and if the soldiers of 'little Belgium' could be heroic, so could and should the men of the Great Republic.

Finally, having travelled 80,000 kilometres the Belgians landed in Bordeaux. They had expected to rejoin the Belgian front in Flanders but by now it was November 1918 and the unit was disbanded and the men reassigned or sent home. It had been quite an adventure, which some even compared with Xenophon's classic account of a military expedition (in *Anabasis*).

6

Occupation

Apart from the coastal region and the rear area – land immediately behind the front, controlled directly by the army, called the *Etappengebiet*, the access to which was severely restricted – the whole of the country was placed under military administration, the *Generalgouvernement*. Three successive governors held the top job: *Generalfeldmarshall Freiherr* (Baron) Colmar von der Goltz who had held command in the August 1914 campaign briefly held the governorship. In November 1914, *Generaloberst* (Colonel General) Moritz Ferdinand von Bissing was made *Generalgouverneur*, a job he held until he died of pneumonia in Belgium in April 1917.

Von Bissing, who was thus to preside over the country's destiny the longest, encouraged Flemish separatism and generally tried to curry favour with the Flemings, as when he decreed the administrative separation of Flanders and Wallonia, and reopened Ghent university. He was the one who signed the death warrants of Edith Cavell and many Belgians. He also tried to control the activities of the International Red Cross, vital for the exchange of information on soldiers when they were listed KIA, WIA or POW, and for the meagre correspondence between the Belgian soldiers at the front and their families, but Geneva very firmly put its foot down and he did not insist.

At his death von Bissing was replaced by Ludwig von Falkenhausen, a veteran of the Franco-Prussian war of 1870, who remained until the Germans evacuated Belgium. In fact his being sent to Brussels was a demotion, as he had held a high command against the British and Canadians at the front and had been found wanting during the Battles of the Scarpe and Vimy Ridge. His nephew was to hold the same job during most of the second occupation (1940–44) and would be arrested by the Nazis for sympathizing with the plotters against Hitler.[1]

All three governors were retired general officers who had been called up when hostilities began. Their attitudes were different but in step with the evolving situation. Von der Goltz, who presided only briefly, let it be known the Belgians were not required to renege on their patriotic feelings. All that was required was that they did nothing to hamper the operations of the German army and obeyed the occupying authorities. Von Bissing had a more proactive attitude and encouraged Flemish separatism, but resisted Hindenburg's orders when Germany started plundering Belgium outright. Von Falkenhausen however, obeyed the orders to requisition whatever he could and to make preparations for whatever Germany had in store for Belgium after the war, whether as a protectorate or even full annexation.

The universities were closed for the duration, the main institution, Louvain, being sacked anyway. Some form of censorship was imposed even in schools.

Compulsory identity cards were introduced as was German currency, of course at a forced exchange rate which made purchases by the occupiers very cheap. Heavy war taxes ('war contributions') levied on the central state as well as municipalities made economic life ever more difficult. From forty million Belgian francs a month at the beginning of the war, the taxes were progressively ramped up to fifty then sixty million, massive sums at the time.

German time was also imposed and a story the author has been unable to verify states that when French intelligence had word the Kaiser would inspect his troops in Flanders on a certain day and hour, an aerial strafing expedition was mounted to machine gun his motorcade, only to miss him by an hour because of a mix-up about the local time…

Berthe J. and her family spent a lot of time at the family chateau some distance south of Bruges. At one point, a son of the Kaiser came to stay and they were confined to the basement. One day she noticed water cascading down the stairs. She went up and saw the prince, whose hobby was photography, had forgotten to turn off the water tap that allowed the photo-sensitive glass panes to be immersed in basins. At that moment the Kaiser's son came back and Berthe started angrily yelling at him, along the lines of, 'You turn us out of our house and now you cause inundations and depredations! You should be ashamed!' The prince without a word called orderlies, who quickly cleaned up the mess. On another occasion a properly uniformed German officer complete with pointed helmet rang the doorbell of their Bruges home and asked if he could escort her to Sunday Mass. 'Never with a German!' was the uncompromising answer. My grandmother was very pleased with these stories, which she often recalled, including once in a Weinstube, a wine-proving bar in the Mosel Valley when I was posted in Germany with NATO. We had to hush her up when she began repeating in a loud voice, 'Avec un Allemand, jamais!' The Germans make good wines.

The electric Iron Curtain

Fifty years before the Iron Curtain went up across Central Europe dividing Germany in two, another deadly barrier was established between Belgium and its northern neighbour. As the number of Belgians seeking to join the army, allied soldiers escaping captivity, spies and German deserters was increasingly using the porous Dutch border, a German captain of engineers came up with the idea of installing an electric fence along the Belgian–Dutch border. Governor von Bissing approved, the Dutch government in The Hague was officially informed by the German ambassador there, and a copper wire fence, through which a 2,000 volt current passed, was erected between Aachen, where the three borders meet, all along the 300 km border, to Knokke, on the North Sea, at the Scheldt estuary.[2] At regular intervals watchtowers and searchlights were built, diesel generators set up to provide the current that was fed to the multi-layered wires, and sirens that went off when it was tampered with. Ordinary, non-electrified steel warning wires to prevent the patrolling Dutch and German soldiers from harm were strung in parallel and at a distance. The *Elektrozaun* is reckoned to have accounted for 2,000 victims, though it is estimated as many as 20,000 managed to cross it successfully. This was done by various methods: corrupting the guards, using empty wooden casks to keep the wires apart through which you could crawl, thick rubber sheets (but rubber was difficult to get hold of), cutting the wire with insulated plyers and shunting the cut with wires. Professional *passeurs* would help you across for a fee but very gruesome pictures exist of some who lost their lives trying, including one Belgian agent working for the Allies.

Public opinion in Belgium

After the fighting stabilized in the extreme west of the country, the population took stock. Naturally the first reaction was shock and indignation at the brutality of the unexpected, unprovoked German attack on Belgian neutrality, the massacre of thousands of civilians, the burning down and plundering of a number of medium-sized cities. No one had expected a civilized neighbour, with whom the country had no quarrel – for whom many even professed admiration – to behave like this. A regime of military occupation was immediately installed. For the Belgian civilian population a period of isolation from the rest of the world, of repression, misinformation and enforced silence was beginning. It would last four and a half years and would become gradually worse.

As for most peoples suffering alien occupation the main preoccupation became to survive, to find food for one's family, in a country that produced only a reduced part of its needs.

Another side-effect was a surge of patriotic feeling, triggered by all that was being done to the country and unheard of in peacetime, the Belgian propensity for self-mockery and lack of chauvinism being legendary.

Unlike in the second occupation twenty-five years later, the King, to whom loyalty was felt by almost the whole population, and the army, wherein many families had members who were known to be resisting and fighting on behind the Yser River, were very popular. The army, previously unpopular because of compulsory military service, suddenly became the darling of the nation. The legal government was known to be in exile in France, even if little was heard of it. The rumble of artillery, especially during offensives, could be heard in most of Flanders and Hainault, a clear indication that the war was not over. Thus the German invasion and long occupation was recognized and perceived by the overwhelming part of the Belgian population as exactly what it was: a foreign army that had violated the country's neutrality, had committed numerous atrocities on civilians during the invasion, imposed ever harsher requisition of food and other goods and even at a later stage deported part of the labour force to work in Germany. Obviously there was ill feeling towards those responsible for all this misery, the brutal neighbours bent on pursuing their own interest. And whereas at the beginning of the war no particular sympathy was felt for any of the belligerents, this rapidly changed and the Allies attempting to liberate Belgium became the hope and the favourites of Belgian public opinion. By their decision to trample on Belgian neutrality for purely military reasons (which did not even bring them the quick victory over France they had hoped to achieve) the Germans unsurprisingly alienated any friendship or admiration their peacetime achievements had inspired. With the exception of a small number of Flemish activists, the populace felt nothing but contempt and hatred. The occupiers could count on little sympathy from those of lower incomes, who were forced to ever harder work and hunger by their requisitions, from the middle class who saw their income shrink through inflation, or from the rich bourgeoisie and aristocracy who, with a very few exceptions, cold-shouldered them. This was so even when family links existed, which was not unusual and was the case with the royal family, as we have seen with Princess Stéphanie, daughter of Leopold II, thus King Albert's first cousin and widow of Rudolf of Habsburg, who committed suicide in Mayerling (see note 1, for ch. 1, Part I, and chapters 2–5).

Another member of the Belgian royal family, Princess Charlotte, daughter of Leopold I had also married into the Austrian imperial family. Her husband, Archduke Maximilian briefly reigned as emperor over Mexico before being executed on the orders of Benito Juarez. Charlotte went mad, came back to live in Belgium and spent her last years at the chateau of Bouchout, north of Brussels. Recognizing her as an Austrian archduchess, the Germans posted a guard of honour at her chateau. A few Belgian families of high birth possessed land in Germany and had dual nationality, which created a tricky situation. The Dukes of Arenberg were to pay heavily after the war for having chosen the wrong side, seeing their assets either confiscated like the Palais d'Egmont in central Brussels, now a part of the Ministry of Foreign Affairs, or being forced to sell their chateau of Heverlee outside Louvain (where they had sheltered refugees during that city's sack). As a whole, and unlike in the second occupation when extreme right parties both in Wallonia and Flanders sided with the Nazis, the Kaiser's men had next to no sympathizers, certainly not in Wallonia, very few if any in Flanders and certainly none among the French-speaking elites in Flanders, who had everything to lose from a 'germanization' of Belgium.

6.1 Feeding the Belgians: Of Ships, Sealing Wax, Cabbages and Kings

The strategic importance of the British naval blockade of Germany in 1914–19 (as a means of pressure it lasted until the Versailles Treaty was signed) is often underrated by historians, especially non-British ones. It was a far more important factor in the Great War than is generally appreciated, as attention is commonly focused on the land battles. Its effects on Germany and Belgium were significant. Germany (like Belgium) had recently heavily industrialized its economy, but needed to import ores, coals, and chemicals for industry, as well as foodstuff and fertilizers for agriculture. Occupied Belgium, having suffered invasion and the execution of citizens was now threatened by another looming catastrophe, mass starvation, since its own agriculture could only cover 20–25 per cent of the population's needs while the German occupiers continued to make massive requisitions of all goods, including food, livestock and farm horses. The situation would go from bad to worse towards the end of the war and we should now look at it in more detail.

Realizing what was happening, a group of prominent Belgians including industry tycoons, Nobel Prize winners and academicians, notably Ernest Solvay and Emile Francqui, met to see what could be done. They in turn contacted the embassies of neutral countries in Brussels, in particular Don

Rodrigo, Marquis de Villa Lobar, envoy of the Spanish King, Mijnheer Van Vollenhoven representing the Dutch Queen and especially Brand Withlock, the American representative. (It should noted that at the time diplomatic representations in smaller countries were known as legations and headed by ministers; only larger countries sent and received ambassadors. Later, all became embassies and for simplification's sake this is the word I use.) Future president Herbert Hoover happened to be in occupied Belgium to take care of American interests and citizens, and unhesitatingly joined the efforts to save the Belgians from starvation by setting up food shipments from the United States to come in via neutral Holland. The two most interested belligerents, Germany and Britain, were reluctant and mistrusted each other at first, but then realized it would be better for their images to relent and enter into the agreement creating the Commission for Relief of Belgium (CRB), of which Hoover became the President.[3] Von Bissing tried to exercise some control over the CRB but was forced to back down by the neutral embassies, the importance of whose role in Brussels during the occupation cannot be overrated. After the war, Hoover, Brand Withlock, Villa Lobar and Van Vollenhoven were all made honorary citizens of Brussels and had streets named after them.

On the basis of predominantly private donations, clearly marked cargo ships conveyed flour, canned milk, meat, bacon, apricots and other dried fruit, salmon and so on, as well as clothing and toys. Some packages held concealed encouraging messages 'from American mothers to Belgian mothers'. Vegetables could be grown locally and many flowerbeds were sacrificed both in private gardens and public parks. Empty bags of flour embroidered by Belgians women with elaborate 'Thank you' messages, with crossed Belgian and American flags, were sent back to the United States as tokens of gratitude. Teachers made Belgian schoolchildren write moving letters to America, decorated with drawings: *Without you we would have died of hunger*, wrote a (rather precocious) five-year-old girl from Ghent. The American Library of Congress holds about 8,500 of these letters.

Thus Belgium escaped famine during the First World War thanks to a massive surge of generosity from the United States, under the auspices of the Commission for Relief in Belgium. Shipments started in October 1914 and almost 3.2 million tonnes of food and clothing were sent to Belgium from the US and Canadian ports between January 1915 and December 1918, carried in about 2,300 specially chartered ships. And though (despite **'Relief for Belgium'** being painted in white on their hulls) a number of ships were sunk by U-boats on the high seas (twelve in 1917 alone), broadly speaking both the British and the Germans respected their parts of the accord, the Germans never attempting to seize the shipments being sent by barge or lorries to Belgium from Rotterdam, where special facilities were provided in the port, docks and warehouses rented for the purpose. At the beginning of the war, the American representatives of the CRB operated freely in occupied Belgium. Aid was distributed through local committees with the assistance of Belgian auxiliaries. Part of the food was distributed to the parts of northern France that were also occupied. US embassy motorcars wore large American flags and were allowed to go about by the Germans. After the US entered the war the other neutrals took over.

Most of the help was paid for by private donations amounting to 750 million dollars, while the US government added 370 million dollars. The Belgian government in exile also chipped in. Families of Belgian soldiers who could not receive the pay of their menfolk had to be helped also.

Sugar and butter became rare luxuries, but if you knew a farmer, sometimes a rabbit, some ham, bacon or eggs would find their way into your cooking pot. Of course there was a flourishing black market with astronomical prices.

6.2 Enslaving and Robbing the Belgians: Plundering and getting rid of Competition

Germany (and Britain too as we shall see when covering Versailles) always considered the smaller but vigorous Belgian economy as a competitor, its prices being often lower for equivalent products like steel and glass. This explains in part what follows but of course the main reason for plundering the country and deporting its working force was to contribute to its war effort, ever more hampered by the British naval blockade.

Enslaving

In 1916–17 the Germans started using French, Russian and Belgian POWs to dig trenches, underground shelters and artillery dumps, and to work on narrow gauge railways, telephone lines, dugouts and tree felling behind their front.[4] This was barely legal as the Hague Conventions state POWs have to be kept far enough from the combat zone to be out of harm's way (Article 19). Using Belgian and French civilians for the same purposes was absolutely illegal but began at about the same time. Worse was to come: French civilians from the occupied part of their country were brought in to Belgium to work on farms or in factories, another internationally illegal measure.

In 1916 alone, 55,000 Belgians were taken to Germany and 47,000 forced to work at the front. According to the Germans 15,000 of those had volunteered, but they did not bother to pretend the others had. That the Belgian civilians working at the front were certainly in harm's way is demonstrated by the fact that some were provided with gas masks. All this created an international incident: the Dutch government had promised Belgians, based on a promise von der Goltz had made, that nothing untoward would happen to refugees who had taken refuge in its territory if they returned home. This had been intended to lighten the burden of feeding and housing them in Holland – but the Germans promptly deported some of those people, breaking the Dutch government's word. At an early stage the Germans tried to voluntarily enrol the unemployed, describing the 'idyllic' conditions and fat wages they would have, but this was quickly abandoned for lack of success and replaced by forcible removal, with men sometimes simply being plucked off the street and their families not even allowed to go to the railway station to say their farewells. In Luxembourg province even women were put to work felling trees in the forests.

By the end of 1917, 120,000 Belgians had been deported illegally (out of a total population of seven million), of whom 2,600 died. In Belgium, in a rare show of unity, the Catholic Church and the freemasons protested in unison and appealed to their German brethren.

The Belgian government in exile sent a mission to the US to inform the government and general public there of the deportations, King Albert wrote to President Wilson, the king of Spain and the Pope, who all protested to the Germans. None of this helped much, and though Wilhelm II suspended the measure after receiving letters from King Alfonso XIII of Spain, the deportations soon started again. It seems the Kaiser and Bethmann Hollweg were in a kind of denial, despite the international outcry. German industry expressed its satisfaction at the dismantling of competition, but even German trade unions were dismayed at the state of affairs. One Belgian put to work in a munitions factory in the Berlin area fled to the American embassy there and the ambassador asked to see Bethmann Hollweg or offered to take him to the factory, but the Chancellor refused. By then the army already reigned supreme in Germany.

Von Bissing also remarked this ran counter to the *Flamenpolitik*.

Plundering

By 1917, potatoes cost fifteen times more than the price in 1914 and practically all foodstuffs had followed the same trend, in large part due to

German plundering. They also took away church bells and all non-ferrous metals like silver, copper and brass. Machine tools and rolling stock were taken away and coals bought at artificially low prices to be sold at a large profit to the Netherlands.

Even family heirlooms were transported to Germany for scrap to feed the armaments industry, as well as of course, coals, chemicals, glass and rubber. Soldiers would demand entry to your home and take away silver and brass, clocks, even mattresses for the wool. Of course people began to conceal what they could and the searches became more unpleasant and destructive.

Berthe buried the family silver under a tree in their garden.

Dismantling the Belgian industrial infrastructure had a dual purpose, the most obvious being to acquire strategic goods or means of production. However, the destruction and dismantling of Belgian industry became far more intense from mid-1917 to November 1918, and was intended to protect Germany's own means of production later.

Von Bissing realized there was more to be gained by letting the Belgian economy work alongside the German and his reports made use of metaphors, such as that dead cows don't give milk and that you can only squeeze so much juice out of a lemon. He also reported the enormous amount of unemployment all this had created and entered a tug of war with Hindenburg and Ludendorff for Wilhelm II's ear about it, but to no avail as for the two real masters of Germany, this was of minimal importance, a swift and complete victory for Germany the only true goal.

From 1917 onwards, but especially when the German army retreated in 1918, the plundering became outright, systematic destruction, the application of *terre brûlée*, or scorched earth policy.

It was as merciless as it was systematic. Telegraph and telephone poles were torn down, the wires taken away. Trees were felled, sometimes whole forests, livestock halved, horses, even stud stallions and bulls seized. There was systematic destruction of 700 kilometres of railway track, practically the whole network, bridges collapsed, and the rails themselves taken to Germany, the wooden sleepers being cut or burned. From 1918 to 1919 it took Belgian engineers months to rebuild a single line from the front to the German border. When the Germans left, only nine out of sixty blast furnaces were left intact, most rolling mills destroyed. Often the Germans had used unskilled Russian POWs who simply destroyed rather than dismantled the hangars, warehouses and factories producing steel, glass, chemicals, bricks, and textiles.

Industrial production was crippled. In 1913, Belgium produced 2.5 million tons of pig iron, in 1915 a mere 28 tons. Textile production fell from 200,000 tons in 1913 to just 9 tons in 1918. Steel production in 1919 was 10 per cent of what it had been in 1913.

The German army even started inundating the coal mines, allowing rivers to flow into them, but this was stopped when the neutrals strongly protested. However, damage was already done and restoring the mines would have cost a great deal of time and money. President Wilson had earlier strongly warned the Germans against the destruction of the Belgian and French coalmines when it had come to his attention they were intending to blow the shafts up. To all this should be added that a large part of the territory was inundated by salt water in the Yser region and that all of the Ypres/Passchendaele area was completely flattened, turned into a mud desert pockmarked with shell holes, with here and there wooden stumps where a forest or wood had once stood. Rusting barbed wire, wrecked tanks and pillboxes were all that could be seen. The city of Ypres was completely destroyed, as were Dixmude, Nieuport and others. Today one is struck when visiting the region, that not a single building predates 1919.

In 1914, Belgium was rated sixth of the world's economies – a place it never recovered, partly because of German plundering and partly because the 'great powers', Britain and France, did so little to help it at Versailles.

6.3 Dividing the Belgians: The *Flamenpolitik*

As we have seen some 'Flemish feeling' people had entertained contacts before the war with the Pangermanists (see ch. 3, Part I, note 1). The latter were mainly to be found in German universities and had long had their eye on Flanders as one of the territories with Germanic-speaking people who would one day 'return home to the Reich', *Heimkehr ins Reich*.[5] Until 1914 there was practically no official German support for the Flemish cause apart from the university-based Pangermanists, who could not deliver anything concrete anyway. The executions in August 1914 in Aarschot and Dendermonde, the sack of Louvain, all Flemish cities, did not make the Germans popular to say the least. In August 1914, all Flemings stood behind King Albert, united with their French-speaking compatriots in indignation at seeing their land trampled upon by a brutal invader who had been given no reason to quarrel with it or complain about it. This state of affairs remained largely unchanged for the rest of the war, even though a small proportion of Flemish opinion did gradually begin to express sympathy for the German cause as we shall see.

When it was realized that the occupation of Belgium was destined to last for some while, the German authorities in both Brussels and Berlin gave some thought to what should be done about Flanders and its nascent nationalist movement and cultural aspirations. As all previous empires had found, from the Roman to the British, the cardinal rule was of course to divide and rule, *Divide et impera*. Some Flemish activists were not slow in contacting the German governor and his staff, who already knew what they wanted anyway and were lavish with their promises. It should be stressed however, that all through the war the vast majority of Flemings continued to have serious doubts about accepting favours from the occupying power, whose eventual victory was far from certain anyway, and felt that in doing so their movement would be tainted with infamy.

The Germans never made their intentions for Belgium after the war quite clear. In fact probably not much thought and certainly no firm decisions about it were ever made.[6] And expediency in terms of what could be given away in negotiations would have taken precedence over promises anyway. We know, however, through the exchanges that took place when peace feelers were made, that in the best of cases Belgium would have been reduced at least in Hindenburg and Ludendorff's vision to a vassal state, with controls over its fortresses, ports, and railways, in a customs union with Germany. In fact the rejection of those peace feelers by the Allies in 1916 and the failure of those of Albert I in 1917, came about in large part because they involved the evacuation of Belgium as a condition for the Germans keeping control over it. At the very least the Germans saw it as a pawn to be exchanged for the recovery of their overseas colonies. Vague promises of autonomy or independence and revised frontiers, to include cities in northern France which had until the eighteenth century belonged to the old county of Flanders,[7] were made to the Flemish activists.

As the war dragged on the German occupiers and their masters in Berlin saw the Flemish cause ever more as a wedge they could use to divide and rule the Belgians. Activist newspapers were allowed to be published. But still the leading Flemish activists gave the promises made by the Germans a chilly response and remained overwhelmingly loyal to Belgium. In April 1915, Chancellor Bethmann Hollweg made a statement in the Reichstag supporting the Flemish cause.

The Flemish population was certainly not spared the massive deportations to Germany later in the war and this also helps to explain why so little sympathy was felt in Flanders for the invaders and occupiers from the east – though the German occupying authorities in Belgium itself, in particular Governor von Bissing, did oppose these measures, in vain it should be added.

As we have seen, two of the principal claims of the Flemish activists were access to higher education in the Dutch language and political autonomy. The German occupation authorities did take important but obviously divisive decisions about both.

Ghent University was, at the outbreak of war, bilingual in the sense that a part of the lectures were given in Dutch and a part also of the examinations for degrees could be taken in that language. But the French language continued to coexist in the alma mater and this was felt as a thorn in the side of Flemish activists because they saw, not without reason that most aspiring young men were more attracted to the French-language curricula. At the invasion in 1914 all teaching stopped, then in 1915 the Germans asked the professors if they were prepared to resume teaching, but only in Dutch. All but five refused. Two of those who refused, including historian Henri Pirenne, were deported to Germany. In March 1916, the Germans announced the University of Ghent would reopen as a unilingual Dutch-speaking institution. With a dearth of Flemish Belgian professors the Germans were compelled to call on Dutch, Luxemburgers and Germans to fill the gap. When the 'von Bissing University' as it was promptly dubbed (solemnly) opened, a mere 110 students had enrolled. From Sainte Adresse, the Belgian government let it be known the degrees awarded would not be officially recognized and those who agreed to teach would be dismissed. Frans van Cauwelaert, a leading Flemish activist who had taken refuge in the Netherlands, made every effort to dissuade anyone from cooperating with the Germans, seeing clearly that no good could come from such a poisoned chalice.

In another important move on 21 March 1917 the Germans announced the official administrative division of Belgium: all ministries, agriculture, public works, industry and home affairs, were split into Flemish and Walloon parts, the latter having to move with all their civil servants, archives *et al.* to Namur, which they did with deliberate slowness, whilst the Flemish halves stayed in Brussels. In fact, since economic activity was much reduced it had only limited impact and if the success of the split was much mitigated in Flanders, it was a pathetic failure in Wallonia.

The previous year, on 4 February 1916, an unelected political body known as the Council of Flanders (*Raad van Vlaanderen*) was allowed to be set up, with nine ministers, including the arch collaborator August Borms, who would face a firing squad after the Second World War, named as the 'minister for defence'.

Two years later, on 8 February 1918, Borms and another activist were arrested at their homes by a Belgian investigating magistrate on the basis of existing Belgian laws of high treason. The pair were quickly freed by a German officer backed by troops and it was the Belgian judge who found himself in jail, on his way to deportation in Germany. Borms gave the Germans a list of persons he thought they should arrest though they actually took only a few of them into custody. As a consequence all Belgian courts stopped hearing cases and legal professionals stopped assisting clients. Governor von Falkenhausen wrote a conciliatory letter, to which the Brussels Court of Appeals replied invoking the principle of separation of powers.

This 'judicial strike' continued, but in the interest of public safety the courts did continue to prosecute common criminals.

On the whole, the Germans overestimated the influence of Flemish activists who were prepared to work with them. In Berlin where he visited the German parliament and was lavishly entertained (whilst most Flemings were close to starving), Borms admitted candidly to German politician Erzberger that only about 5 per cent of the Flemish population was behind him. Borms' wrath was mainly directed at the *Franskiljons* or *Bastaardvlamingen*, the French-speaking Flemish elite, rather than the Walloons. A misjudgement the Germans made was seeing these French-speaking Flemings as counterparts of the German speakers of German stock in Bohemia and Poznania, whereas they were in fact Flemings who had adopted the French language.

Borms wrote many articles for the papers still allowed by the Germans, encouraged desertions in the Belgian army, visited the front on the German side as well as Belgian POW camps in Germany to incite the Flemish soldiers there to join a Flemish Gendarmerie (without success, he was shouted down as a traitor) and never expressed any concern over the deportations or destruction in his homeland. One can only imagine how the magistrates he had had deported by the Germans (and their families) felt about him. The visit to Berlin of his *Raad van Vlaanderen*, quickly dubbed *Verraad van Vlaanderen*, that is 'Treason of Flanders', was also a bad political mistake.

A more complete relation of the life and death of August Borms can be found in the companion volume to this book.[8]

7

Resistance: A Merchant Navy Captain, Edith Cavell, Gabrielle Petit, a White Lady, a Cardinal, a Burgomaster, a Professor and others

The term or concept of 'the Resistance' is most often associated with the Second World War, where such movements sprang up in practically every continental European country that was occupied by Nazi Germany. However, there was significant resistance during the first world conflict, when Luxembourg, almost the whole Belgian territory and a large part of northern France were occupied by the Kaiser's army.

The Belgians resented seeing their country's neutrality violated, having been dragged into a long war through no fault of their own. They hated the Germans for the atrocities and destructions visited on them in the summer of 1914 and the increasing plundering of their wealth by an ever more desperate belligerent, economically strangled by the colossal expense of a long dragging war and by the British naval blockade. The main motivation of the resisting Belgians seems to have been simple patriotism, but some inevitably also worked for money, or to fight boredom, a factor that would probably have made them dangerous to work with. And the Resistance started from almost the very beginning of those four and a half long years.

It took many forms. Some prominent figures resisted just by stating openly their mistrust and opposition to the occupiers, like Cardinal Mercier who denied their legitimacy, the Burgomaster of Brussels whom the Germans deported or famous historian Henri Pirenne, until 1914 an admirer of Germany, who met the same fate. This could be called moral resistance and its impact on the general population should not be underestimated, as the Germans well knew. Others resisted more actively, spying or helping soldiers get to the other side to (re)join the Belgian or Allied armies, still others by getting themselves to the neutral Netherlands to join the Belgian army there, or by printing clandestine papers and pamphlets. Many paid the ultimate price, by execution or electrocution.

On 21 July 1915, the first Belgian National Day after occupation, a spontaneous demonstration took place in Brussels at the Place des Martyrs, where heroes of the Belgian Revolution against the Dutch in 1830 are buried. Smaller demonstrations were held in other cities across the country. In Antwerp there was a strike. The Germans cleverly and maliciously organized a (noisy) military parade of their own that same day. By then the bloody excesses that had been perpetrated in August 1914 were known to all and the indignation at being occupied, for the foreseeable future, was beginning to sink in. Stripping of infrastructure and the forced removal of labour to Germany were still to come, but a genuine hatred for the occupier was there already. One of the first actions of the unwanted guests had been to impose German time on occupied Belgium, one hour ahead of that used before the war. This led some to comment it would at least be one hour less until the Germans would finally leave...

Identity cards were introduced to better control the comings and goings of all, as well as travel restrictions especially to the coastal zones or close to the front, where an Etappengebiet (rear area) with a special status was introduced and military control absolute. All over Belgium, men of military age or who had served in the army had to report once a month at a German office, as did nationals of the countries at war with Germany who had not been interned. At first, the German authorities kept up a pretence that apart from what they obviously wanted to control directly themselves for military reasons, for example rail transport, they would leave Belgian institutions and laws unchanged. They quickly had to change tack however when Belgian judges, applying state laws, started prosecuting collaborators for high treason.

Illustrative of Belgian defiance is the anecdote mentioned by former British Prime Minister Gordon Brown, in the chapter on Edith Cavell in his book *Courage: Eight Portraits*. In a Brussels tramway a German in uniform asks a Belgian for a light. The Belgian gives it to him, then throws away the rest of his cigar unsmoked. Others would stick little 'scraps of paper' to their lapels on the anniversary of the invasion, on national or King's Days etc. Flying the Belgian flag was forbidden but women would try to dress in combinations of black, yellow and red, and children would fly kites made with paper of the same colours. When the registration of dogs became compulsory many declared their animals' names to be 'Kaiser' or 'Willy'.

One of the first expressions of active resistance was the underground press. Dozens of papers appeared and disappeared, throughout the occupation. They gave factual news of the military operations and political developments gleaned from Dutch or Swiss newspapers that had found their way into the country, reminded the Belgians of their resistance against other foreign occupiers in the past like the Spanish, the Austrians and the French, or poked fun at the Germans and their militaristic, arrogant ways, the absurdities of their bureaucracy, the German emperor's moustache and so forth. Some clandestine papers lasted a very short while, others managed to find paper and printing presses for several months which was no mean feat. There were papers in both languages: *La Patrie* and *L'Âme belge* were in French and *De Vlaamsche Leeuw* ('The Flemish Lion') was in Dutch. Some would disappear when the journalists or presses were discovered, only to reappear later in another guise. Most famous of all was *La Libre Belgique*, which had replaced the censored *La Belgique*. There appear to have been 171 issues (some sources say 200) of *La Libre* (for short), with a print run of 20,000 copies for some of them. The responsible editor was of course Peter Pan and his official address was that of the *Kommandantur* in central Brussels. It was said Governor von Bissing would find a new copy on his desk every morning and a cartoon showed him with the following caption: 'Notre cher Gouverneur, écoeuré par les mensonges qu'il lit dans la presse censurée cherche la vérité dans *La Libre Belgique*.' ('Our dear Governor, disgusted by the lies he reads in the censored press, seeks the truth in *La Libre Belgique*.') This paper, which followed a similar path in the Second World War, exists to this day.[1]

The subject of *francs-tireurs*, or rather the absence thereof, we have already addressed in this book. It should be noted that at no time (and contrary to the Second World War) did Belgians out of uniform use weapons against the occupier, nor did they become guerrilla fighters. This was confirmed in a report to the Pope by his Nuncio. Some acts of sabotage however did take place, like the blocking of a tunnel on the vital Aachen–Liège railway. And some daring boys put calcium carbide, used for lighting, or sugar if they could find it, in the tanks of unattended German motor vehicles, disabling the engines.

If one compares resistance in the two wars, that of the first occupation was more focused on intelligence gathering and less ideological, sentiments like patriotism aside. Resistance against the Nazis was more ideologically orientated (fighting against a dictatorship for democracy and freedom, there was by now an important, organized communist party, some groups were protecting the Jews, etc.) and if intelligence gathering was extremely important in Belgium in the Second World War (its importance recognized in his memoirs by no less than Churchill) acts of violence like assassinations and sabotage were far more numerous than in 1914–18. Some networks that had worked against the occupier in the earlier conflict were reactivated in

1940–45. Many Belgians who had engaged in this type of activity in the First World War prudently destroyed their relevant archives in 1940. And some started again as we shall see.

It has been estimated that about 7–8,000 people worked for Belgian or Allied intelligence at one time or another between 1914 and 1918, maybe 30 per cent of them women. About 300 groups and 40 larger networks worked for Belgian, British and French military intelligence services. Their main task was to gather as much information as possible on German military movements, what units were stationed where, especially when large build-ups of troops and supplies were indicative of preparations for an offensive. The identification of units and ranking officers, the monitoring of railway stations, lines and movements, of barracks and airfields, the importance and location of ammunition or food dumps, the building of defensive works or of large underground shelters to protect troops from artillery were naturally focused on. The ports of Bruges, Ostend and Zeebrugge were the object of special attention and as we have seen even the Imperial Navy officers' messes in Bruges were infiltrated. Transmission of the gathered information was (and always has been) a problem because radios, or what was then called wireless was in its infancy and practically no one in Belgium at the time possessed transmitters. Pigeon racing has always been a national pastime in Belgium but the Germans quickly requisitioned most of the birds. Others, some of them priceless, simply had their necks wrung by German patrols visiting the dovecotes. Troops at the front were issued with fowling pieces to shoot them down. Contrary to what happened in the second conflict, the Netherlands were neutral and many secret messages went that way, usually written on very thin 'onion paper'.

By whatever means, important intelligence somehow reached Sainte Adresse, Paris or London, like the plans Admiral Tirpitz drew up for the building of newer submarines, in the German naval cypher that was used by the British, according to some sources, to decode the (in)famous Zimmermann telegram. Other sources state it was found by Russian naval personnel on a sinking German warship and passed to the British,[2] and included the German naval staff list and many data on the personnel, materiel, arrangements, missions, defences etc. of the German navy's ports in Flanders like Zeebrugge, the German spy network in the Netherlands, von Bissing's directives as to how to address and encourage Flemish separatism, information on the peace negotiations between Germany and the new Soviet regime in Russia and more. The most important intelligence gathering effort by far focused on German troop deployments in Belgium, a task at which Walthère Dewé's *La Dame Blanche* ('White Lady') network excelled and which will be examined in detail later.

If their motivation was not in doubt, the professionalism of the Belgian and other agents who worked in occupied Belgium was certainly lacking. Amateurism and naiveté were the rule rather than the exception, making infiltration and eventual undoing relatively easy, with the predictable catastrophic results at the hands of a ruthless foe.

As might be expected, the reaction of the occupiers was extreme repression. The usual well known methods of infiltration, interrogation and eventual execution or deportation in less 'serious' cases were used. Executions were usually announced by posters. This had the (for the Germans, desired) effect of deterring others, but also intensified the hatred against them. The number of those executed is generally estimated to have been approximately 300,[3] although some sources give more than three times as many, 1,135 (though that number may include Germans executed in Belgium for desertion, rape, etc). Still another source[4] states 500 death sentences were passed, of which 277 were executed. Dutch papers of the epoch mentioned 300 executions and 2,600 deaths in deportation, this including those taken to Germany and forced to work there. There were roughly the same number of executions in Wallonia as in Flanders.

German counter-intelligence units were set up in every major city, and even in some Dutch towns like Maastricht or The Hague, where Belgian refugees were concentrated, or at places where those having fled Belgium on their way to the western front were passing. Some collaborators were infiltrated into the escape networks posing as volunteers to join the Belgian army via the Netherlands, so as to uncover the individuals and methods involved. It has been estimated that about 7,000 people worked for German intelligence in occupied Belgium. Not all were German military or Belgian collaborators, there were also a large number of Germans who had been living in Belgium before the war and whose knowledge of the country and its people, and fluency in French and Dutch, were put to good use. This played a large role in their eventual expulsion after the war.

A mysterious character called Prebisch Lincoln, said by some to have been a former member of the British Parliament and by others to be an adventurer, set up a 'peace school' in Maastricht, apparently a base for spying in nearby occupied Belgium. There were doubts about where his real loyalties lay and after the war he was incarcerated in Britain, then deprived of British citizenship and deported, and finally he fled to the USA.

Cardinal Mercier

Désiré Mercier was born in 1851 and had six siblings. Three of his sisters became nuns. He became a priest in 1874 and taught theology at Louvain (Leuven) Catholic University. Remarkably he had a Native American connection, since his uncle was a missionary in an Indian reservation in Oregon and his cousin, Joseph Croquet, joined his father (Mercier's uncle) and married there. Today, there are several thousand of Joseph's descendants with Native American background in the Pacific northwest, with the surname Crocket. Father Mercier became a monsignor in 1887 and wrote several books on the philosophy of St Thomas Aquinas, metaphysics and psychology, many of which were translated into other languages. In 1906, Pope Pius X appointed him Archbishop of Mechelen (Malines) and thus Primate of Belgium and the following year he was made a cardinal. War and the invasion of his country found Cardinal Mercier in Rome to attend the funeral of the late Pius X and participate in the following conclave that elected Benedict XV.

When he returned to his archdiocese, the Mechelen Cathedral had been partially destroyed and thirteen of the priests in Mercier's diocese, which includes Louvain, had been killed, as well as many civilians. At Christmas, the outraged Mercier's defiant pastoral letter *Patriotism and Endurance*, was distributed to be read aloud in all Belgian churches, reminding the congregations that Germany had violated its solemn word to respect Belgium's neutrality, denying any legitimacy to the German occupiers and stating that no respect, attachment or obedience was owed them. It was approved by practically all, not only the Catholics. After that he was kept under house arrest by the Germans, and many priests who had read the letter aloud in public were also arrested, though the Germans, mindful of the international outcry this would have provoked, including in Rome, never dared to deport him. Several more pastoral letters in the same vein followed, to the great fury of the successive German governors who had Berlin make representations to the Holy See to silence him. Instead Pope Benedict XV, though he was accused by some allies of having sympathy for Catholic Austria and the Catholic element of Germany, sent him a letter of total support. This is worth noting because comments had been made in Paris and London doubting the Pope's impartiality, noting his appeals for peace always came when the central empires were in difficulties or when the Allies were preparing an offensive, rarely the other way round. Monsignor Eugenio Pacelli, later Pope Pius XII, who knew Germany very well because he had served as Nuncio (papal ambassador) to Munich and Berlin, and later as the Vatican's foreign minister, was said to favour a *status quo ante* peace, which would have meant France had to renounce Alsace Lorraine, its main war aim. This of course put Mercier in an awkward position, even though as mentioned earlier Belgian war aims were quite different to those of France.

It seems the German officer corps in Belgium could not help feeling a certain respect and admiration for him.

After the letters were banned, clandestine copies began to circulate, quickly followed by other anti-German pamphlets and even short newspapers. These originated with the secret press that was to flourish all through the occupation.

Cardinal Mercier always kept in contact with King Albert and his uncompromising attitude contributed to the sympathy felt in Allied and neutral countries for occupied Belgium, also helping to raise the morale of the overwhelmingly Catholic Belgian population. His encouragement also extended to the Belgian soldiers at the front and those in captivity in Germany, POWs and deported civilians.

When the war was over, he undertook a successful trip to the USA to raise funds to rebuild and stock a new library for the sacked Louvain University. He also encouraged friends to study Einstein's theories being published at the time.

Cardinal Mercier died in 1926 and there is a statue of him outside Brussels Cathedral. He was also known to be strongly opposed to the aspirations of the Flemings for cultural and linguistic equality. Because of this and some statements he might or might not have made in this context he was called by some a *Vlaminghater*, a hater of the Flemings.

Adolphe Max

The Burgomaster (*Maire*) of Brussels in 1914 had to witness the humiliating entry of the invading troops to his city in August, assembling on the famous Grand-Place right in front of the much admired Gothic-style Town Hall. After arrogantly parading their troops through the streets, the Germans announced the imposition of an 'occupation tax' on the city – at which Burgomaster Max understandably protested. This and other successive protests led to him being deported to Germany as early as September, where he was to languish for the rest of the war. Politically this may have been a mistake because it made a martyr of him, the Germans being seen to remove a legitimate elected representative to be replaced by a German military administration. He was however able to resume his duties in 1918 and to welcome the Sovereign and other allied dignitaries. He remained Burgomaster until 1939.

One of the main thoroughfares in central Brussels is named after him, Boulevard Adolphe Max.

Henri Pirenne

Pirenne is considered to be Belgium's leading historian. Specializing in medieval history, his books *Mohamed et Charlemagne*, *Histoire de l'Europe* and *Histoire de Belgique* remain valued reference works to this day, especially the last in which he convincingly demonstrates there was a Belgian people with most attributes of a nation long before Belgium became independent in 1830. His explanation is that its different constituent parts (the counties of Flanders, Hainault and Namur, the duchies of Brabant and Luxemburg etc.) were ruled by the same distant monarchs, the kings of Spain or emperors of Austria who granted them autonomy, thus creating a national solidarity, expressed in numerous common revolts throughout the centuries, including during the later French and Dutch occupations.[5]

Pirenne, teaching in French at Ghent University, had studied in Germany and corresponded with German colleagues as well as historians from other countries. He professed a genuine admiration for Germany and its culture. This was to change completely after what happened in August 1914 and he tirelessly criticized the occupiers and what they did to his country. He steadfastly refused to teach at his alma mater, which the Germans had transformed into a monolingual Dutch-speaking university. His son Pierre was killed in action at the Battle of the Yser. On 18 March 1916, Pirenne was called in to the *Kommandantur*. He was interrogated and the German officer asked him why he persisted in answering in French, since he was known to speak excellent German, with doctorates from both Leipzig and Berlin Universities. Pirenne replied, 'I have forgotten German since 3 August 1914.' He was arrested and immediately shipped to Germany without even being allowed to go home, pick up any belongings or say his goodbyes.

Henri Pirenne was imprisoned in different cities in Germany until November 1918, when he returned home. In exile, he learned Russian from fellow prisoners from that country. Refused books, he nevertheless began writing his *History of Medieval Europe* from memory. The Dutch and Spanish governments had intervened in vain to have him liberated.

After his return home, he wrote a book about Belgium in the war[6] and admitted he recognized that from being a Germanophile he had become a Germanophobe and had lost his objectivity.

Captain Fryatt

On 25 June 1916, two destroyers of the German navy captured the British merchant ship SS *Brussels* belonging to the Great Eastern Railway steamship company, off the Belgian coast. The *Brussels* had been sailing twice a week from Harwich in Britain to Holland. Fryatt and his crew were arrested and taken to Ruhleben prison camp outside Berlin. Later transported to Belgium to stand trial, Fryatt was accused of acting as a 'pirate' because earlier that year, on 28 March, when his ship came under attack by a German U-boat Fryatt apparently turned the *Brussels* around and attempted to ram it. The submarine fled, and Fryatt's courageous conduct was honoured with a gold watch. The Germans deemed this piracy.

Some uncertainty surrounds the situation, but the attitude of the German navy seems to have been ugly towards British seamen because about that time Winston Churchill, the First Sea Lord, had given orders not to save German sailors even after they had surrendered, or even if they were in the water after having their U-boat sunk under them. This version contradicts a Belgian source, which states that Captain Fryatt was offered a drink at the naval officers' mess in Bruges. According to an even more shaky source (which I nevertheless chose to mention because of its outlandishness), he would have been recognized as being the captain who had tried to ram the U-boat in March, the Germans spotting the watch he wore, the one presented to him by British merchant interests as a token of gratitude. This story is in turn contradicted by Fryatt's widow, who affirmed he had left the watch at home. It is more likely the Germans found out about his previous involvement with the German submarine through an article in a Dutch newspaper, as Fryatt used to sail regularly from England to the Dutch coast. He was brought back to Bruges from the internment camp in Germany and put on trial, under the predictable charge of being a *franc-tireur*, not being a member of the armed forces and having attempted to destroy a German warship. Fryatt was sentenced to death and executed by firing squad in Bruges on 27 July 1917, causing an international outcry not only in the Allied countries but also in neutral ones like the Netherlands and Switzerland.

In 1919 his body was returned to Britain, a memorial service was held in London and Captain Fryatt was reburied in British soil at Dovercourt. Belgium made him a Knight of the Order of Leopold. A hospital is named after him in Harwich and there is a plaque to his memory at the Liverpool Street station in London.

In April 1918, under the command of Admiral Keyes, the Royal Navy made a brave attempt to sink block ships in Zeebrugge harbour; SS *Brussels* was still there moored to the mole.

Edith Cavell

The story of Nurse Cavell is well known both in the UK and in Belgium. Unlike poor Captain Fryatt, whose name seems largely forgotten, she is still commemorated in both countries and considered in Belgium to have died for this country as well as for her own.

Since many books and articles have been written about her and lectures and commemorations held in both countries, I have chosen to concentrate on the 'Belgian' phase of her life, less known to Anglo-Saxon readers. Cavell, the daughter of a Norfolk clergyman, came to Belgium in 1900 to look after the children of a Brussels lawyer and to learn French. She was inspired by her visit to a hospital in Bavaria and went back to Britain to study nursing. Through the well-known industrialist Ernest Solvay she was put in contact with Dr Antoine Depage, who had noticed that in Belgium nursing was carried out by nuns, who knew little of modern hygiene. So in 1907 the Berkendael Institute was opened in Brussels to train aspirant nurses, mostly Belgian but some German girls also enlisting. The first class numbered sixty. August 1914 found Edith Cavell in England, but she hurried back to Belgium and spirited the German girls away to safety. Dr Depage followed the Belgian army in retreat and went on to found the military hospital in De Panne (La Panne).

Cavell witnessed the entry of the Germans to Brussels and her nurses tended German as well as Belgian wounded. Right after the retreat from Mons, Cavell was contacted by a British colonel and a NCO who had been cut off and were dressed as civilians. She managed to smuggle them to the Netherlands and, one thing leading to another, a complex network developed to which hundreds of people eventually belonged, such as architect Philippe Baucq, Louise Thuilier, Louise de Bettignies, Prince and Princess Reginald and Marie de Croy and many others, from different walks of life, varying political and religious persuasions, including schoolteachers, publicans and postmen. The network extended to northern occupied France and is known to have exfiltrated some 200 British, French and Belgian soldiers or volunteers via the Netherlands. Some sources mention a far higher number. Ambulances and safe houses were used. It seems probable some military intelligence gathering and transmitting[7] was also done, though at their trial

Cavell and her consorts were not charged with espionage. Baucq and de Croy were also involved in distributing *La Libre Belgique* and passing messages to Belgian soldiers at the front. Suspicion of what was afoot eventually mounted with the Germans. *Leutnant* Bergham of the German counter-intelligence eventually uncovered the network and had about 35 people, including Cavell and Baucq, arrested and locked up at Saint Gilles prison in Brussels, in July and August 1915. Address books were seized. Marie de Croy who had used the anagram 'Yorc' in her correspondence, managed to flee. Cavell was interrogated for several weeks and eventually confessed. The Germans did not torture the accused, but used the trick of persuading some the others had already confessed, in conjunction with promises of leniency. Baucq managed not to give anything away and some members of the network remained undetected. The trial took place in the Belgian Senate, adjudicated by five German officers. Hugh Gibson of the American embassy sat as an observer. Cavell chose to appear in civilian garb, not in a nurse's uniform. Most of the accused received very heavy sentences. Baucq, Cavell and three others were given the death sentence and were shot on 12 October 1915 at the former Belgian army rifle shooting range in Brussels, Tir National, transformed into an execution ground, despite persistent attempts at intervention by the American and Spanish ambassadors in Brussels, Withlock and de Villa Lobar. The Kaiser, probably mindful of the propaganda disaster a nurse's execution would cause, is also said to have argued, in vain, for all except Baucq to be spared. Several accounts, more or less fantasy, were printed at the time of the details of Cavell's execution, such as that she was forced to witness Baucq's shooting first, and so forth. She seems to have been struck by three bullets in the chest and one in the forehead, killing her outright.

Her dog was adopted by a Belgian lady.

Edith Cavell was buried at the execution grounds, but after the war her body was taken to England, with Belgian and British guards of honour, and buried outside Norwich Cathedral after a service at Westminster Abbey. A member of the Belgian embassy usually attends the annual service at Norwich, as well as the wreath laying at the Cenotaph in Whitehall that was inaugurated in 1920. There is a plaque at the Belgian Senate, a Rue Edith Cavell in Brussels and a private clinic called after her in the same street. In Ostend there is an Edith Cavell Straat. There is a monument to her in Brussels and even one in Inverness, Scotland. Cell number 23 where she was held at Saint Gilles prison, is preserved as she left it and never afterwards used out of respect. The famous French singer Edith Piaf was named after her.

Louise Thuilier and Marie de Croy were eventually caught by the Germans and detained at Siegburg prison in Germany with Louise de Bettignies, until the end of the war. Both the former later wrote memoirs.

In all eleven lives were lost, including a Belgian woman who committed suicide after having served as an infiltrator for the Germans.

With rather extraordinary callousness the Germans went on to use the Tir National shooting range for executions again in the Second World War.

Louise de Bettignies

Frenchwoman Louise de Bettignies, well connected and a polyglot (French, German, English and Italian), travelled widely before the war. Interestingly she met Crown Prince Rupprecht of Bavaria, a fact that might ultimately have saved her from the execution post. She was also offered the job of looking after the children of Archduke Franz Ferdinand, the same who was assassinated at Sarajevo. Finding herself in the occupied part of France, she became involved quite early in resistance work, both in smuggling stranded soldiers out and in gathering and passing on intelligence. At one point she was able to signal the exact date and hour of a visit to the front by Kaiser Wilhelm. Two British planes tried unsuccessfully to attack his convoy. She also tried but did not succeed in warning the French about the preparation for the Verdun offensive. Later she became a member of the Belgian *Dame Blanche* network. Arrested by the Germans in Tournai on 20 October 1915, she was sentenced to death in Brussels on 16 March 1916, but this was reduced to hard labour for life by Governor von Bissing. Taken to Siegburg jail in Germany she fell ill and died for lack of adequate treatment in Cologne, on 28 September 1918.

Gabrielle Petit

Gabrielle Petit was a Belgian woman, born in Tournai on 20 February 1893. Her widowed father placed her in a Catholic orphanage run by nuns, where she was reported to be a playful child. She later worked in a shop.

When war broke out she joined the Red Cross, where she was recruited by British intelligence to gather information on the Germans in the Tournai region and the north of France. She wrote the information on very fine cigarette paper and pasted the pieces under the lifted surface of illustrated postcards.

The last of these she was never able to send because she was arrested; it mentioned that a German Zeppelin had fallen near a small village in the south of Belgium. Betrayed by a double agent she was arrested, charged with espionage and though she resisted interrogation, condemned to death.

She spent her last days in a cell at the Saint-Gilles prison and was shot by the Germans at the age of only twenty-three, at Tir National in Brussels on 1 April 1916. Her patriotism and Catholic convictions gave her moral strength and she had refused to sign a clemency appeal. Her younger sister Hélène was allowed to visit her on the eve of her execution. In an interview with the Belgian radio RTBF in March 1966, she described their last meeting: 'I said, "Gaby, my God, it's for tomorrow." She immediately understood and blushed. I could not speak. She told me she was expecting it, because others had left the prison in the morning and she was sure it would be soon, but she was not afraid of death.'

After her execution, she became a symbol of resistance in the occupied country. In 1919, she was given a state funeral. Statues and monuments were erected to her memory in Tournai and central Brussels. It is possible the Germans would have spared her life had she signed the clemency appeal.

Margriet Ballegeer

Young Margriet Ballegeer, born in 1890, was the daughter of a police chief constable and lived in the village of Kontich, between Brussels and Antwerp. At the start of the war she fled to the Netherlands, where she joined the Red Cross and helped her compatriot refugees. She did not seem destined to play a hero's role, but circumstances change things. Soon back in Belgium, aged only twenty-four, she joined a local resistance group and became part of a wider network of spies run by the British intelligence service from Rotterdam, acting as a courier. She also helped young men escape from Belgium and got them false papers. Through her father who was working at the town administration, she acquired false identity papers and passports. This ultimately proved her undoing because the Germans found her out by tracking where the false papers they seized had come from. After capture in 1915 she spent six months in jail for forging documents, but the Germans then released her.

She now joined a larger resistance group. She and her partner Henri Van Bergen gathered information on German troop movements in Belgium and passed the details to British agents in Rotterdam. In 1917, she was arrested a second time and interrogated by the Germans after being betrayed by one of her recruits, a fellow villager. This time she was interrogated very roughly, charged with spying and sentenced to death, the sentence being however commuted to deportation to Germany. Her lover, Henri Van Bergen however was executed by firing squad near Antwerp.

Liberated after the war, she had to identify Van Bergen's body. After all these traumatic experiences she could not settle in Belgium, where too much reminded her of her suffering and her murdered partner. She decided to go and live in Britain, where she eventually died in 1980. A school in Mons is named after her.

The White Lady of Walthère Dewé

The largest and most successful intelligence gathering cell was Walthère Dewé's *'Dame Blanche'*. The name itself is interesting. Dewé, an engineer from Liège, chose it first of all because there was an ancient prediction that the appearance of a white lady would precede the end of the House of Hohenzollern, the German Imperial family. It is also the name of a popular Belgian dessert (molten chocolate poured over vanilla ice cream). *Dame Blanche* eventually numbered 1,300 members, a large proportion of them women, organized like an army in regiments, companies and platoons, each entrusted with a particular sector of the occupied territory. Its territorial observers were tasked mainly with reporting anything of interest about the German armed forces, with special emphasis on rail transport. It was probably the most important intelligence services run by any Allied government in any occupied territory in the First World War. Through its help, British military intelligence was able to accurately predict coming German offensives in Flanders and northern France. About three-quarters of all the military intelligence received by the Allies seems to have come from *Dame Blanche*. Gathered information made its way to the top of the hierarchy and was transmitted via a variety of creative means: hollowed out broomsticks and soap bars, dictionaries, buttons, fountain pens, underwear etc. were all used to conceal messages on their way to the neutral Netherlands.

Apart from trainspotting, *Dame Blanche* was also involved in smuggling in goods the Germans would have objected to and in facilitating the escape networks of young men of military age or other persons seeking to leave Belgium clandestinely.

Dewé's cousin Dieudonné Lambrecht was executed at Liège in 1916 and Laure Tandel, a schoolmistress who spied on railways served one year in jail. Young Louis Antony Collard was caught and tortured and spent four months in detention, but Dewé himself was never caught. He wrote his memoirs after the war. During the Nazi occupation, rather incredibly seeing as his book revealed what he had done earlier, the Germans did nothing about him and he started a new network, 'Clarence', to which several former members of *Dame Blanche* and the author's father belonged. Escaping after being arrested he was shot dead in a Brussels street, on 14 January 1944.

The Atlas V

As we have seen, the Germans erected an electric fence along the Dutch border to prevent would be recruits for the Belgian army or others from crossing into that neutral country. Many still did, obviously at great risk.

Some in Liège spotted a weak spot: the Meuse River flows north from Liège, through Visé and then into Dutch territory at Maastricht. The flow goes the right way and pushes craft north. Of course the Germans had noted this and erected a barrier across the river just before the border. However on 5 December 1916, 42 people sailed into Holland aboard the *Anna*. The skipper was an Alsatian, Joseph Zilliox, a soldier drafted against his will into the German army, who was later shot in 1917 for treason and desertion. The barrage on the Meuse was reinforced soon after this incident.

However a craft strong and heavy enough, like a river tugboat, could overcome the boom defence if its occupants were protected from the inevitable small arms fire. The 23.5 m tug *Atlas V*, lying in Liège, was thus fitted with steel plates around its wheelhouse and set sail around midnight on 3 January 1917, with 107 would-be Belgian soldiers aboard; she moved swiftly downstream. The German guards at Visé were surprised at first but quickly opened fire with rifles and machine guns, helped by powerful spotlights. A German armed motorboat capsized in the heavy wake of the tug. *Atlas V* crashed into a bridge near Visé, which partly collapsed on to its quarterdeck and went on to tear apart the chain and the electrified wires that barred the river. It sank a pontoon armed with machine guns and escaped an intensive fusillade. Slowed but undeterred by the extra load aft, the valiant boat pushed on and crossed the border. With cheers of 'Vive le Roi!' and 'Vive la Belgique!', to the sound of La Brabançonne and with the Belgian flag flying, *Atlas V* docked in the Netherlands at about one o'clock in the morning.

The family of Captain Jules Hentjens, suspected of complicity, were arrested and sentenced to heavy prison sentences. Hentjens did not see them again until the end of the war.

The boat was returned and later gave its name to one of the Liège bridges near the place of embarkation: the Pont Atlas or the Atlas Bridge. A small stone monument on the bridge recalls the fact.

Two films about the escapade were made after the war.

And many others

There were many other such stories, too numerous to tell, of heroes and villains, patriots and traitors. Like that of Franz Merjay, shot in Charleroi in May 1917 aged sixty-five, a father of nine with three sons at the front and whose courage impressed even the German soldiers of the firing squad. Or Mathieu Bodson who met the same fate as Edith Cavell, at the same place on 14 September 1914 and for the same reason.

Leon Trulin was shot on 8 November for working for the British. In his correspondence he had used an anagram of his name, Noel Lurtin.

Amédée Gilkinet was a journalist and teacher. In 1914 he was a stretcher bearer at Fort d'Embourg when Liège was besieged. He withdrew to the Yser with the rest of the army but agreed to go back to Belgium and was also involved in smuggling people over the Dutch border. Betrayed and arrested he was shot in Liège on 16 June 1916.

The most extraordinary story must be that of Irma Van Meersche. After her husband was executed she agreed with the Germans to go to jail herself, and to infiltrate and betray the network her own brother-in-law had set up! In 1918 she fled to the Netherlands and thence to Germany.

8

Belgium and the Propaganda War

Real Atrocities and Propaganda

In *Mein Kampf*, Hitler himself conceded that the Kaiser's Germany had lost the propaganda war; it would be difficult to overstate the role Belgium played in that defeat. Nothing had prepared this small, highly industrialized country to play such an important part in the propaganda war, waged in parallel to the military operations, to win hearts and minds, as the usual definition goes. This role it played in part directly, through its own efforts at swaying international public opinion in its favour, but mainly indirectly by the use the Allied propaganda machine made of its misfortunes. The international position of Belgium before the war, when it hosted humanitarian and scientific meetings like the Solvay science conferences, the Socialist Internationale and so on, was of considerable significance. In the late nineteenth century, several political refugees found asylum in Belgium, such as Karl Marx and opponents of Napoleon III like the poet Victor Hugo. Today Belgium still plays host to two of the most important international institutions, NATO and the EU, but attacking Belgium in 1914 should rather be seen as equivalent to an attack on Switzerland today.

The violation of its neutrality gave Belgium the moral high ground. It also provided the Entente with a marvellous weapon to use against Germany.

Both reality and fiction were used by the sophisticated Allied propaganda machine. The well-known slogans, 'Belgium's martyrdom', 'Remember Belgium', 'Ruined Belgium', 'Belgium the Glorious' and even the ridiculous 'Belgium, the Christ of Nations', played a vital role in Allied propaganda, while the actions taken by Germany that caused it are on a par with other propaganda disasters or 'own goals' Berlin scored, like the 'scrap of paper' (Belgian neutrality or rather the treaty guaranteeing it to which Germany was a signatory), the execution of Edith Cavell (in Belgium), the sinking of RMS *Lusitania* (with the Belgian nurse Mrs Depage among the victims), the foolish Zimmermann telegram and so on. The real atrocities duly documented by neutral observers like members of the American embassy (in Brussels until 1917) offered too good an opportunity to miss and were duly put to good use in the Allied war effort.

There is an ancient tradition in Anglo-Saxon countries of press owners influencing public opinion, like William Randolph Hearst having a decisive role in starting the Spanish-American war, and British press barons Lords Beaverbrook, Rothermere and Northcliffe playing important political roles in their day. This state of public opinion being strongly influenced by press ownership still exists in Britain. Thus, Fleet Street was not slow to stoke up public indignation in the first months of the war when there were still significant numbers of the public who had doubts about going to war; it kept up the pressure to bring in a steady supply of volunteers for Kitchener's new army; and, when the war had become an exhausting never-ending slogging match the like of which the world had never seen, continued with the aim of inciting the neutrals, especially the USA, to join the Allied camp.

The starvation and deportation of the Belgians and the plundering of their industrial infrastructure and general wealth were reported, but with less intensity than the shooting, looting and vandalism of 1914 had been.

In fact, as well as the real atrocities, blatant exaggerations like babies being thrown up and stuck on bayonets, serial rapes or other particularly gruesome but far-fetched reports by Allied propagandists of German atrocities that did not in fact take place, had an adverse effect. It led to a dulling of perception of the real crimes and to an eventual dismissal of all atrocities as propaganda. The events described in section 2.2 were real enough, but later exaggerations led to denials from almost all Germans and of course, later, complete denial by the Nazis. As we shall see the Belgians had established a list of war criminals to face trial after the war and secured such dispositions at Versailles, but German war criminals did escape justice and accountability at the Leipzig farce, which will be described later (see Part III, Chapter 2).[1]

Today's Germany is a tolerant society, an exemplary democracy. Its hard-working people and efficient economy are Belgium's first commercial partner and the two countries enjoy excellent bilateral political relations, besides being partners in the EU and NATO, organizations on which both governments have always held similar views. When based in Bonn before German reunification, I was often told that the Germans appreciated that after the Second World War and its atrocities, which almost all Germans recognize, the Belgians had been the first of their neighbours to extend the hand of friendship and reconciliation to the new Germany that Adenauer was rebuilding.[2]

When the German Minister in Brussels, von Below, delivered his ultimatum asking for free passage only to see it refused, a German journalist based there was heard expostulating, 'The poor things, they don't know what they are in for. I know the German army, they will be steamrolled!' Indeed, little did the Belgians expect the fate in store for them, especially for the population of small or mid-sized towns in the path of the German Imperial army in August 1914. It is indeed shocking that a country that has produced Goethe, Kant, and Beethoven; that prided itself at the time for its *Kultur* and unrivalled number of Nobel Prize winners, could possess an army that behaved in such a barbaric way – more akin to the legendary Huns of the Dark Ages or the Turks or Mongols of the sixteenth century. The more so that it was not unruly soldiers temporarily escaping the control of their officers who committed the outrages described in a previous chapter, but rather that they were almost always directed by officers from an educated background, often aristocrats. That these officers were arrogant to a point unheard of in other countries is well recorded. Those wearing the Kaiser's uniform (*Kaiserrock*) would expect civilians to yield passage when they met on a narrow sidewalk and an American diplomat accompanied by his wife at a Berlin theatre, who had left their seats during the intermission, saw their places taken by a young officer and a lady, who refused to give up the seats the Americans had paid for. Only by making a big fuss and showing his diplomatic passport could the outraged American regain their seats. Duelling was common and rejecting a challenge could see the officer in question expelled from the army for cowardice. Discipline was harsh. In the army of Frederic II, king of Prussia in the eighteenth century, enlisted men were supposed to be more afraid of their officers than of the enemy and that had not completely disappeared by 1914. Insubordinate or simply stupid enlisted men could expect an *Ohrfeige*, a heavy slap on the ear, from their officer, sometimes so brutal it shattered the offender's eardrum. This type of punishment was of course banned in the British, French and Belgian armies; only the Tsar's officers treated their men worse than the Germans.

There were never *francs-tireurs* in Belgium in 1914. Enough testimonies, including that of the Papal Nuncio, have confirmed it. The Belgian government and all other official institutions, before, during or after the invasion of 1914, absolutely abstained from arming or organizing armed bands of irregulars, which in the restricted space of Belgian territory would not have made any military sense. Indeed, the government and many, even most, municipalities insistently appealed to the populace by way of posters and announcements to abstain from any hostile acts against the German army. During the two occupations, each lasting four years, the Germans had time enough to investigate any archives, interrogate people possibly involved and enquire, yet never came up with any convincing evidence of their existence. French *francs-tireurs* had existed during the Franco-Prussian war of 1870 and indeed in some parts of Germany and Austria like the Tyrol, during the Napoleonic wars against France. It must have been a recurring conversational theme in German officers' messes and barrack rooms before 1914. Unfortunately for about 7,000 Belgian civilians, German soldiers did believe there were *francs-tireurs*. Alcohol abuse, of which there are several reliable reports, and even deliberate actions by some German officers to make their men believe they were shot at by civilians and seeking by subsequent executions to create 'shock and awe' (to use a modern concept), played a part. So did disappointment at seeing the Belgian army resist, when the contrary had been expected, and also the reports in German newspapers. In some cases where the German press stated *francs-tireurs* had been at work in the very town they were in, though they had seen nothing with their own eyes, soldiers believed them. It is also possible that Belgian soldiers in uniform, some of whom had top-hat like headgear (the *Carabiniers*), were mistaken for civilians. The fact green troops were fighting in a strange environment and being fired upon in anger for the first time played a role too, as well as echoes of shots in the streets. And if possibly a farmer or two were foolish enough to discharge a hunting gun to vent their frustrations, it is nevertheless a historical fact that no official organization of armed civilian resistance ever existed in Belgium during the First World War.

In 1914, the Belgian government in exile published a Grey Paper listing all the atrocities the invading army had committed. In answer, Germany published a White Book signed by ninety-three intellectuals including Max Planck and twelve other German Nobel Prize winners (Einstein refused and wrote a dissenting paper with two others), who justified the invasion of Belgium, as well as the executions of civilians in August/September 1914 with the usual rationales (presence of *francs-tireurs* etc.). The general gist of the paper was 'How could we civilized Germans have committed the unspeakable atrocities we are accused of?' – precisely what astonished the world. The atrocities provided an argument for Irish nationalist Redmont to recruit Irish volunteers for the British army and for four years Regiments of Irish Catholics fought bravely side by side with Ulstermen in Flanders.

Examples of German clumsiness that were God-sent for Allied propaganda abound: on 4 August 1914, von Bethmann Hollweg himself recognized in the Reichstag that the invasion of Belgium was a breach of international law. The expression 'scrap of paper' was used by him in conversation with the British ambassador in Berlin, while lamenting that Britain was going to war with Germany just for the sake of the 1839 Treaty. Neither utterance of course did anything to help Germany's cause. Among other examples of German diplomatic ineptitude, we can count the occasion when the German ambassador discussed with Belgian authorities the reasons his country had had to invade Belgium. The German diplomat stated as a fact that French officers in mufti had crossed the border into Belgium in a motorcar and also that French dirigibles had already started to drop bombs. Asked where this bombing had taken place, the German replied that it was in Germany. The Belgians understandably demanded to know how this could be blamed on Belgium, leaving only the (doubtful) presence of French officers in civilian clothes as Germany's reason for going to war…

The executions of several women, including that of the female nurse Edith Cavell, showed similarly poor judgement, her case being probably the most emblematic. In terms of anti-German propaganda, Captain Fryatt's trial and execution undoubtedly also worked in the Allies' favour: in the still neutral United States, *The New York Times* called his death a 'deliberate murder'. As a Canadian civilian who had been studying music in Germany when war broke out and who had been interned at Ruhleben camp, near Berlin, with Fryatt and his crew, recalled: 'The judicial murder of a man who had lived with us caused deep shock and anger, and brought the war home to the camp as nothing had done before.'

At the time, it is possible the German authorities hoped that executing Edith Cavell would have a deterrent effect, discouraging people from assisting young Belgian men and Allied soldiers cross into the neutral Netherlands, but shooting a nurse was, to be slightly cynical, too good an occasion for Allied propaganda to miss. Indeed, news of Cavell's execution stimulated enlistment in Britain. And the use of the Belgian Senate as a courtroom might not have been a good idea either, as it shocked Belgian public opinion. As they did for other women, the Germans would have been wiser to condemn her to a stiff prison sentence or commute her death sentence and then take her to captivity in Germany, where several other women captives eventually died of illness. After the Cavell furore, which he read about in the British papers that were sent to him via neutral countries, the Kaiser forbade execution of women without his express permission.

Of course, the French also executed women; including two German female spies and the most famous case of all, Mata Hari. She might well have been a double agent sacrificed by the Germans to the French to compensate for the Cavell propaganda disaster, in order to demonstrate that not only Germany shot female civilians. There seems indeed to have been a radio message sent by the Germans and intercepted by the Eiffel Tower radio receiver announcing Mata Hari's arrival time in a code the Germans knew the French had deciphered, and with a code name for her that was easy to identify.

Publications like *La Belgique héroïque* ('Glorious Belgium') were printed by the Sainte Adresse government and widely distributed via the embassies in Allied and neutral countries. It contained reports and articles on the destructions visited on the country, as well as justification of its moral stand and political points of view. Among these was a long article by Paul Hymans, then ambassador in London, recalling the events of August 1914 and their international political context.

In 1914 the image of Belgium in Britain was not very good, because of Leopold II's actions in the Congo. But as we have seen, the British press barons saw to it that changed rapidly. Another very successful propaganda instrument, also mentioned in a previous chapter, was the *King Albert Book*, published by the *Daily Telegraph* before Christmas 1914, which soon could be seen in every British drawing room. It was a collection of very flattering articles and poems. Some of their authors, like Arthur Conan Doyle had not spared Albert's uncle, Leopold II a few years earlier. The literary value of its contents is variable, its propaganda value incontestable.

German propaganda staff of course dug deep in the archives of occupied Belgium and made much play with the records of conversations Colonel Bernardiston, the British military attaché in Brussels before the war, had had with senior Belgian military personalities about contingencies in time of war. Belgian defence of neutrality was strictly restated on that occasion by the Belgian government though it is doubtful it made a lasting impression on neutral opinion.

In **France** numerous books, publications and articles, all extremely flattering towards Albert, *le Roi Chevalier* ('the Knight King'), his Queen and his heroic army saw the light of day throughout the conflict. It was all part and parcel of what was called *le bourrage de crâne*, 'brain stuffing' – another term for propaganda.

Allied Propaganda in Neutral Countries

Italy's long hesitation and soul searching before it finally joined the Allies is well known and outside the subject of this book. The calamities that befell Belgium were not without influence on that country's public opinion though.

To encourage sympathy further, the Belgian government in exile decided in the autumn of 1914 to send a mission of prominent Belgian politicians to the Peninsula. Since Italian political life was intensely divided and the Catholics for example more inclined to side with the Central Powers than with anticlerical France and Protestant Britain, whereas it was the opposite for the Italian Liberals, the delegation was carefully composed of politicians from the Belgian Catholic Party, the Belgian Liberals and the Socialists, each of them tasked to try to influence their opposite numbers in the Italian political landscape, as well as the Vatican for the Catholics.

United States

It is of course difficult to assess how much 'Belgium' played a role in the American decision to declare war on Germany, or rather to finally put an end to Wilson's hesitations and procrastinations. The influence of the large German-American and Irish-American communities, each with its own reasons to be more pro-German, should neither be over- nor underestimated. Of course, the U-boat war, especially the sinking of RMS *Lusitania* and the incredible blunder that was the Zimmermann telegram, or factors like the debts owed to American creditors by the Allies, played equally important if not more determining roles. The August 1914 massacres and burning down of Louvain library, duly documented by its embassy in Brussels, was severely condemned by the US government and public opinion. But all these factors probably varied in time and location, the Zimmermann telegram logically being resented far more in California, Arizona or Texas. One remembers the 'roar that came out of Texas' described in Barbara Tuchmann's excellent book about the Zimmermann telegram[3] and the *Lusitania* and Belgian atrocities were probably more discussed on the east coast and especially New England.[4]

The Netherlands had relatively little sympathy for Britain, before the Great War broke out. Not only was the economy, especially the seaports of Rotterdam and Amsterdam strongly intertwined with and dependent on German trade and transit, but the population had to a man taken the side of the Dutch-speaking Boer Republics. When these eventually fell, a Dutch navy warship fetched President Kruger to spend the rest of his life in exile in Holland. The rough handling of their southern neighbour by the German army, reported at first hand by Dutch journalists who were well placed to find out what had been happening, for example at Visé, which is within walking distance of Maastricht, changed public perceptions and the hundreds of thousands of Belgian refugees, some of whom had horrendous tales to tell, only added to the misgivings about Germany.

Spain, Portugal and Latin America

Portugal, Brazil and a few other Latin American countries joined the Allies later in the war, while Spain remained neutral. In every case, both the Sainte Adresse government and the Allies were careful to dispense as much data about the Belgian atrocities as possible, their efforts being directed mainly towards the local press.

9

Liberation: The Emperor's Battle and the King's Flanders Army Group

The year 1917 was a year of disappointments for both sides. Passchendaele, or Third Ypres, had turned into a gigantic bloodbath in the mud with no significant progress either way, Russia had abandoned its Allies, Italy was again on the brink of collapse, and Romania was being knocked out of the war. For Germany things did not look very rosy either: as was expected the unrestricted submarine war, coming after so many other provocations, had finally brought the United States into the war and due to the Royal Navy blockade the German economy was close to choking, significant numbers of its population near starving. Hindenburg and Ludendorff, who now controlled everything in Germany and its occupied territories, decided the spring of 1918 would be the best moment for a last throw of the dice, a series of important land attacks directed especially at the British army – this after they had had time to withdraw the troops that had been fighting Russia and were now freed by the Brest Litowsk peace with the Soviets, but before the US had had time to train and deploy its full military might on the Western Front, an effort that was taking the Americans more time than they had expected. This was to be combined with the all-out submarine offensive, designed to bring Britain to its knees by starving it of imports.

Thus the *Kaiserschlacht,* the 'Emperor's battle' was launched against the British with new tactics: small lightly armed (grenades, light machine guns and flamethrowers) groups of well-trained and motivated German troops would go around heavily defended posts and go straight ahead, aiming for the jugular instead of trying to maintain an aligned straight front pushing back the enemy. The British army just south of the Belgian front received several heavy blows. Part of it, including a Portuguese division, completely collapsed and the Germans found themselves having almost taken Mt Kemmel (which can be seen from the Eurostar between Lille and Calais), which was practically surrounded. The Belgian army now lent its support with artillery and by attacking at the Battle of Merkem on 17 April 1918, at the point where the Belgian and British fronts met, a link which had been extended south at the British and French request. The Belgians attacked with 23 battalions and 200 guns. Some 20 German officers and 768 other ranks were made prisoner; total figures were 254 KIA, 1,211 WIA and 789 POW. The Belgians lost 155 KIA, 354 WIA, and 449 MIA, but their morale was given a boost by this action. The Germans were not invincible! However, between 17 and 29 April there were renewed and successful German attacks against Mt Kemmel and its surroundings. The British had to evacuate Passchendaele and withdraw to the immediate outskirts of Ypres. As they had been asked to do by the Allies, the Belgians agreed to extend to the south the part of the front they held, to relieve the hard-pressed British. However, had the *Kaiserschlacht* managed to completely overrun the British positions, the Belgian army would have found itself in a very perilous situation – the Germans would have pushed the British to the Channel ports and the Belgians would have been trapped between the North Sea and the enemy. They would have been forced to surrender.

In the south, the Kaiser's troops were on the Marne River again, close to Paris, four years after the famous battle there. To his horror, Haig realized Pétain was allowing the French front to be separated from the British lines, to protect Paris. This would have left him with no alternative but to run for the Channel ports, a scenario that would have resembled Dunkirk twenty years before it actually happened. However, the German troops now began to show their exhaustion too and some troops, even officers, paused to plunder Allied depots and wine cellars, losing precious time. The German attacks petered out and a series of counterstrokes led by new Generalissimo Foch in (nominal) command of all Western (French, British and Commonwealth, Belgian, American and Italians brought to France) troops pushed the Germans back. On 8 August, the 'day of mourning of the German army', as Ludendorff described it, he realized all was lost, suffered a breakdown and soon after even offered the Kaiser his resignation. By 25 and 26 September, the Germans had lost about 100,000 men and 1,000 guns and it was clear the end was in sight. In preparation of the *Kaiserschlacht*, the German GHQ had moved to Spa, in the Ardennes,[1] where long conferences, even shouting matches between the Kaiser, Hindenburg, Ludendorff, the Austrian Emperor and others were held at the Hotel Britannique (now a boys' boarding school) close to the city centre. The news from Bulgaria, Turkey and even Austria-Hungary was very bad. The Americans, who were taking their time organizing themselves and who insisted on having a continuous American sector like the British and French, began to realize this dillydallying might cause their allies to collapse and make their coming 'over here' pointless…

At this point also, both the French Prime Minister Clémenceau and Generalissimo Foch paid King Albert visits and asked him for help. To overturn the Belgian constitutional prohibition of having Belgian troops under foreign command and be able to integrate them in a larger unit, they proposed King Albert himself be given command of a newly created Army Group Flanders, in which French, British and American troops would be added to the Belgian army. This group, with Albert flanked by French General Degoutte, would be strong enough to move on from the Yser front and the Ypres Salient and conquer Flanders. Albert agreed. So far, he had been very wary of international arrangements involving his troops for reasons already explained, but felt this time there was a real chance to reconquer the country – it would have been unthinkable for the Belgians not to participate in the liberation of their country and the chance to drive away the enemy oppressing the soldiers' families. Thus the Flanders Army Group consisted of the six infantry and one cavalry division of the Belgian Army (CO General Gillain), with the British 2nd Army (General Plumer), the 7th French Army Corps (General Massenet), the 2nd French Cavalry Corps (General Robillot), the 34th French Army Corps (General Nudant), the 30th French army Corps (General Penet), the 37th US Division (General Farnsworth) and the 91st US Division (General Johnson). On 11 September, King Albert took command of the Flanders Army Group.[2]

The Belgian army itself had been built into a strong, well-trained and well-equipped (including artillery and aircraft) instrument, about which the French and British military attachés reported positively. Via the Netherlands or from elsewhere about 30,000 volunteers had joined, the total strength now being 170,000 men, about 1,000 guns and 100 planes. Its six army divisions (*Divisions d'Armée*), each with two infantry divisions and auxiliaries, were commanded respectively by Lieutenant Generals Bernheim, Drubbel, Jacques, Michel, Rucquoy, and Biebuyck, while General Major De Blauwe commanded the cavalry Division.[3]

Preparations started early in September, ranging from the usual staff and logistics work, the launching of access paths and small gauge railways to the lines of attack, and the provision of large quantities of wooden planks or duckboards to haul artillery and supplies over the former, devastated Passchendaele battlefield that had to be crossed, with great difficulty. Most preparations took place at night to remain undetected and over day the combined air forces tried to interdict German reconnaissance flights. About 100,000 men and 1,000 guns

Liberation: The Emperor's Battle and the King's Flanders Army Group

were ready. Flanders Army Group was divided into three operational groups, the most northerly having the most difficult task of conquering the fortified Houthulst Forest, where German artillery had been firing at the Belgian front for four years by now.

Facing the Flanders Army Group the Germans had built a succession of three strong defensive lines, each with parallel subsidiaries. Around the Houthulst Forest where the heavy artillery and ammunition was hidden and parallel to the canal linking the Yser to Ypres, were three parallel lines about 5 km apart, stretching about 15 km behind the front. Together they formed the *Preussen Stellung* (the Prussian Line). Behind and parallel to the *Preussen Stellung* were the *Flandern II Stellung* and the *Flandern I Stellung*.

As was customary in the Allied armies, the men were offered strong drink before the attacks. Some took it, others did not.

First Phase

On the night of 25 to 26 September at 0530 hrs, the artillery preparation commenced. After 'treating' the forward German positions, the bombardment lifted and was transformed into a creeping barrage. Belgian and Allied infantry left their trenches but encountered only light resistance. The creeping bombardment continued, lifting a hundred metres every three minutes until it reached the core of the *Preussen Stellung*. After a lull of 15 minutes, the creeping barrage fired at 100 metres every 5 minutes. The Houthulst Forest was reached but not taken, as the Belgians hit unforeseen resistance and counter-attacks from Staden, from where they clearly could be observed and fired at by machine guns and mortars.

On 28 September, Commandant Robert V. stormed the Houthulst Forest at the head of his company, part of his Regiment and of the 1st Division d'Armée. Once inside the Forest he stopped on a little knoll and took out his field glasses to observe the enemy. At this point a German machine gun no one had spotted opened fire quite close. Two bullets struck Robert. One went straight through his (empty) binocular case without harming him but the other one went through the side of one thigh and stopped in the other thigh. He was evacuated and later taken by hospital train to the Hôpital Albert 1er in Paris.

Many other infantry officers and troops were lost, and Belgian air ace Willy Coppens was severely wounded during the attack, losing his leg to an explosive bullet (see Chapter 3.1).

On 28 September in the afternoon, the southern group advancing astride Ypres took the area where Third Ypres had been fought. The *Flandern II*

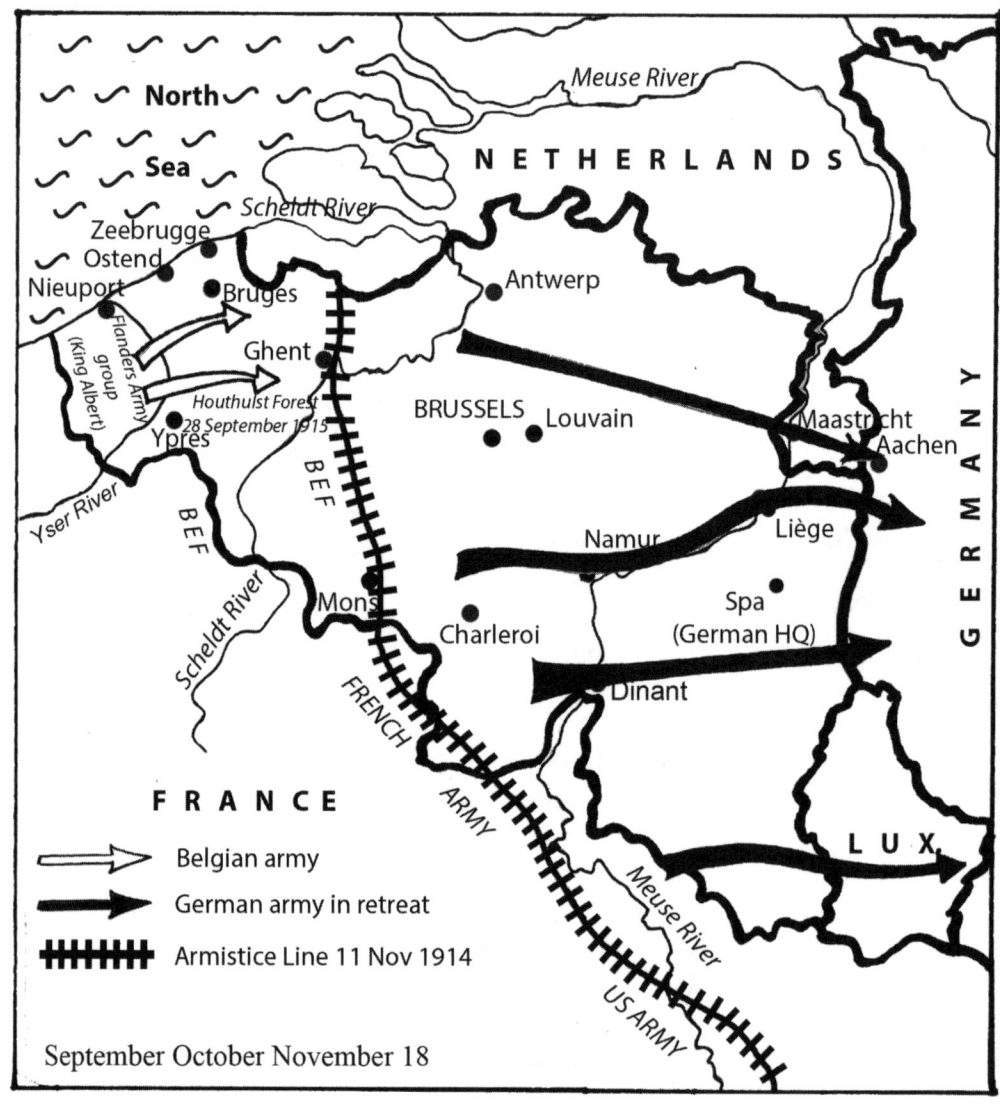

4. Final offensive, 1918

Stellung was reached and partly taken. Poelcapelle and Passchendaele were taken by Belgian troops who went further in a single day than the British had advanced in four months during third Ypres in 1917. Of course the circumstances, including the weather, were very different and the German defences now much weaker.

Meanwhile the very able General Plumer was making good progress towards the Lys (Leie) River, where he was met by Belgian troops.

On 28 September, the northern group also managed to take Dixmude.

Liberation: The Emperor's Battle and the King's Flanders Army Group

But the Flanders Army group had taken heavy losses, about one fifth of its force. Those still fighting were tired and there were, as foreseen, great difficulties in crossing and bringing up supplies over the terrain devastated by former battles or where inundation had taken place.

On 5 October, the Germans reinforced the part of the *Flandern Stellung* that was still under their control. The 36th German Division replaced the 16th Bavarian Division and the *Ersatz Garde* Division replaced the exhausted 36th Reserve Division, where it linked with a 1st Bavarian Division. Crown Prince Rupprecht of Bavaria did little to hide his pessimism. On 14 October, Ludendorff himself gloomily noted growing signs of poor morale and discipline in the German army, including among the officers who were either increasingly disrespected or sided with those of their men who thought all the sacrifices were in vain… In short, the morale of the German army had begun to crack.

Second Phase

The same day, 14 October, the second phase started. At 0230 hrs the 'softening' bombardment opened all along the Belgian line. Progress of about 15 kilometres was made but lots of problems of supply in the muddy conditions had to be resolved. Long-buried bodies were sometimes exhumed by artillery.

The entirely Belgian northern group forced the Germans out of the Nieuport/Dixmude sector. The *Kaiserliche Marinekorps*, who did not play an important role in the fighting, evacuated by river barge all the German logistics in north-western Flanders and abandoned the submarine ports after their complete sabotage. What could not be moved was destroyed, including the ports of Zeebrugge and Ostend.

It was also during these weeks that the complete plundering of Belgian infrastructures and factories described in Chapter 6.2 occurred.

Third Phase

The third and last phase started without artillery preparation, and in undestroyed terrain the Belgian and French troops of the southern group left their trenches in silence and attacked in the direction of Ghent. A few days later the three German defensive lines were completely conquered, including the last, the *Flandern I Stellung*. Confusion reigned supreme among the German troops, who had received news of mutinies in Kiel and Brussels. Negotiations were meanwhile underway behind the scenes via Switzerland and President Wilson.

On 11 November, Armistice Day found the Flanders Army Group roughly on a line Ghent to Mons, with further south the Allied lines on the upper Meuse valley and Sedan. There everything stopped. The war was over, at least in terms of fighting. Now the new goal was to win the peace, as Clémenceau said. By 27 November, German troops had completely evacuated Belgian territory. Some columns used neutral Dutch territory and the Maastricht bridges (see Map 5 on page 184). The Dutch said they had allowed this (and withdrawn their troops) to facilitate the evacuation, but the Allies and the Belgians were dismayed at the Dutch thus violating their neutrality.

A few days earlier Berthe J. was strolling in the garden of her parent's chateau south of Bruges. Suddenly she beheld two soldiers on horseback in a khaki uniform she had not seen before. They were Belgian cavalry scout officers, the first Belgian soldiers she had seen since 1914. They trotted up to her and the trio found they knew lots of people in common. So, she asked them about all the young men she had known before the war who were in the army. Finally, she dared to ask them about Captain V. 'Oh!' said one of the Belgians, obviously unaware of their engagement, 'V. is a Commandant now,[4] or rather was, for I heard he has been killed at Houthulst.' The author remembers his grandmother, now in her eighties telling him this in the 1960s. She said, ' For four years I had waited for him, only to hear this! So, I wished them both well, went up to my room, locked the door and just cried and cried.' After so many decades it was a moving story to hear. My grandfather of course was only severely wounded, not dead.

On 10 November Kaiser Wilhelm, realizing everything was lost, boarded his imperial train at Spa and headed for Liège. There the party disembarked and took to less conspicuous motorcars. A stop was possibly made at the Château de Wodémont for refreshments and then the cars headed for the Dutch border at Lixhe, just north of Visé, where the German troops had behaved so barbarously in 1914. The Kaiser's aides went to the Dutch border post at Eijsden and asked for political asylum for their master. This decision was of course far above the local border guard pay grade and he had to spend several hours on the phone with The Hague to obtain a positive answer. And so, Wilhelm II, King of Prussia and last Emperor of Germany went into Dutch exile, there to remain until his death in 1941. Not without having, in 1940, congratulated Hitler for having conquered the country that had given him asylum! He was first buried in a mausoleum in the grounds of Doorn Château (Huis Doorn) where he ended his life and where a trainload of furniture was sent from his Berlin Palace, but has been recently reinterred in Germany.

'Mummy there is a soldier outside'

Parades of Belgian troops, followed by their allies, were held in all liberated Belgian cities – Bruges, Ghent, Brussels, Antwerp, Liège, everywhere the welcome was rapturous. In Ghent the Flemish French speakers were slightly too vocal in their acclamation of the French troops, almost more than for the Belgians themselves, which prompted the King to ask for the dissolution of the Flanders Army Group.

Soldiers who had not seen their families for years were allowed short home leave. At a small Flemish village, a little girl ran to her mother in the kitchen telling her excitedly there was a soldier at the door of their home. Just six years old, she had not recognized her father.

10

Liberation Politics

10.1 Chaos in Brussels

In the first fortnight of November mutinies broke out in the German Navy and in all major German cities. Between 9 and 15 November, this rapidly spread to the German garrisons in occupied Belgium. In Brussels, red flags were hoisted, *Soldatenräte* (soldiers' soviet-style councils) constituted and machine guns installed at street crossings; soldiers started disrespecting their officers, tearing off their rank insignia when they did not execute them outright, though some sided with the mutineers. The mutinous German soldiers tried to fraternize with the local Belgian populace, but all especially the socialists kept their distance from what had become mob rule, from which they could expect little. There were thousands of deserters and cases of pilferage and arson. Common criminals were freed from jail and here and there fights erupted between 'red' soldiers and troops who had remained loyal to the Kaiser and were on their way to Germany. Eventually the 'uninvited guests' all disappeared.

On 22 November, King Albert entered Brussels at the head of his army and the other, British, French and American contingents of the Flanders Army Group. He went straight to the Belgian Parliament he had last addressed on 4 August 1914 and received, to rapturous acclamation, the salute of the Belgian army arriving from the Yser. The army had lost 1,100 officers and 29,000 other ranks between killed and wounded in the last liberation offensive.

10.2 Lophem

En route to Brussels, King Albert stayed a few days at the Lophem (Loppem) chateau just outside Bruges, a nineteenth-century neo-gothic affair. Here he received various political individuals from Brussels, some of whom it has later been said painted a blacker description of the situation in the capital than was the case. However, the economic reality was stark enough: 850,000 jobless, two million living on hand-outs from overseas. On the other hand, a chasm had inevitably opened over the years between the Sainte Adresse government and King Albert. The latter was better informed and more aware of both the internal situation in occupied Belgium and the evolution of the international context. The government in exile had done good work in some respects, but with plenty of time on their hands could and should have done more both to prepare for the liberation and the post-war reconstruction period and its positions for the peace conference.

Albert felt strongly that this was the victory of the ordinary man, the Walloon and Flemish soldier in the trenches, and that something ought to be done in recognition of their resilience and courage during all these years. So, when the leftist Liberal and Socialist politicians proposed a reform of the electoral system towards universal suffrage, 'one man, one vote', he agreed. The rightist Catholic party did not raise very strong objections and this reform was seen as a way to both appease and recognize the social aspirations of the Walloon factory workers and the cultural aspirations of the Flemish. Of course, this was a constitutional matter, and not for the King alone to decide, but Albert's support was a determining factor in giving all male Belgians one vote. War widows and mothers of soldiers who had lost their lives were also given the vote, but other women had to wait until after the Second World War.

Occupation in Germany

In the last days of November the Belgian army entered Aachen, the city that had been the gateway for the August 1914 invasion and occupied it, as well as other cities on the west bank of the Rhine and bridgeheads on the east banks, all directed and coordinated with the other allies and belligerents under the overall coordination of French Generalissimo Foch. It rankled with some Germans to see the troops of their 'small' enemy, Belgium, whom they had defeated in Liège, occupying the *Kaiserstadt* Aachen, Emperor Charlemagne's capital. But Clémenceau made a very acute *bon mot* when the German delegates protested at the severity of the Versailles Treaty – to their aggrieved, 'What will the historians of the future say of this?' he replied, 'One thing the historians of the future will not say is that Belgium invaded Germany in 1914!'

Five Belgian divisions took part in the occupation of the Rhineland immediately after the war (not to be confused with that of the Ruhr in 1924), along with 21 French, 10 British and 7 American divisions.

The standing of the well-trained Belgian army was very high with its allies. German planes, captured, abandoned or delivered were used by the *Aéronautique militaire*. Modern French planes were also acquired. The French also helped set up a small navy during the war, consisting of torpedo boats, the crews being trained in France. At the end of the war, with lots of surplus ships, German (abandoned or ceded as reparations) or Allied available, this fleet expanded and even the small French cruiser *Entrecasteaux* was ceded and based in Bruges. In 1927 however, the *Détachement des Torpilleurs et Marins* fell victim to a defence review and the sailors became soldiers. The *Entrecasteaux* was given back to France to join other rusty buckets due to be scrapped. It was not until the Second World War that the Belgian-manned Flower-class corvettes of the Royal Navy would form the embryo of the modern Belgian Navy.

Part III

AFTERMATH

1

Disappointing an Immense Minister

Attitudes

'La Belgique est petite mais son Ministre est immense!' (Belgium is small, but its Minister is immense) was another *bon mot* that did the rounds in Paris during the preparations for the signing of the Versailles Treaty. The pun was that Minister Hymans' surname, originally Flemish, when pronounced in the French way sounds like the French word for 'immense'. Like the other delegations the three senior Belgian delegates, Paul Hymans, from the Liberal Party, Socialist Emile Vandervelde and Catholic van den Heuvel plus numerous diplomats, clerks and other civil servants, set up shop in a Paris hotel for the duration.

Initially, they thought their position was strong. The Declaration of Sainte Adresse (which promised no separate peace without Belgium and gave it priority in reparations, see Chapter 4), plus the moral high ground achieved through Belgium's heroic defence and martyrdom during the war, would assure them significant priority in the reparations and the fulfilment of their (long) list of aspirations. Or so they thought.

The well-known principle that might is (usually) right, tried and tested by Germany in 1914, seems to have been adopted by Britain and France for their diplomacy in 1918–19, to the disadvantage of the lesser powers. Clémenceau and Lloyd George divided the (tens of) delegations present in Paris into 'powers of general interest', that meant in fact France, Britain, the US, Italy and Japan, and the others 'of limited interest' on the other hand. The 'Big Five' worked things out among themselves at first and a ridiculous situation arose wherein Japan, which had played virtually no role in military operations, certainly not in Europe, was given a bigger role at Versailles than Belgium, even in matters that concerned Belgium directly, like the future of the regions on the Belgian borders. Committees and working groups there were aplenty on all imaginable subjects. Italy and Japan sat on committees deciding the future of the Rhineland, directly adjacent to Belgium and where it had stationed occupation troops, while Belgium was absent. Italy and Japan of course had no troops anywhere near.

In one of the institutions, Brazil which had only sent some warships as far north as Gibraltar (the Royal Navy had said no thanks, they were not really interested in seeing the two Brazilian battleships, though built in Britain, join the home fleet and instead asked them to patrol the African coast between Gibraltar and Dakar), got three seats and Belgium only two. This was reversed after a strong Belgian protest by Hymans to Clémenceau. A Royal Navy messenger being told to bring a despatch to the 'the Belgian committee' not unnaturally delivered it to the Belgian delegation, not knowing there was actually a committee discussing Belgian affairs that was off limits to the Belgians! Still not unnaturally, the Belgians opened the envelope and read that the Admiralty was opposed to giving Belgium the southern bank of the Scheldt River, one of the Belgian claims.

After a while, Japan and Italy, disappointed by what they were offered by the other 'big three' fell out with them and dropped off from the Committee of Five. They were later to become Germany's allies.

Lloyd George who, by withholding 450,000 trained troops back in England instead of sending them to Haig, almost lost the *Kaiserschlacht* and thereby the war,[1] took frankly rude attitudes towards the Belgian delegation. 'It is understood that Mr Hymans, like all good children shall be seen and not heard', he was heard to declare! In fact, according to American historian Sally Marks, he was allergic to everything Belgian including the climate, food and the central heating,[2] even refusing to allow some special conferences and meetings to be held in Brussels.

Britain was fearful of French hegemony on the Continent after Germany's defeat, and wanted the erstwhile enemy to rebuild its strength as a traditional balance to France. Moreover, it was fearful (without much reason) that Belgium would become a vassal state of France. Lloyd George seems mainly to have been preoccupied expanding the British Empire through League of Nations mandates and refused to enter a French/Belgian military alliance, being bent on helping Germany recover to prevent the French growing too strong, the traditional British attitude. In the Middle East too, Britain tried to thwart French influence, securing the oil rich provinces of Iraq as the Royal Navy started using oil for fuel.

Belgium had some friends in the British delegation. As well as Lord Keyes, Balfour tried to help them. Lord Curzon was a personal friend of King Albert but had no real control over the Foreign Office at the time because of interference from Lloyd George, who constantly changed his mind and was motivated by short-term political interests like the perceived competition between Belgian and British industry.

Clémenceau, whose only aim in 'winning the peace' seems to have been to make Germany pay as much as possible ('L'Allemagne paiera!'*)* and who was inspired by wrath against that country which he had seen invade his own twice (1870/1914), was determined to keep Germany down, poor and weak. As for Belgium's plight, it interested him so much he usually fell asleep when Belgian delegates were allowed to speak in session. He treated Hymans with rudeness and contempt.[3]

The American president, Woodrow Wilson, was a dreamer weakened by the internal political situation in the US and later by his own failing health. His adviser, Colonel House, was disgusted at British and to a lesser degree French, indifference to Belgium's economic state and instructed the American delegation to hold firm. But there was only so much the Americans could do when confronted with British and French cynicism.

In a sense, promises made to Belgium in 1914–15 were weakened by the unexpectedly long duration of the war. One has the impression that subconsciously Britain became embittered by the catastrophic losses it incurred in coming to the aid of 'Brave little Belgium' in August 1914. Such losses could hardly have been foreseen at the time, but nor could they be blamed on the Belgians... At Versailles the atrocities suffered by the Belgians, useful for the Entente's propaganda, were forgotten and didn't weigh as much as computations that were now made of the ratio of soldiers killed, wounded or missing versus soldiers under arms. These were 1:6 for France, but only 1:50 for Belgium. In absolute numbers respective losses were, according to official sources (such statistics are always difficult to establish and the Spanish flu epidemic further complicated matters):

Belgium: 53,000 KIA/MIA (including the Belgian Congolese troops)
France: 1,390,000
Russia: 2,000,000 (?)
Great Britain: 1,100,000 (including 200,000 Empire troops)
United States: 91,000
Germany: 1,800,000

There again, who could blame the French and other losses at Verdun, Passchendaele, the Somme and Chemin des Dames on the Belgians?

Apart obviously from the Germans, who were to make use of its harshness skilfully in the 1930s, Versailles (and its parallel treaties with the different allies of Germany) disappointed also Italy, China and Japan, the Belgians, the Kurds (who to this day are denied a homeland), the Arabs and many others. The French historian Jacques Bainville in *The Political Consequences of Peace*, a title designed to counterbalance Keynes' famous and very useful work, *The Economic Consequences of Peace*, predicted very accurately in 1920 all that would happen between 1920 and 1940 and commented that Versailles was too hard where it should have been soft (like the reparations issue, the sums being in fact unpayable), and too soft where it should have been hard (e.g. re the military limitations).

Austria-Hungary was destroyed and replaced with states that all had reasons to quarrel with each other over territory and minorities and, especially Yugoslavia, with Italy. Borders were designated with pencil, ruler and rubber in back rooms by civil servants, who duly took into account the principles of nationality when applied to victors like Romania, but not to the vanquished like Hungary or Bulgaria. These borders were 'sold', usually without much discussion, to ignorant politicians, as with the (militarily sensible but ethnically nonsensical) boundaries of Czechoslovakia. Of Foreign Minister Aristide Briand it was said he knew nothing but understood everything, and of his predecessor, old Alexandre Ribot, senile and usually fast asleep during sessions, that he knew everything but understood nothing.

That the United States were not party to these negotiations is understandable for well-known reasons, but it weakened the whole, including the nascent League of Nations.

As soon as he was able, Commandant Robert V. made his way back to Bruges, to his sisters and other family and, first of all to Berthe J. who was faithfully waiting for him. They were married on 10 July 1919 and on Bastille Day attended the great Victory Parade on the Champs Élysées, where contingents from all the victorious nations marched behind their respective flags. The Belgian detachment was given rapturous applause. They spent their honeymoon in northern Italy. Robert's health however was giving him trouble: the two flesh wounds on the thigh that had been shot through healed easily, but not so the other thigh, where it was found the bullet had stopped close to the femoral artery and it was deemed wiser not to remove it. The wound never healed completely, but Robert resumed his duties at the head of his old company in 4ème de Ligne Regiment stationed in Bruges. They lived close to the barracks and the couple had four sons, the eldest being my father. On 30 March 1921, he was made a major. He also, in addition to his previous wartime decorations, was made an Officer in the Order of Leopold and received Italian and Polish medals as well.

In 1923–24 he took part in the occupation of the Ruhr, Belgium and France, having decided it was the only way to force Germany to start paying the reparations stipulated in the Versailles Treaty. One of the barracks there was called Camp Termonde, in remembrance of one of the Belgian cities where the Germans had executed civilians in 1914.

Nevertheless the fact that four of his men had deserted during the war slowed his promotion. When it was announced that the officers who had spent most of the war in captivity, even those taken as early as 1914, would be given the rank they would have attained had they not been taken prisoners, General Bernheim, former CO of the 1st Division wrote an indignant letter to the powers that be to the effect that V. was certainly qualified for command of a battalion or a regiment, that he had been given a justifiable dressing down when his men had deserted but that it would be profoundly unfair to promote officers who had spent the war in relative safety, while Major V. had had an exemplary war and had been seriously wounded. There matters stood when Robert died, in a matter of hours, on 9 April 1926, his wound having got the better of him. He was fifty-six. My father was six years old, my youngest uncle, still alive today, just a few months old. Five generals and several other officers attended his funeral, as well as troops from several units apart from his own. Two aeroplanes performed a fly past.

My grandmother was left to raise her four sons. She was very active in the local Red Cross and Veterans' Association, as well the Association of War Widows. When there was famine in Germany she sent food parcels to ladies she had known long before when a pupil at a school in Bruges, the English Convent. She lived on through the second occupation and died in 1984, at the advanced age of ninety-nine years and nine months. Bureaucracy (again) prevented her being buried alongside her husband.

Belgian Claims

Belgian public opinion was divided as to what the country wanted at the Paris Peace Conference. The government in exile clung to the Sainte Adresse declaration and Wilson's Fourteen Points (one of which specifically mentioned Belgium's restoration) and gave it more importance than it proved eventually to have. Most opinion in Belgium itself was mainly concerned about the total wreck the Germans had left behind in the country and wanted reconstruction and the (financial and material) means to effect it. The Sainte Adresse government during its years of partial idleness had also elaborated on territorial concessions to the detriment of Germany and more surprisingly the Netherlands. These were supported by the active newspaper tycoon, Fernand Neuray, whom we have already come across as an enemy of the 'Flemish feelers'. The King himself was far from enthusiastic about territorial annexations, because he recognized they would only create bones of contention.

The reasons for some Belgians wanting Dutch territory were that the compromise peace treaty with the Netherlands in the late 1830s had hived off Belgian territory, making half of the Belgian province of Luxembourg into the independent Grand Duchy of that name and giving the Dutch province of Limburg (with the strategically important city of Maastricht and its Meuse River bridges), as well as the southern bank of the Scheldt River (*Zeeuws Vlaanderen*), to the Netherlands (see Map 5, page 184). The idea, when France was still seen as a threat by Britain a century earlier, had been to make Belgium difficult to defend if France invaded it, as Napoleon had done before Waterloo. In 1919, of course the situation was completely different, and the aggressor had come from the east, not the south. The Belgians themselves were not all of one mind. The Belgian army was against annexing the Grand Duchy of Luxembourg, which was difficult to defend against Germany, but it had strategically important railways and a thriving coal and steel industry. However, the greatest problem about annexing Luxembourg was that France was also interested. As to annexing Dutch territory in general, the difficulty was that Holland had remained neutral in the war, so it would be morally indefensible to take land, though some Belgians toyed with the idea of giving the Netherlands some German territory adjacent to its own in compensation. In the case of the Dutch southern bank of the Scheldt River it made sense for Belgium to have it, as it would allow Belgian warships and merchant shipping to sail to Antwerp while remaining in Belgian territorial waters, which was not the case at the time. In 1918, the Netherlands' image had deteriorated somewhat. The Belgians were grateful to the Dutch for having accepted thousands of Belgian civilian refugees (700,000 in 1914, of whom 100,000 were still there in 1918), but in the meantime the Dutch had made huge profits trading with and selling supplies to both sides, allowing Dutch plane manufacturer Anthony Fokker to relocate all his factories and stock by train to the Netherlands, out of reach of the Allied Armistice disarmament commission. They refused to extradite the Kaiser, who was wanted by the Allies as a war criminal, and allowed some of the retreating German troops in November 1918 to cross Dutch territory and the Maastricht bridges as a short cut, taking their arms and some of the plunder from Belgium back to Germany. A few thousand more German POWs would have come in useful to clean up the mess they had left behind in Belgium. The Dutch troops were even told to retire from the area to avoid incidents.

But Lloyd George seemed to be more grateful to the Dutch for remaining neutral and allowing the Germans to retreat through their territory in 1918, than to the Belgians for having fought and upheld their neutrality in 1914.

Dutch coffers were full, while the Belgians were ruined and, this, allied to some skilful diplomacy by The Hague (as opposed to the rather clumsy efforts by the Belgians, who played their hand badly) helped turned the tide. The Dutch delegation in Paris was very keen to follow up developments and finally managed to avoid the talk of Belgian annexation of any of their territory, in part because they could offer the British and French credits for reconstruction – exactly the opposite of the Belgians, whose economy was on its knees. With some chutzpah, the Dutch at one point even declared all of Belgium's 3 miles of coastal waters to be part of their territorial waters, including the approaches to the Belgian ports of Ostend and Zeebrugge, on the grounds that it was all part of the approach to the Scheldt River!

Flemish public opinion was generally opposed to the annexation of Luxembourg, but in favour of annexation of the south bank of the Scheldt River, directly adjacent to Flanders and where Dutch was spoken. At one time there was talk of a more personal union between Belgium and Luxembourg, with King Albert I of the Belgians becoming also Grand Duke of Luxembourg, thus avoiding outright annexation – the more so since the Grand Duchess was said to have had pro-German sympathies (or at least her court had) and she was deposed. But eventually, her younger sister became (a very popular) Grand Duchess and the Luxembourgers remained, as they are fond of saying, as they are.

Further Belgian claims included the abandonment of imposed compulsory neutrality, which implied the revision of the 1839 treaties. A lot of energy was wasted on that, which was in a way self-evident.

Reparations

A far more complicated problem was that of the reparations to be paid by Germany and what part would be apportioned as a priority to Belgium's reconstruction. Belgian claims amounted to $3.2 billion in damages, war debts, pensions and so on. The Versailles Treaty provided for Belgium, in accordance with the Sainte Adresse Declaration, to take a certain priority in the matter of reparations. What that priority would amount to led to endless bickering between Lloyd George and Clémenceau on one side and Hymans on the other, details of which it is not necessary to go into here. Suffice it to say that relations became so bad, and refusal by the British and French to talk to the Belgians about it so bitter and constant, that Hymans saw no recourse but to ask King Albert himself to come to Paris. Not even Clémenceau and Lloyd George could refuse to see the *Roi Chevalier* and Albert duly came (he flew) to Paris to put facts and figures on the table. Belgium was accorded a $500 million priority over German reparations. If it was ever paid is another matter as the Reparations question in the 1920s and 1930s is an incredibly complicated matter. According to some sources, up to the end of 1922 Belgium should have received 31 billion francs but had actually only received a paltry 4.5 billion francs. Anyway, in April 1922 Germany decided to stop making payments and the following year France decided to occupy the Ruhr and help itself to the coal, in which it was joined by Belgium.

Major Robert V was among the occupying troops.
This occupation became unpopular in Belgium because it resulted in a lengthening of compulsory national service. Some Belgian agents also encouraged German separatists in the Rhineland, especially in the Aachen area.

There were those in Belgium who thought Hymans spent too much energy and goodwill on the forlorn hope of annexations and too little on the far more important question of reparations. Belgium did not fare well in the reconstruction payments, which is as much due to British and French obstructionism as to German unwillingness to pay up. Overall, maybe Belgium got about 30 or 35 per cent of what should have come its way, in money, locomotives and rolling stock, armaments, coals, pig iron etc. Even French historians have agreed that Belgium was very modestly compensated at Versailles for the sacrifices it had made for the common cause. And apart from the nibbling away by the French and British at what should have been its fair share of the compensation paid by the Germans, Belgian export would be hard hit by their protectionism. It should also be remembered that during the war Belgium had lost a large part of its merchant navy and the millions it had invested in pre-communist Russia, for example in the railways, tramways and heavy industry there.

The final results of Versailles for Belgium

To cut a long story short the final results for Belgium of the Versailles Treaty were, apart from the Reparations that never were paid in full:

1. In 1921, Belgium and Luxembourg entered into a monetary and customs union (*Union Économique Belgo Luxembourgeoise,* UEBL) of which the main effects were a customs union and the fact that Belgian and

Luxembourg francs, though still separate currencies, became legal tender in both countries. (This of course no longer applies since their membership of the EU and the introduction of the euro in both countries.)
2. The cities of **Eupen** and **Malmédy** and lesser territories at the border with Germany were annexed by Belgium. They had belonged until 1815 to what was then Belgium (known as the Austrian Netherlands), up to the French invasion and Waterloo. A local referendum was now organized and out of 63,000 persons registered to vote only 271 voted to remain German. The boundaries were marked out by delegates sent from the Versailles conference, who after dark in the winter months would repair to a local auberge where a good fire and hot punch were available, only the Japanese delegates continuing to brave the cold to fulfil their duty. In Eupen the local language is German, though most people are bilingual, whilst Malmédy is mainly French speaking. Recently given a largely autonomous administration, they are known as the *Cantons de l'Est* or *Communauté Germanophone de Belgique* or rather *Deutschsprachige Gemeinschaft Belgiens*. Apart from the period between the wars (when there was a local Nazi party) there has never been a serious movement for becoming German again and the locals seem happy in their bi-cultural environment. Some local traditions are more German than Belgian, however, such as the way Carnival is observed.
3. **Ruanda-Urundi**: these two African kingdoms, populated mostly by Hutus but ruled by the aristocratic Nilotic Tutsis, are small but very populous and situated in the eastern highlands, formerly part of German East Africa (*Deutsch Ost Afrika*, DOA), and as we have seen the Belgian Congolese army had played an important part in conquering that German colony. After the war it suited Whitehall fine to have the Belgians occupying more than a third of the DOA for about three years, as British troops were needed elsewhere, even in Russia, after the war was officially over. Its future was another matter as the Colonial Office wanted all the former German colonies for Britain, without exception. DOA was the largest and richest German colony and the old fantastic dream of building a Cape to Cairo railway finally seemed in sight (it never materialized because roads and aircraft were already taking over). Belgium certainly did not want the whole of DOA (today's Tanzania), only Ruanda and Urundi. In fact, Brussels would have preferred the Portuguese enclave north of the Congo, on the Atlantic, because its coastline was very short, and envisaged possibly compensating Portugal with a slice of DOA annexed to northern Mozambique. But nothing

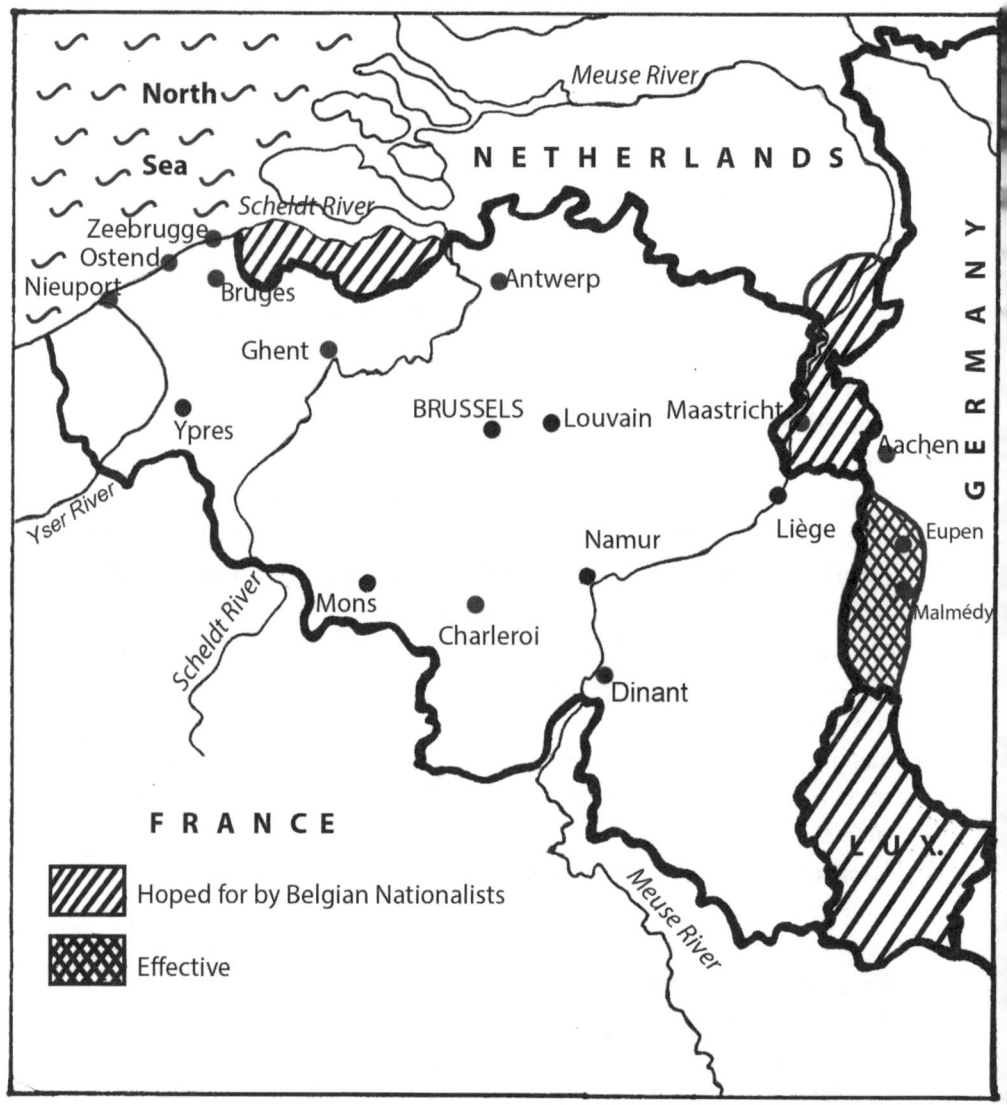

5. Annexations

came of that. Belgian territorial claims in Europe were weakened by Wilson's Fourteen Points, while in Africa it played its best card badly. Here again, Lloyd George was his usual self and belittled the Belgian contribution (to this day it is hardly mentioned in British literature), denying or minimizing the important military participation of the Belgians and Congolese and feigning ignorance of the fact that they still occupied a large part of the territory, also conveniently forgetting it had been the British who asked very insistently after their initial fiasco and von Lettow's stubborn resistance, for Belgium to send military aid.

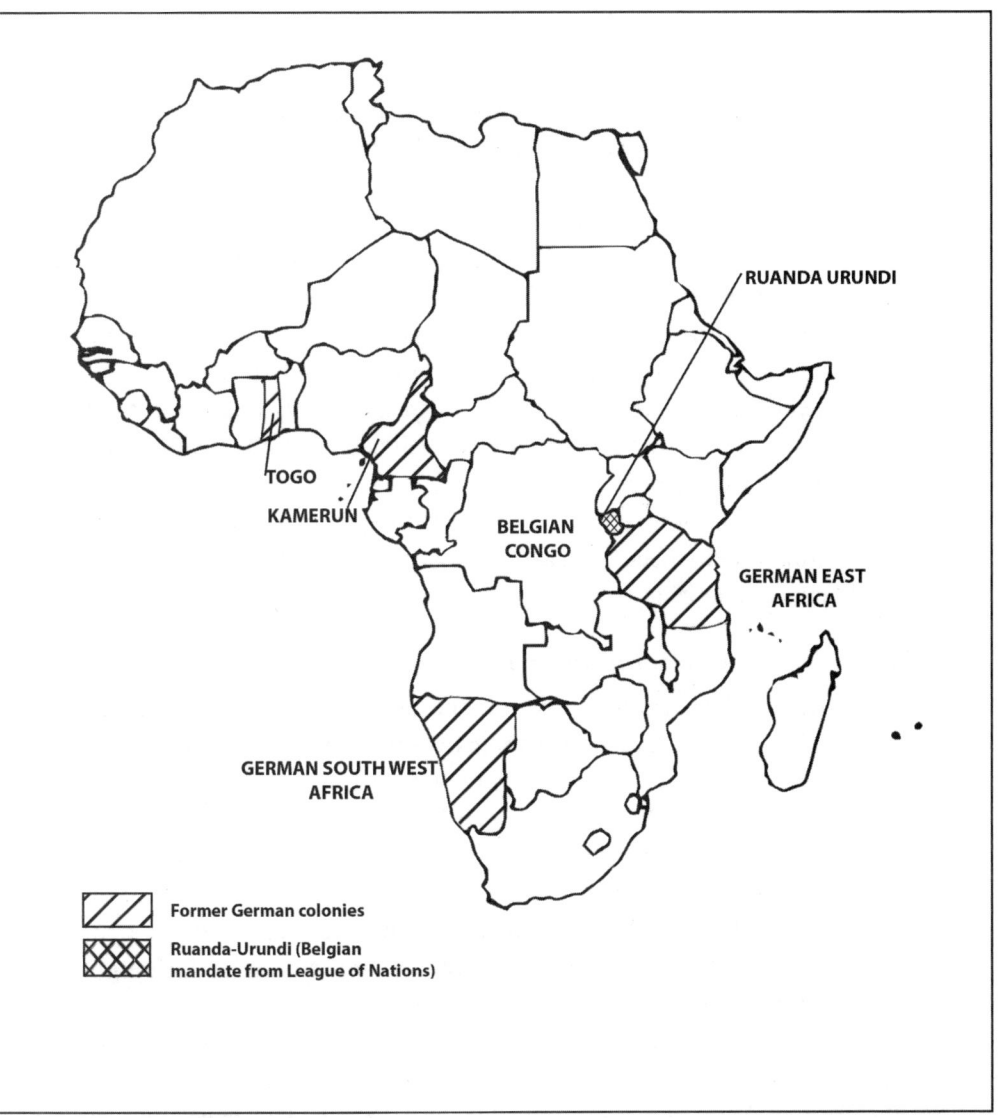

6. League of Nations mandates

In the end, Belgium got Ruanda and Urundi as Mandates of the League of Nations. They were to have a very troubled and bloody history and since 1962 have been separate countries, Rwanda and Burundi.

Belgium also obtained tax-free and customs-free use of roads and railways from the Belgian Congo to the Indian Ocean ports, later extended to land and air transit through the new British Mandate territory of Tanganyika.

4. Some thought was given, and newspaper articles written to the idea of entrusting **Palestine**, which General Allenby had conquered from the Turks, to Belgium as a League of Nations Mandate, Albert's prestige being a factor. Fortunately for Belgium nothing came of it; we are now all too aware that what at the time seemed the future of the Holy Land would have given Belgium a lot of headaches. For once Belgium might have owed some thanks to Britain for having thwarted its colonial ambitions. Prime Minister de Broqueville and Cardinal Mercier were in favour.
5. A wishy-washy article of the Versailles treaty gave Belgium a say in the trial of German **war criminals**. We shall see what effectively came of that in the next chapter.
6. Finally, Belgium was relieved of its **compulsory neutrality** and free to enter military alliances as it saw fit. This put an end to the articles of the 1839 peace treaties to that effect.

King Albert and Queen Elisabeth after the War

In 1919, King Albert could reflect on the fact that most other European monarchs, his cousins, had all lost their thrones, while by a twist of fate he himself, though from a German family and with a Bavarian-born queen, Elisabeth, had accidentally found himself in the company of the French and American republics. Only Britain, Italy, Serbia, Romania and Japan were monarchies and in the victors' camp. Breaking with a long tradition of welcoming exiled monarchs like Louis-Philippe and Napoleon III, Britain did not allow Tsar Nicolas II and his family to come to England, though he had been a faithful ally and was the cousin of King George V.

The prestige of Brave little Belgium, its army, its King were running extremely high. The monarch and his wife were to embark on several visits to the former Allies, including the US and Brazil, who specially sent a battleship, the *São Paulo* to fetch them from Zeebrugge in 1921. Everywhere Albert and Elisabeth were given a rapturous welcome. Monuments, statues and plaques were erected all over Europe and beyond. Schools, streets, mountain peaks, even dishes were named after them.

In the USA, Albert obtained massive support from American universities for their Belgian counterparts, especially the ruined Louvain institution. Presiding over his country's reconstruction, everywhere he went he tried to encourage foreign investment in Belgium or, for example in Brazil, Belgian/Luxembourg investment in the nascent local steel industry.

A keen mountaineer, Albert was fated to die a victim of his favourite sport which he often enjoyed in Switzerland and Italy. On the evening of

16 February 1935, he managed to get away for a few hours to climb, on his own, a cliff on the Meuse bank near Namur. When he failed to return to the waiting car the driver raised the alarm and his fallen body was eventually found, fatally wounded in the head. His funeral in Brussels was a grandiose affair attended by several heads of state and senior generals from the war. Several countries sent military detachments. The mountain guides from the Italian Dolomites were also there with their Alpenstocks.

His son Leopold succeeded him to the throne, becoming Leopold III.

One of the last initiatives Albert I took before his untimely death was to encourage meetings in Brussels between a select group of French, German, Belgian and Luxembourg diplomats and businessmen. All had the backing of their respective governments and their brief was to try to iron out the differences existing between Germany and her immediate western neighbours: that is, the Reparations, the size of the future German army, and the Polish–German border, especially the Danzig Corridor. All this took place against the background of rising xenophobia, antisemitism and nationalism personified by the advance of the Nazi party. The timing at which these informal talks, which might have led to a peace saving agreement, were held, is particularly ironic: December 1932 and the first weeks of January 1933. On 30 January, the negotiators were having their lunchbreak together in a Brussels restaurant when the German head delegate received a telegram informing him Hitler had just become chancellor. They all agreed it was, however sadly, pointless to carry on.

Both while Albert was still alive and during Elisabeth's widowhood, the Brussels Palace was often visited by scientists and artists, both Belgian and from abroad. A regular guest was Albert Einstein, with whom Elisabeth would play the violin. Her taste for sculpture and especially music was always strong, and she instituted musical contests that are very well attended to this day and are now named after her.

Elisabeth died in 1965, aged 89, not without having been at odds with the government on a few occasions, such as the time she visited Moscow and Mao Tse Tung when the Cold War was in full swing.

The Flemish Movement after 1918

In November 1918, many Flemish activists including the members of the infamous *Raad van Vlaanderen* fled to the Netherlands or Germany, and Borms himself went to Cologne. Most stayed abroad at least until 1940 but Borms, coming back under an assumed name, was picked up and condemned to death. He then had his sentence commuted to ten years which he sat out, refusing every conditional release. In 1928 while still in jail, he was elected to the Belgian parliament for Antwerp with 83,000 votes, but never took his seat as that house voted to invalidate his election. Unlike what happened after the Second World War, no one was executed for treason after the First World War.

2

Settling Accounts and the Leipzig Farce

The German community in Belgium, especially strong in Antwerp, was expelled. Some would later claim they were transported in cattle boxcars smelling of horse manure. If so at least they were not forced to work upon arrival, as had been the case for many Belgians who had gone the same way earlier and were now returning. Among the Germans 'asked to leave' was a young woman called Magda Quandt, whose complicated family life had seen her mother married for a time to a German Jew called Friedländer, who probably died in Buchenwald in 1939. She had been living in Antwerp with her mother and another stepfather and had been sent to boarding schools run by Ursuline nuns, first outside Antwerp and later at Vilvoorde, just north of Brussels. She later recalled that when arriving in Germany in 1919, a gypsy had looked at the palm of her hand and predicted she would become a kind of queen, but that the end of her story would be terrible. Some unconfirmed sources indicate she had an affair with Chaïm Arlosoroff (of all people!), who was a leading Zionist and one of the founders of the modern state of Israel, later assassinated in Tel Aviv. Magda got a job as a clerk for a German newspaper in Berlin, where she met her future husband, Joseph Goebbels. Hitler's minister for propaganda had himself been arrested and released twice by the Belgians during the occupation of the Ruhr. If the prediction of a ghastly end really was made, it certainly materialized, because Magda Quandt became Magda Goebbels in 1931. And her husband shot her dead on 1 May 1945, outside the Reich chancery, after they had poisoned their children and just before committing suicide himself. They were among the last few who remained with the Führer to the end.

Streets named after German cities or even the ones just called Rue d'Allemagne had their names changed, usually renamed after victorious generals, executed heros or politicians, Belgian or Allied. A popular hot drink, café bavarois, became café liégeois and German shepherd dogs became Alsatians.

In October 1918, a law was passed putting all enemy-owned goods under sequester. The Palais d'Egmont in central Brussels, belonging to the d'Arenberg family, became an exhibition hall displaying evidence of the German atrocities committed during occupation. It later became part of the Belgian Ministry of Foreign Affairs and it was there that Prime Minister Edward Heath signed Britain's entry papers to the then EEC, in 1972.

In international recognition of the role Belgium had played, its legations became embassies and the larger countries transformed their legations in Brussels into embassies. Ministers leading legations became ambassadors, and this was later extended to every country with a diplomatic presence.

War Criminals

Articles 227 to 230 of the Treaty of Versailles stipulated the arrest and trial of German officials defined as war criminals by the Allied governments. Article 227 made provision for the establishment of a special tribunal, presided over by a judge from each one of the major Allied powers, namely Britain, France, Italy, the United States and Japan. This tribunal identified the former Kaiser Wilhelm II as a war criminal, and demanded that an extradition request be addressed to the Dutch government, which had given him asylum. This was eventually refused by The Hague. Article 228 allowed the Allied governments to try German war criminals in their military tribunals.

On 3 February 1920, the Allies submitted a list of 900 names of individuals accused of committing alleged war crimes to the German government. However, the Germans refused to extradite any German citizens to Allied governments and suggested instead trying them within the German justice system in Leipzig. This proposal was accepted by the Allied leaders, and in May 1920 they handed the German government a reduced list of only 45 accused. Not all these people could be traced and in the end only 12 individuals were brought to trial between 23 May and 16 July 1921. Among them was a Max Ramdohr, charged with crimes against the civilian non-combatants in occupied Belgium who unsurprisingly was found not guilty. Many more individuals whom the Belgians had identified as clearly responsible for the August/September 1914 atrocities, or as having been involved in organizing the internationally illegal deportations of civilians, were listed also, without any result.

Others were naval officers based in Flanders who had, for example, sunk hospital ships or machine-gunned survivors in lifeboats or in the water. They drew jail sentences yet it is not certain they served even a part of them.

Outside Germany, especially in Belgium the Leipzig trials were considered a farce because of the small number of cases tried and the leniency of the court, which of course was to be expected. Inside Germany, on the other hand, they were perceived as unfair because of all the belligerents only German servicemen were being tried, though numerous Allied servicemen were also accused of war crimes. The Anglo-Saxons quickly lost interest; US Secretary of State Lansing openly stalled the proceedings and the British, as we have said, did not want to be too harsh or weaken Germany and humiliate it too much at this time. They considered Belgium's insistence on justice a pretentious nuisance. On 15 January 1922, a commission of Allied jurists, appointed to inquire into the trials, concluded that it was useless to proceed with them any further, and preparations for the Locarno Treaties, introducing a new spirit of reconciliation, definitively sounded their death knell.

Although largely regarded as a failure at the time, the Leipzig trials were the first attempt to organize prosecution for serious violations of international law. This trend was renewed during the Second World War, as even before the conflict was over the Allied governments announced they would try defeated Axis leaders for war crimes. The practice was ratified at the Nuremberg Trials and the International Military Tribunal for the Far East in Tokyo.

Following the end of the Cold War, the same rationale led to the establishment of the International Criminal Court in 2002.

3

Cleaning up, Rebuilding and Remembering

Disposal of unexploded ammunition

It is estimated 1.5 billion shells were fired during the First World War on the Western Front, concentrated on a strip of land about four or five kilometres wide. Every year between 250 and 300 tons are made harmless by the dedicated unit of the Belgian army called SEDEE/DOVO *(Section Enlèvement Destruction d'Engins Explosifs / Dienst voor Opruiming en Vernietiging van Ontploffingstuigen)*. The company in charge of the Flanders battlefield is based in Poelcapelle, more precisely in the Houthulst Forest where its main installation for making safe unexploded ordnance from the 1914–18 period is sited. Other units dispose of contemporary terrorist bombs and SEDEE/DOVO personnel have also been assigned to Iraq, Mali and Afghanistan. In 2016 alone, 217 tons of explosive devices were dealt with, of which 190 were at the Poelcapelle facility. On an average day (such as the occasion of my visit), three lorryloads of unexploded ammunition, mainly shells, were trucked in. The company base in Poelcapelle is on a 24/7 standby. Usually farmers find shells while tilling their fields. They call the police, who in turn call SEDEE/DOVO. About 30 per cent of the shells are unexploded duds and this can be explained by several factors: first, many POWs were working in the munitions factories on both sides and sabotage was frequent, second, there was no real quality control, and third, in some battles like Passchendaele, the soil had turned to mud and was not hard enough for the fuse to detonate on impact. Ten per cent of shells contain poisoned gas and it is imperative to identify this as the process of destruction is different for high explosive and gas. One identification error in 2012 led to an explosion and the bomb disposal facility was out of commission for four years. Surprisingly enough, the men in charge first use a hammer to (gently) remove the mud clinging to the shell. It is then usually X-rayed or put in a neutron ionizing machine, the analysis of the spectrogram identifying, for example, mustard gas. The decision to destroy by explosion or otherwise make safe is then made. Green crosses were painted on phosgene shells, but after a hundred years the paint is hardly visible. Other gases were used that made the soldiers vomit in their masks, thus choking them.

Spontaneous explosions are very rare, as are aerial bombs.[1]

Belgium and a few other countries have of course exemptions from the international treaties forbidding the handling and transportation of chemical weapons. Interns from various countries come regularly to Poelcapelle to study the methods and equipment used. Considering the huge quantities that are still being found a century after the war, the men and women working in the SEDEE/DOVO unit and their successors will still be needed for many years to come. They are both brave and competent.

When General Plumer conquered the Messines ridge in the opening phase of the Battle of Passchendaele, twenty mines had been placed by tunnel diggers under the German-held ridge. The attack was a complete success, due in large part to the buried mines. However only eighteen actually exploded (the din was heard in London – the vast craters are still visible and serve as waterholes for cattle), which means two failed to detonate. One did so (harmlessly) in the 1950s during a thunderstorm, but the other, with its tons of amatol, is still there, the exact location unknown.

Rebuilding the Economy

With tenacity the Belgians reconstructed their ruined country, mainly with their own resources and finance. Special funds were allocated for the rebuilding of destroyed dwellings and factories, railways and roads. The central bank managed to control monetary circulation, keeping the increasing Belgian exports competitive and controlling the amount of credit private banks were allowed to provide. The global financial instability that prevailed in the 1920s, followed by the 1929 crisis, hit Belgian reconstruction hard, but by the mid-1930s it had reached pre-1914 levels again. The completely devastated and inundated sector of Flanders was drained and rebuilt, and the merchant navy brought back up to strength. The ports of Antwerp and Ghent were relatively intact but those of Ostend and Zeebrugge had been completely destroyed. In 1914, there were 36 Belgian merchant ships displacing 164,000 TDW belonging to the principal Antwerp shipping line. Thirteen ships were lost through U-boat action causing 139 sailors to lose their lives. Several of these ships had brought in a large part of the food for the Belgian population during the occupation.

Universities

Nobody was ever tried for war crimes committed by the German army in 1914, but Belgium's universities did benefit from the impact the sack of Louvain (Leuven) had on world opinion – American universities gave massive amounts of help for their rebuilding.

King Albert managed to bring Princeton alumnus Woodrow Wilson to Belgium, the only place the president visited outside Paris whilst he was in Europe, and that may also have had an effect. American universities literally showered their Belgian counterparts, especially Louvain, with aid for reconstruction, donations of books, equipment and so on. This continued well after the war. The surplus funds were used to create the University Foundation and the Belgian American Educational Foundation (BAEF), which still awards scholarships to Belgian and American students who want to study across the Atlantic. The Universities of Brussels, Louvain, Ghent and Liège each received $ 3.8 million. Even the Malines (Mechelen) school for bell-tower-clock ringers received 3,000 dollars!

Lest We Forget

All over Belgium, even in small villages, monuments were erected with the names of the local victims, military or civilian, who had perished in the greatest conflict the country had ever known. Larger monuments or statues were also put up at Liège, Loncin, Haelen, Nieuport, to the victims of executions in towns like Dinant. After King Albert's death several statues of him and others in homage to his army, were erected, including one in Paris close to Place de la Concorde.

The Belgians, British, Dominions and colonies (now Commonwealth), Americans and French, built large cemeteries. Notable are the Tyne Cot British cemetery (with 11,952 graves, the largest Commonwealth cemetery in the world), the French cemeteries of Potyze and Mount Kemmel, and the Belgian Houthulst Forest Cemetery which contains the graves of 1,723 Belgian soldiers, most of them killed during the liberation offensive of 1918. There are also 81 Italian soldiers buried there, POWs used as forced labour by the Germans.

Apart from these in the Yser/Ypres region, there are several hundred more wartime burial grounds in Belgium.

It is a profound experience to walk the beautifully kept alleys and to see the youth and often the faraway origins of these soldiers. At the German cemetery of Langemarck stand the twin statues by Käthe Kollwitz, a deeply moving depiction of 'the grieving parents'.

The Last Post ceremony in Ypres

At the Menin Gate in Ypres, where the names of 54,896 British and Commonwealth personnel listed as missing in action are inscribed on the walls, every day at 2000 hrs the local police stop the traffic and buglers from the local fire brigade play the Last Post. This is done with more solemnity on special occasions, but since its inception has only been discontinued during the second German occupation, in 1928.[2] Apart from this moving ceremony, one should also mention the lighting of the torch at Westminster Abbey every year, in remembrance of the fact that after the Second World War the eternal flame at the memorial to the Unknown Soldier in Brussels was relit.

The Belgian Cenotaph Parade

When King Albert was killed in an accident in 1934, King George V gave the Belgian army the privilege of being the only non-Commonwealth army to parade each year bearing its arms at the Cenotaph in Whitehall and then to march to Horse Guards Parade, in homage to the 'King-Knight', his army and their heroic conduct during the First World War. This tradition has been kept up every year since in July by a detachment, usually from the Belgian Navy.

As a token of thanks for the sacrifices of the British, Commonwealth and Dominion people who liberated their country, Belgians presented them with a monument that now stands on the London Embankment.

During the 1940–44 occupation, the Germans left the First War cemeteries and most of these monuments alone. One NCO was punished for having urinated at the Menin Gate while drunk. However, they removed or blew up the monuments that carried more offensive inscriptions referring to 'German barbarism' or 'Teutonic savagery', some in cities where massacres had occurred in 1914 or those referring to the burning down of central Louvain. Since they never admitted to their first use of poison gas, the monument at Steenstraete that clearly referred to this was blown up.

Belgium had lost about 18 per cent of its wealth, but more importantly had 105,000 dead out of a population of 7 million, about equal numbers of military and civilian losses – this being very different from the other Western countries where practically no civilian losses were incurred.

Belgium (and the Congo) were forever changed by the experience in many ways, some of them for the better. Women went on to play a larger part in society, socialist aspirations for fairer treatment of workers, and Flemish cultural aspirations were given more attention. Belgium and the whole of western Europe, indeed the world, emerged from the conflict a very different place. In all senses it had been the Great War.

Notes

Prelude: The Fall of Fort de Loncin

1. The exact hour is disputed, some have said the explosion occurred at 1715 hrs or 1745 hrs.
2. http://fortdeloncin.be/page.php?pagID=34. There is a small museum with an interesting working model whose top lifts up, revealing the fort's inner galleries and installations. For a good description of the Forts on the Meuse see *The Forts of the Meuse in World War I* by Clayton Donnell.

PART I: NEUTRAL BELGIUM

1: Waterloo and All That

1. Leopold I, born in 1790, first King of the Belgians (1831–65) was the brother of Queen Victoria's mother and arranged for his nephew Albert to marry Victoria. His Saxe-Coburg-Gotha family made a series of dynastic marriages:
   - Ferdinand, another nephew, married Queen Maria II of Portugal
   - Ferdinand, his great nephew, became king of Bulgaria
   - August married the daughter of Emperor Pedro II of Brazil.
   - Charlotte, his daughter married the ill-fated Maximilian of Habsburg who briefly reigned over Mexico
   - Leopold, his eldest son, married Archduchess Maria Henrietta of Austria, also a Habsburg
   - Philippe, his other son, married Marie of Hohenzollern. They were the parents of King Albert I of the Belgians
   - His granddaughter Stéphanie married Rudolf, son of Emperor Franz-Josef of Austria and of Elisabeth, Duchess of Bavaria (the famous Sissi, who was assassinated in Geneva by an Italian anarchist), and would have inherited his father's throne had he not committed suicide in Mayerling.

2: Leopold II, Brialmont and Ordinary Politicians

1. The campaign against the actions of Leopold II's agents was partly justified, as was attested by neutral observers in a report published in 1906 by independent

Belgian and foreign experts, but also inspired by his competitors, the Liverpool merchant class, jealous and disappointed at having seen themselves excluded from the lucrative ivory and rubber trade at the turn of the century. Before being hanged as a traitor in 1916 for having helped the Germans ship arms to the IRA, one of Leopold II's severest detractors, Sir Roger Casement declared the behaviour of the Belgians in the Congo Free State was certainly not worse than that of the British rubber companies in South America, which he also reported on. Serious historians agree that after it was taken over from Leopold II and became a Belgian colony, on the whole the Congo was run neither better nor worse than the neighbouring colonies in British, French, German or Portuguese Africa, as was also reported by visiting American journalists like John Gunther in his 1955 book *Inside Africa*.

2. It has been said but never proved that the French General Weygand who was to play an important role in both world wars and whose parents were unknown, was Charlotte of Belgium's natural son, possibly by the Belgian General van der Smissen. When young, van der Smissen had served in the French Foreign Legion in Algeria. After the Mexican expedition, protected by Leopold II, he made a career in the Belgian army and became a general, later committing suicide. Maxime Weygand was born in Brussels in 1867 'of unknown parents', a technically illegal formula in Belgian law, which stipulates that at least the name of the mother should appear on the birth certificate. Young Maxime (note Charlotte's husband's first name was Maximilian) studied at French military academies, the expenses being covered by persons unknown, some say the Belgian royal family. He was adopted by a certain Mr Weygand and eventually attained the rank of general in the French army, working closely with Marshal Foch and commanding all Allied forces in June 1940. The theory he might be the son of van der Smissen and Empress Charlotte is sustained by pictures of the two men at similar ages, which bear a striking resemblance, as well as the facts that we know Charlotte was in Belgium when Weygand was born, and details of confidences made by both Leopold III and Charles de Gaulle. There is however no documented proof and might well never be.

3. The *Maison du Peuple/Volkshuis* literally 'People's Houses' were built by the Belgian Socialist party in every major town. They included a meeting hall, meeting rooms where for example reading classes could be given, offices and a café. The Brussels Maison du Peuple was built by internationally renowned architect Victor Horta in the Art Nouveau style. Unfortunately it was dismantled in the 1960s, but then partially rebuilt and some of its elaborate ironwork saved.

4. At the time smaller countries had ministers, heading legations, whilst larger countries had ambassadors and embassies. For clarity's sake however, only the word 'ambassador' is used in this book.

3: The Flemish Movement before 1914

1. The Pangermanist movement that appeared in the nineteenth century sought to unify, under German dominance, all Germanic-speaking people in Germany, Austria, the Low Countries and Scandinavia. Some of their ideas would be taken over by the Nazis.

PART II: BRAVE LITTLE BELGIUM

2: Invasion

1. The *Garde civique*, or Belgian Civic Guard, comparable to the American National Guard, had existed since Belgium's independence, but was composed of 'weekend soldiers' who paid for their own uniforms, and it was better known for the pot bellies of some of its bourgeois officers than for rigorous training and marksmanship. Its members had been used to guard bridges, banks and the like, and were also supposed to catch spies. The Germans hanged a few, not recognizing them as armed combatants, another good reason to abolish the institution altogether.
2. See Larry Zuckermann, *The Rape of Belgium*.
3. Koenigsberg used to be the capital of East Prussia, the easternmost part of Germany at that earlier time. Today the city no longer exists as such. It is called Kaliningrad, and was annexed by the Soviet Union (now Russia), together with a part of East Prussia. The rest of East Prussia is now part of Poland.
4. The priceless golden reliquary of St Hadelin (617–690), dating from 1046, which had escaped the Burgundians, the Calvinist iconoclasts and the French revolutionaries, was well hidden and survived the fire started by the German troops on 11 August that completely gutted the gothic collegiate church. According to tradition the first church on this site was built by Charlemagne's daughter.
5. A monument to de Gaulle was recently erected at the spot and the bridge is now named after him.
6. See relevant books on this subject by Jeff Lipkes, *Rehearsals: The German Army in Belgium, August 1914* and Terence Zuber, *Ten Days in August*.
7. Herstal is where the world famous Fabrique Nationale (FN) small arms manufacturer has its main plant.
8. The street where this incident occurred is now named after him.

9. Contrary to what some authors have written it does not seem that the Austro-Hungarian Skoda 305 mm guns were used against the Liège forts, but only later against Namur and Antwerp. The German 420 mm Kurze Marine Kanone super-heavy guns had been developed in great secrecy by Professor Rauchenberger and *Hauptmann* (Captain) Becker around 1910 for the Krupp Werk. Trials took place in 1911 and they were ready by 1913. They were transported on five flatcar railway wagons, weighing 42.5 tons and were manned by a 280-man crew. The shells weighed more than 820 kg (this could vary) and the propellant charge 50 kg. Their range was at least 9 km but also depended on variables like wind etc. They were usually shot at four-minute intervals. Rauchenberger was later to design the famous Krupp Paris gun with a range of 120 km. The shell would penetrate the stratosphere before starting its descent. Several Krupp guns were dubbed 'Grosse [big in German, fat in French] Bertha' after Krupp's daughter.
10. There is an island called Namur in the Pacific Ocean, commemorating its fall to French King Louis XIV in the seventeenth century.
11. It was to be reconstituted and in the 1930s converted into the Chasseurs Ardennais, whose colours carry the 'Namur' battle honour.
12. The Stroobants family now run the Silver Helmets Museum where there was also fighting.
13. The Death's Head cap badge was later taken over by the SS.
14. See Hugh Gibson, Secretary of the American Legation in Brussels, 'A Trip to the Haelen Battlefield' in his published diary.
15. The battlefield can easily be visited today, starting from the local museum. Halen, as it appears on road signs, can be reached from Brussels in about 45 minutes by motorway. The visit should include the Silver Helmets Museum (see note 12 above), the Ijzerwinning Farm and the Haelen Belgian military cemetery where 181 Belgian soldiers rest. The closest medium-sized city is Diest. Visitors should check the museum's website, as it regularly organizes battlefield tours, starting and finishing at its premises, when after the tour coffee and cookies are served. The museum boasts an impressive collection of shining cavalry German helmets and a comprehensive map of the battle.
16. She died in Hungary in 1945, after having been remarried to a nobleman from that country. Her daughter by Rudolf became known as the 'red Archduchess' for her sympathy for the communist cause in Hungary after the Great War.
17. Most of these forts, or rather what is left of them can be visited today.
18. The Germans tried to send an armoured train on a raid to the Channel ports but Belgian engineers thwarted its progress by destroying the railway switches.

19. General Pau was a veteran of the 1870 Franco-Prussian war where he had lost an arm. He used to give the military salute with his left arm.
20. See note 1, this chapter, on the Belgian Civic Guard.
21. There is a Belgian military cemetery in Ramskapelle.
22. A large warship currently serving in the French Navy is named after Dixmude. Appropriately it is a landing ship and as such carries *Fusiliers Marins*.
23. Such a trick was also used in May and June 1940 with Belgian civilians and POWs.
24. In Belgium as well as in France and unlike in the Anglo-Saxon countries, relations between freemasonry and the (Catholic) Church are bad.
25. After the Battle of the Marne, a row developed between Generalissimo Joffre and General Gallieni who had famously ordered and executed a flanking movement out of Paris against von Kluck's exposed right flank, using the Paris taxi service to transport part of its garrison to the battlefield. The former said: 'I don't know who won the Battle of the Marne but I b....y well know who would have lost it!'
26. Farmers have to keep the ditches and moats free of weed at the peril of heavy fines and landowners pay a special 'poldertax', which goes to the administration, called appropriately the Wateringen.
27. Gheeraert's mother was a Veranneman.
28. General Thys, hailing from Dalhem in the Pays de Herve, built the first railway in the Congo, from the coast to the new capital Leopoldville, across a mountain range. A city in that country was named after him, but it is now known as Mbanza Gunzu.
29. See the website at: http://tourisme.diksmuide.be/product/1084/boyau-de-la-mort.
30. The embankment is no longer used by the railway but has been turned into a bicycle path.
31. There is an interesting and very accurate wall painting of that visit at Lancaster House in London.

3: Stabilization: Mud and Misery, Dogs and Rats, Flies, Lice and Ice

1. The Mauser rifle was of course a German design, but had been manufactured under licence in Belgium before the war. Since the Belgian soldiers had been trained on them and a number were still serviceable it was thought more expedient to have new ones made in France rather than switch to another French or British type. No royalties were paid to Germany.
2. See in particular *La boue des Flandres* by Max Deauville.
3. This kind of nickname probably has its origin in the long greatcoats the Belgian soldiers started using, called a *Jas* in Dutch.

4. Haber was to win the Nobel Prize after the war, but the ceremony was boycotted by many.
5. The Germans always denied they had been the first to use gas. During the 1940–44 occupation they destroyed a monument at Steenstraete that said so. Though it is now undisputed that the Germans did make the first use, it might not have been in Belgium but in Russia, since some warnings were given by Tsarist Russia to the Allies.
6. Brasschaat to this day hosts a large Belgian military camp. It was later used by the Artillery and a fine collection of guns can be seen there.
7. Captain Guynemer, still in his early twenties, had a tally of 50 when he died but the highest French score was that of Colonel René Fonck: 75.
8. The Brussels Royal Army and Military Museum hosts a large collection of military planes, most having been used by the Belgian air force, including a Nieuport, a SPAD and a Sopwith Camel, others the result of exchanges with museums around the world. Remarkably, since very few have survived the two world conflicts, there are also authentic German First World War planes. The museum is certainly worth a visit for any aviation enthusiast.
9. A part of the German coastal defences has been preserved and can be seen at the Atlantic Wall Museum outside Ostend.
10. It has been stated by German sources that the *Lusitania*, *Mauretania* and *Olympic* (the last being *Titanic*'s sister ship) were listed as armed merchant cruisers by the RN. The author checked with the 1914 edition of *Jane's Fighting Ships*, the recognized reference, but this is not the case. They are indeed mentioned in that compendium of warships, but under the heading 'British Liners', after the list of RN ships. With a few others they are the only such vessels mentioned in this publication, which is dedicated to warships, not merchant marine. See Fürbringer's (interesting) memoirs in the Bibliography.
11. See Marie-Rose Thielemans in the Bibliography.
12. See Fürbringer.

4: King Albert, his Bavarian Queen, a Post Office and a Saintly Address

1. I was surprised to read in a book recently written by an Oxford professor that 'The Belgians (had) turned the Congo into a slave colony', as in fact exactly the opposite occurred when the Belgian government took over the administration of that vast territory.
2. In the Second World War she would use her German connections to save Jews in occupied Belgium and was accordingly distinguished with the title of 'Righteous among the Nations' by Israel. She was one of only two members of European royal families to be so honoured, the other being a Greek princess,

Alice of Battenburg, the mother of Prince Philip, Duke of Edinburgh. In May 1940, when Belgium was invaded she stayed behind at the Brussels Royal Palace, which had been turned into a military hospital when her son King Leopold was with the army. When the German army burst into it they found Elisabeth nursing the wounded of both sides.

3. Readers wanting to have a deeper understanding of King Albert's ideas and mentality should read: *Albert 1er, Carnets et Correspondance de Guerre* by Marie-Rose Thielemans, compiled from Albert's personal wartime notes, recently opened by the Brussels Royal Palace.
4. The murderers, who included the officer later found to be behind the Sarajevo murder, had been supported by France and Russia. Despite his bad impressions, King Albert reluctantly agreed to a visit from the Karageorgevic Crown Prince of Serbia.
5. Known at the time as the Head of Cabinet.
6. The International Court at The Hague had ruled that a neutral suffering aggression without provocation and defending itself could not be considered to be at war.
7. Eugenio Pacelli later became Pope Pius XII.
8. This brother, Felix de Bourbon-Parme would later become Prince Consort of Luxembourg.
9. Karl lost his throne in 1918. After unsuccessful attempts to reconquer it, he retired to the Portuguese island of Madeira, where he died of pneumonia in 1922 and is still buried. A devout Catholic, he was beatified by Pope John Paul II in 2004. His son Archduke Otto, later came to live in Belgium and was a longterm member of the European Parliament. Once asked if he had watched the Austria-Hungary football game the evening before, he asked, 'Whom were they playing against?' He was given a state funeral in 2011 in Vienna and buried with his Imperial ancestors in the famous croft of the Capuchin church there.
10. I am indebted for the coverage of these matters to Prof. John Rogister FSA, FRHist, who recently published the very interesting article, based on his lecture, 'King Albert I: The Legend and Reality.'
11. F. Stevens, *Naar aanleiding van de Verhouding tussen de taalgroepen in het Ijzerleger* BTMG, XX-7 MRA, Brussels 1976. See also Laurence van Yperseele (section 10.1), Sophie de Schaepdrijver, and Anne Morelli in Bibliography.
12. Christine Van Everbroeck 'Une conscience née dans le Feu' Divergences à propos du pourcentage de victimes flamandes de la Première Guerre mondiale, in *Les Grands Mythes de l'Histoire de Belgique, de Flandre et de Wallonie*. (See Anne Morelli in Bibliography)

13. In the companion volume to this, *Belgium in the Second World War* (Pen & Sword, 2014) I have given a description of the life and eventual execution of arch collaborator August Borms.
14. See companion volume, as in note 13.
15. President Woodrow Wilson made the Fourteen Points speech to Congress on 8 January 1918. He said the First World War was being fought for a moral cause and called for peace in Europe. The speech was the basis for a peace programme, suggesting that a League of Nations be established to help guarantee the self-determination of countries (point 10).
16. The word *Flamingant* is sometimes used to designate these persons. It has, however, recently acquired a pejorative sense it did not originally have.
17. July 11 is now the national day of the Flanders region of Belgium.
18. For more on this subject see, *The Birtley Belgians*, Schlesinger et al., in the Bibliography.

5: Out of Africa and around the World

1. In the sixteenth century, the Portuguese exploring the African coast contacted the Kongo kingdom and eventually exchanged ambassadors with them. When Queen Nzinga went to visit the Portuguese governor of Luanda she was denied a seat. The proud lady called for one of her slaves, who was told to get down on all fours for the queen to sit on his back.
2. The 'Etat Indépendant du Congo' (EIC) or Congo Free State was an enormous area in the Congo River basin privately acquired by King Leopold II of the Belgians in the last decades of the nineteenth century. At the end of that century a persistent campaign protested against the way his agents, Belgians and those from other European countries, treated the natives to make them produce as much rubber as possible. It is undeniable that serious abuses were committed, reported by both Belgian and international experts. This prompted a worried Belgian government to transform Leopold's domain into a colony in 1908. Most abuses then stopped, as observed by several non-Belgians who visited the Congo, which became no worse and no better than the neighbouring colonies run by France or Britain, but probably better than those of Germany or Portugal. Some authors, even modern ones, have largely exaggerated the abuses and there is no evidence, as an American author has recently claimed, that 'millions' lost their lives.
3. One black soldier was taken prisoner by the Germans in Namur.
4. The two motor launches had originally been built by Thornycroft & Co., for a Greek order, but were commandeered when war broke out. They were each 40 ft long and could make 19 knots. They were shipped on the SS *Union Castle*

to Cape Town, thence by train to Elisabethville (now Lubumbashi) in the Belgian Congo, and then pulled by steam-powered locomobiles (wood-fuelled, wheeled locomotives, specifically designed for use on roads not rails) which took them across very difficult mountainous terrain to the Lualaba River (in fact the name for the Congo River in this part of the country) and at last by rail again to Lukuya on Lake Tanganyika, where they joined three larger Belgian boats.
5. Refloated after the war, the *Graf von Götzen* was still being used in 2015 as a transport, quite an achievement and a testimony to German engineering. Now more than a century old, she was built in Germany in 1913, packed in numbered crates and reassembled on the lake shore.
6. During the Second World War, a number of Belgian pilots fought in the RAF. One of their Spitfires had 'Usoke' painted on its fuselage, commemorating this battle.
7. *Javary, Madeira* and *Solimões*, all names of rivers of the Amazon basin, were gunboats originally built for Brazil at the Vickers shipyard in Barrow-in-Furness, UK, but taken over by the Royal Navy and renamed HMS *Humber*, HMS *Mersey* and HMS *Severn*. They reduced SMS *Königsberg* to a hulk in July 1915. Shortly before this one blockade-breaking ship, sent from Germany disguised as a Danish freighter, managed to reach the DOA shore only to be sunk in an inlet by an RN cruiser. The Germans did manage to salvage part of the coals, arms and ammunition she carried.
8. In the Bantu languages spoken in central Africa, number is distinguished by the prefix *mu* for a singular and *ba* for plural. Thus, one says, 'two *baluba* soldiers and one *mukongo* NCO'.
9. Les Campagnes de l'Afrique de l'Ouest (Force Publique), Special Issue *Memo* 6, see Bibliography.

6: Occupation

1. See *Belgium in the Second World War*, Jean-Michel Veranneman, p. 135 and following.
2. The only other border being the one with Germany, the Belgian territory became thus totally isolated, except for Baarle Hertog, a small village north of Antwerp surrounded by Dutch (neutral) territory the Germans could not cross. Its post office became a very crowded place.
3. The role of the neutral embassies in Belgium was very important during the first occupation.
4. *In 1914 the Château outside Visé where these lines are written was plundered by the Germans. The then owners fled to The Hague. In 1916–17 Russian POWs*

had been put to work on a new railway linking the German border with the Belgian network, from Moresnet to Tongeren. Some managed to escape from their camp at Warsage and lived in an underground shelter they dug in the grounds of the château. Locals would bring them food. A German spy who could speak Russian managed to infiltrate them, pretending also to be an escaped POW and tried to find out where they had their hiding place. However, after a close interrogation by the (real) Russians he was found out. It was decided he could not be spared because he knew both the escaped Russians and the Belgians who helped them, all of whom would be at risk of their lives, since a list of them was found in his possession. The Russians beat him, leaving him for dead and decided to bury him after nightfall. However, when they came back he had disappeared. Following his bloody trail, they found him hiding in a bush and this time it was decided to finish him. In spite of his supplications, lots were drawn, and a Russian had the sinister task of beheading him with a shovel, the executioner becoming sick at the sight. The Germans looked for their man with dogs but never found the body.

5. The Nazis would later pick up where Wilhelm II's Empire had left off and annexe or re-annexe Austria, the Sudetenland and other territories in the east, though never Flanders.
6. The same would be true of the second occupation from May 1940 till September 1944.
7. The old county of Flanders that existed in the Middle Ages did not correspond to today's administrative Region of Flanders, which includes Antwerp, Hasselt and the area around Brussels – these were never part of the old county. But parts of north-eastern France where Dutch was then spoken, including Lille, Roubaix, Dunkirk, Arras, etc., roughly the départements du Nord and Pas-de-Calais, were annexed by King Louis XIV of France.

7: Resistance: A Merchant Navy Captain, Edith Cavell, Gabrielle Petit, a White Lady, a Cardinal, a Burgomaster, a Professor and others

1. Some of these clandestine papers or pamphlets, printed for obvious reasons on bad quality paper, were in danger of disappearing with time and lost to posterity, so have been digitalized. See www.nieuwsvandegrooteoorlog.be
2. Barbara Tuchman, *The Zimmerman Telegram*.
3. See Zuckerman, and Lipkes in Bibliography.
4. Also in Zuckerman, and Lipkes.
5. I was quite surprised to hear a well-known author and Oxford historian stating on BBC television that Belgium was just a piece of Holland glued to a piece of France. One would have expected this learned Scottish gentleman

to know that Flanders and Wallonia were *never* annexed separately to these two neighbouring countries, only together, first by France (1792–1815) and then by the Netherlands (1815–30). The same historian also predicted Donald Trump would never be elected…
6. Pirenne *Belgium and the First World War*, 2014. See Bibliography.
7. Cavell espionage: there is no evidence of this in British archives where some pieces seem to have been destroyed, but some was recently found in Belgian records by former director of MI5 Dame Stella Rimington.

8: Belgium and the Propaganda War
1. See Pirenne in Bibliography.
2. See Pirenne.
3. Barbara Tuchmann, *The Zimmermann Telegram*.
4. See Hickey and Smith, *Seven days to Disaster: The True Story of the Sinking of the Lusitania*.

9: Liberation: The Emperor's Battle and the King's Flanders Army Group
1. The thermal city of Spa, in the Belgian Ardennes, has given its name to all spas around the world. It was especially famed until the 1880s, but its attraction for the Germans was its location not far behind their lines on the western front and its abundance of hotels. Local inhabitants were kept indoors when important visitors roamed the streets. Local place names like Balmoral must have been especially appealing to Wilhelm II, whose love–hate relationship with the country of his mother and grandmother never ceased. The author has sometimes heard Anglo-Saxon historians referring to it on television as 'SCHpa'. The correct pronunciation is of course very simply 'spa', as in Leamington Spa.
2. One of the units attached was the 30th American Infantry Division, Old Hickory. In 1944–45 it fought in Belgium again and there is a memorial monument on a square in Visé, recalling this.
3. He was to be replaced by General Major Lemercier on 12 October.
4. Unlike in the French army where commandant is the equivalent rank of a British or American major, in the Belgian army it is a senior captain.

PART III: AFTERMATH

1: Disappointing an Immense Minister
1. Robin Neillands, *The Great War Generals on the Western Front*, p. 445ff.
2. Sally Marks, *The Innocent Abroad*, 1981.

3. Sally Marks, as previous note.

3: Cleaning up, Rebuilding and Remembering
1. Houthulst Forest itself, where the facility is situated has not been made safe and is dangerous to walk in.
2. Some eyebrows were raised when Sir John French was given the 'victory title' Earl of Ypres in 1922, since a Belgian family could lay claim to that title, which is linked to the Ypres feudal lands.

Bibliography

Bibliographic notes

In the companion volume to this I noted that not a lot has been written about Belgium in the Second World War. Exactly the opposite is true for the earlier conflict. A plethora of publications saw the light of day in the interwar years and even more recently. Interested readers will find hereunder a reference to a publication that was made by the Royal Army Museum of Brussels in 1987 called *La Belgique et la Première Guerre mondiale. Bibliographie.* It is about 600 pages long and its thousands of entries only briefly sum up the author, title, publisher and date of the numerous books and articles written about general subjects, battles, protagonists, incidents, the political or economic context, etc. Some go into details or statistics, or occurrences in one small village, which are of little interest for those interested in the general synthetic picture. Other entries are simple and/or romantic eulogies of, for example, Albert I and/or Queen Elisabeth, sometimes almost childish. This abundance makes it an impossibility to read everything, as this would take about (or more than) a lifetime. Since 1987 and especially, for obvious reasons in and about 2014, a lot more has been written and published, with many interesting contributions to be found on the internet. Therefore, what follows is necessarily a selection, by no means exhaustive.

The books or articles which have been used are organized alphabetically, by chapter of the book.

Part I: NEUTRAL BELGIUM

1. Waterloo and All That

175 Ans de Diplomatie belge Belgian Ministry of Foreign Affairs, 2005.
Bogdan, Henry *Les Hohenzollern, la Dynastie qui a fait l'Allemagne* Perrin, Paris, 2010.
Dumont, G. H. *Histoire de la Belgique* Hachette, Paris, 1977.
Général *** *Plutarque n'a pas menti* La Renaissance du Livre, Paris, 1921.

Gunther, John *Inside Africa*, New York, Harper, 1955.
Hasquin, Hervé (ed.) *Dictionnaire d'Histoire de Belgique* Didier Hattier, Brussels, 1988.
de Launay, Jacques *Les Origines secrètes de la Grande Guerre* In: Histoire de la Diplomatie secrète 1789–1914. Edito-Service, Geneva, 1973.
Liddell Hart, B. H. *A History of the First World War* Pan Books, 1930.
Lousse, Emile and Jacques de Launay *Dictionnaire Biographique d'Histoire contemporaine* Edito-Service, Geneva, 1973.
Mansel, Philip *London, Paris and Brussels. The Prequel: 1787–1830–1839.* Lecture given at the Belgian Embassy in London in 2011.
Marshall, S. L. A. *World War I* American Heritage, Boston, 1987.
de Pierrefeu, Jean *Plutarque a menti* Bernard Grasset, Paris, 1922.
Sondhaus, Lawrence *World War One: The Global Revolution* Cambridge University Press, 2011.
De Visscher, C. and F. Van Langenhove *Documents diplomatiques belges 1920–1940 : La Politique de Sécurité extérieure* Palais des Académies, Brussels, 1964.
De Vos, Luc *De Eerste Wereldoorlog* Davidsfonds, Leuven, 1996.
Van Zuylen, Pierre *Les Mains libres: Politique extérieure de la Belgique 1914–1940* Desclée De Brouwer, Brussels, 1950.
www.rtbf.be/14–18 (website on Belgian French-language radio)

2. Leopold II, Brialmont and Ordinary Politicians

Bainville, Jacques *Bismarck et la France* Haerès, Paris, 1932.
Balace, (Prof.) Francis *1914–1945 Lectures on RTBF* (Belgian French language radio) Liège University.
Bogdan, Henry *Les Hohenzollern: La Dynastie qui a fait l'Allemagne* Perrin, Paris, 2010.
Coolsaet, Rik *België en zijn buitenlandse Politiek* Ed. Van Halewyjk, Leuven, 1998.
de Diesbach, Ghislain *Les Secrets du Gotha* Julliard, Paris, 1962.
Dumont, Georges H. *La Dynastie belge* Elsevier, Brussels, 1959.
Emerson, Barbara *Léopold II: Le Royaume et l'Empire* Duculot, Paris Gembloux, 1980 (original edition Weidenfeld & Nicolson, London, 1979).
de Lys, Frédéric *Cette étonnante Dynastie belge* Editions du Lombard, Brussels, 1978.
Putzger, W. *Historischer Weltatlas* Editions Berlin, 1995.
Roegiers, Patrick *La spectaculaire Histoire des Rois des Belges* Perrin, Paris, 2007.

Part II : BRAVE LITTLE BELGIUM

1. Crisis

Asprey, Robert *The German High Command at War: Hindenburg and Ludendorff and the First World War* Warner Books, London, 1991.

Barnett, Corelli *The Great War* Penguin, 1979.

La Belgique et la Première Guerre mondiale – België en de Eerste Wereldoorlog Bibliografie Editorial directors Patrick Lefevre and Jean Lorette, Centre d'Histoire militaire, Musée royal de l'Armée, Cinquantenaire, Brussels, 1987.

Clark, Christopher *The Sleepwalkers: How Europe went to War in 1914* Harper Collins, London, 2014.

Cuvelier, Joseph *La Belgique et la Guerre. Vol II. L'Invasion allemande.* Foreword by Henri Pirenne. Editions Henri Bertels, Brussels, 1921.

Dinjaert, Raymond (Lt. Col. B. E. M.) *Les Opérations militaires de l'Armée belge au cours de guerre 1914–1918.*

Fouvez, Charles 'L'Armée belge (de 1914–18)' in *Historia 20° Siècle* 126, 1973.

Hastings, Max *Catastrophe: Europe goes to War 1914* Collins, London, 2014.

Kershaw, Ian *To Hell and Back: Europe 1914–1949* Allen Lane (Penguin-Random), 2015.

Neillands, Robin *The Great War Generals on the Western Front 1914–1918* Magpie Books, London, 2004.

Palmer, Alan *The Kaiser: Warlord of the Second Reich* Weidenfeld and Nicolson, London, 1978.

Pirenne Henri *Histoire de Belgique.* Vols III and IV. La Renaissance du Livre, 1907/1911.

Pirenne, Henri *Belgium and the First World War* Foreword by David Nicholas and note by Sarah Keymeulen. Brabant Press, 2014.

Professor Dr Lt. Col. (R) Etienne Rooms, 'Belgium in World War One' Lecture at the Belgian Embassy in London on 4 December 2008.

Schüddekopf, Otto-Ernst *Der Erste Weltkrieg* Bertelsmann Lexicon Verlag, Gutersloh, 1977.

Tuchman, Barbara W. *The Guns of August* Bantam Books, 1962.

Williams, Charles *Pétain* Little, Brown, London, 2005.

Wanty, (General) Emile *L'Art de la Guerre* Marabout University, Verviers, 1967.

Zuber, Terence *Inventing the Schlieffen Plan: German war planning 1871–1914* Oxford University Press, 2002.

2. Invasion

2.1 First Blood

'La Campagne de 1914 de la Brigade de Gendarmerie de Gemmenich' in *Memo, Revue Historique* 7–82.

Foch, (Maréchal) Ferdinand *Mémoires pour servir à l'histoire de la guerre 1914–1918* Plon, Paris, 1931.

Lierneux, Pierre *L'Armée belge dans la Grande Guerre: Uniformes et Equipement* Verlag Militaria, 2015.

Tasnier, (Lt. Col.) Marc and (Maj.) Raoul Van Overstraten *La Belgique et la Guerre. Vol III, L'Histoire militaire belge: Les Opérations militaires*, Editions Henri Bertels, Brussels, 1923.

2.2 The Bloody Harvest of August 1914

Bédier, Joseph *German Atrocities from German Evidence (Letters seized on German POW, documenting atrocities)* Armand Colin, Paris, 1915.

Horne, J. and A. Kramer *German Atrocities 1914: A History of Denial* Yale University Press, New Haven, 2001.

Hutchinson, Walter (ed.) *Belgium the Glorious* (Series) Hutchinson & Co, Paternoster Row, London, 1920.

de Leval, Julien *Le Pays de Herve dans les quinze premiers Jours de la Tourmente Petits Villages dans la Grande Guerre 1914–2014* Commémorations du Centenaire INEA Berneau (Belgium), 2014.

Lipkes, Jeff *Rehearsals: The German Army in Belgium, August 1914* Brabant University Press, 2014.

Tixhon, Axel and Mark Derez *Villes Martyres : Visé, Aarschot, Andenne, Tamines, Dinant, Louvain, Termonde*. Presses universitaires de Namur, 2014.

Zuckerman, Larry *The Rape of Belgium: The Untold Story of World War I*. New York University Press, 2004.

2.3 Resistance of the Forts of Liège and Namur

'La Bataille de Liège 1914' in *Memo, Revue Historique* 7–82.

Brabers, Jules and Rob Lemmens *Luik, De eerste Horde van het Schlieffenplan* Western Front Association Excursiegids, 2008.

Brabers, Jules and Rob Lemmens *Luik Augustus 1914: Zoektocht naar een vergeten Slag* Aspekt, Soesterberg (NL), 2009.

Donnell, Clayton, *The Forts of the Meuse in World War I* Osprey, 2007.

Fort Barchon Honderd Jaar Geschiedenis doorheen twee Wereldoorlogen. Gilbert, Vervier.

The Forts of 1914 and 1940: Tourism and Remembrance in the Province of Liège Liège, 2013 www.ftpl.be

Fürbringer, Werner (*Fips*) *Alarm! Tauchen!! U-Boot in Kampf und Sturm* Ullstein, Berlin 1933. English edition: *Fips: Legendary U-Boat Commander* Pen & Sword Books, 1999.

Hoet, Jean-Claude *Barchon (Fort 1914–1940)* http://users.skynet.be/jchoet/fort/barchon.htm

Hogg, Ian V. *Guns 1914–18: The Artillery War* Ballantine Books, NY, 1971.

Lampaert, Roger *België in Oorlog: De Inval* Uitgeverij De Krijger, Erpe, 1994.

Manchester, William *The Arms of Krupp 1587–1968* Bantam Books, 1968.

Naessens (Colonel) and L. Lombard *Loncin* Editions G. Leens, Verviers, 1937.

'La Province de Liège commémore la Grande Guerre' in: *Notre Province*, December 2013

www.provincedeliege.be

Zuber, Terence, *Ten Days in August: The Siege of Liège 1914* The History Press, 2014.

2.4 Haelen: The Battle of the Silver Helmets

Gibson, Hugh, 'A Trip to the Haelen Battlefield' in: *A Diplomatic Diary*, General Books, 1917.

Guderian, Heinz *Achtung Panzer! (Haelen)* Cassel Military Paperbacks, 1992.

Vanthuyne, H. J. *Halen, 12 Augustus 1914: De Dag dat Cavalerie voor 't laatst storm reed* Editions Museum Slag der Zilveren Helmen, Halen. Fonthill Media, 2015.

2.5 Antwerp

Churchill, Winston S. *The World Crisis Vol I: 1911–1914* Thornton Butterworth, London, 1923–31.

Pawley, R. and P. Lierneux *The Belgian Army in World War I* Osprey, Oxford, 2009.

2.6 The Battle of the Yser River

'Il y a quinze Ans... Les Belges sur l'Yser', article in *L'Illustration*, Paris, 3 August 1929.

Van Pul, Paul *In Flanders' Flooded Fields: Before Ypres there was the Yser* Pen & Sword Books, Barnsley, 2006.

Senesael, Marcel *La Bataille de l'Yser 1914* Private Edition, 1964.

Thys, (Cdt) Robert *Nieuport 1914–1918: Les inondations de l'Yser* Henri Desoer, Liège, 1922.

3. Stabilization

Atkinson, Diane *Elsie and Mairi Go to War: Two extraordinary women on the Western Front* Preface, 2009.

van Bergen, Leo *Zacht en Eervol: Lijden en Sterven in een Grote Oorlog* Standaard Uitgeverij, Antwerp, 1999.

'Le Boyau de la Mort' in *Memo, Revue Historique* 7–82, Yser 1914 – Les Inondations.

van de Casteele, Eric 'De Beerputten van de Groote Oorlog', *Knack* 7 November 2007.

Cave, Nigel *Passchendaele: The fight for the village* Leo Cooper, Pen & Sword, 1997.

De Geest, Joost (ed.) *Couleurs au Front 1914–1918 : Les Peintres au Front belge* Crédit Communal Bruxelles, 1999.

Deauville, Max *La boue des Flandres : Et autres récits de la Grande Guerre.* Editions Labor, 2005.

Forman, Charlie et al. (eds), *Waterways on the Western Front: Untold Stories of WW1* London Canal Museum, 2015.

Holt, T. and V. *Major & Mrs Holt's Battlefield Guide to the Ypres Salient* Pen & Sword, 1997.

Holt T. and V. *The Western Front-North: Major & Mrs Holt's Battlefield Guide* Pen & Sword Books, 2004.

Jacoby, A. *Ouvrez le Ban!* Les Editions de Belgique, Brussels, 1935.

Koene, Prins *Kriegsalbum des Marinekorps: Flandern 1914–1917* Selbsverlag der Marine-Bücherei des Marinekorps.

Laffin, John *Panorama of the Western Front* Alan Sutton Publishing, Stroud, 1993.

do Lago, (Maj.) Correia *Noticia da Guerra Mundial 1914–1918 Front Belga* Editions Leite Ribeiro e Maurillo, Rio de Janeiro, 1920.

Lampaert, Roger *België in Oorlog: Stabilisatie in Vlaanderen* Uitgeverij De Krijger, Erpe, 1995.

Lampaert, Roger *Vuur en Gas in de Loopgraven: Stellingoorlog in Vlaanderen 1915–1916* Uitgeverij De Krijger, Erpe, 1996.

Macdonald, Lyn *They called it Passchendaele* Penguin, 1978.

Vansuyt, Michel and Michel Van den Bogaert *De Militaire Begraafplaatsen vaaan W.O.1 in Vlaanderen: Langemark, Passendale, Eindoffensief* Uigeberij De Krijger, Erpe, 2002.

Wolff, Leon *In Flanders Fields* Reader's Union, Longman, Green & Co, London, 1960.

3.1 In Flanders Skies

Capron, Freddy *L'Aviation belge et nos Souverains* Editions J. M. Collet, Brussels, 1988.

'Gotha Raid on London 25 May 1917' in *Military Heritage* April 2004.

Guttman, Jon *Balloon-bursting Aces of World War I* Osprey, 2005.

'Le Roi Albert 1er et les Ailes belges dans la tourmente de la Grande Guerre' in *Memo, Revue Historique* 9-87.

Longstreet, Stephen *The Canvas Falcons: Pilots and planes of World War I* Ballantine Books, NY, 1970.

O'Connor, Mike *Airfields and Airmen: Ypres* Pen & Sword Books, 2004.

Pacco, John *Militaire Luchtvaart/Aviation militaire: 1910-1929* J.P. Publications, 2000.

Pieters, Walter *Above Flanders Fields: A complete record of the Belgian fighter pilots and their units during the Great War 1914-1918* Grub Street, London, 1998.

3.2 Off Flanders Coast

Fürbringer, W. (Memoir) *FIPS Legendary U-Boat Commander* Leo Cooper, Pen & Sword Books, 1999.

Hickey, Des and Gus Smith *Seven Days to Disaster: The true story of the sinking of the Lusitania* Fontana Collins, Glasgow, 1982.

McGreal, Stephen *Zeebrugge & Ostend Raids* Pen & Sword Books, 2007.

Prince, Stephen *The Blocking of Zeebrugge* Osprey, Oxford, 2010.

Schmalenbach, Paul *Die Deutsche Marine-Luftschiffe: Werden-Wirken-Nachwirken* Koehlers Verlagsgesellschaft MBH, Herford, 1977.

Termote, Tomas *War beneath the Waves: Uboat Flotilla Flandern* University of Chicago Press, 2017.

Thielemans, Marie-Rose (ed.) *Albert Ier: Carnets et Correspondance de Guerre 1914-1918*. Memoirs. Duculot, Paris, Louvain-la-Neuve, 1991.

'Zeebrugge' in *Memo, Revue Historique* 9-83.

4. King Albert, his Bavarian Queen...

King Albert's Book: A Tribute to the Belgian King and People from representative Men and Women throughout the World Published by the Daily Telegraph, 1914.

Bronne, Carlo *Albert Ier, le Roi sans Terre* Plon, Paris, 1935.
Bronne, Carlo *La Légende d'Albert 1er* Plon, Paris, 1965.
Guilleminault, Gilbert *Avant 14: (The fire at the Bazaar de la Charité)* Denoel Livre de Poche, Paris, 1978.
Professor John Rogister FSA, FRHistS, 'King Albert I: The Legend and the Reality.' Lecture given at the Belgian Embassy in London, 2008.
Stengers, Jean *L'Action du Roi en Belgique depuis 1831: Pouvoir et Influence* Duculot, Louvain-la-Neuve, 1992.
Werrie, Paul *La Légende d'Albert 1er Roi des Belges* Dessins de Hergé. Casterman, Tournai-Paris, 1934.
Willequet, Jacques *Albert 1er Roi des Belges* Presses de Belgique, Brussels, 1979.
d'Ydewalle, Charles *Elisabeth de Belgique* Flammarion, Paris, 1964.

4.1 Peace Feelers

de Launay, Jacques *Histoire de la Diplomatie secrète de 1914 à 1918* Marabout Université, Verviers, 1966.
Renouvin, Pierre *Histoire des Relations internationales de 1871 à 1914* Hachette, Paris, 1955.
De Ridder, Alfred *La Belgique et la Guerre: Vol IV Histoire diplomatique 1914–1918* Editions Henri Bertels, Brussels, 1921.

4.2 The *Frontbeweging*

Hermans, Theo et al. *The Flemish Movement 1780–1990* The Athlone Press, London & Atlantic Heights N.J., 1992.
Morelli, Anne (Editorial Director) *Les grands Mythes de l'Histoire de Belgique, de Flandre et de Wallonie* Université libre de Bruxelles, Editions Vie Ouvrière, 1995.
Reyntjens, Annemie *De Ijzertoren ... en de nieuwe Vlaamse Benadering van de Oorlog* Davidsfonds, Leuven, 2014.
Ruys, Manu *De Vlamingen (Een Volk in Beweging, Een natie in Wording)* Lannoo Tielt, Belgium, 1972.
De Schaepdrijver, Sophie *De Groote Oorlog: Het Koninkrijk België tijdens de Eerste Wereldoorlog* Olympus Contact,1997.
Stevens, F. 'Naar aanleiding van de Verhouding tussen de taalgroepen in het Ijzerleger' in *Belgisch Tijdschrift voor Militaire Geschiedenis*, XX-7 MRA, 1976.

Stevens, F. E., L. Schepens and L. De Vos 'Een definitieve Afrekening met de 80% Mythe? Het Belgisch Leger (1914–1918) en de sociale en numerieke Taalverhoudingen onder de Gesneuvelden van lagere Rang' in *Belgisch Tijdschrift voor Militaire Geschiedenis* XXVIII-8 December 1988.

Vanacker, Daniël *De Frontbeweging: De Vlaamse Strijd aan de Ijzer* De Klaproos Brugge, 2000.

4.3 Belgians Abroad

Bygate, John G. *Of Arms and the Heroes: The Story of the 'Birtley Belgians'* Prontaprint, Durham, 2005.

Schlesinger, J., D. McMurtrie and J. Bygate *The Birtley Belgians*, History of Education Project, Revised edn, Durham, 1988.

5. *Out of Africa and around the World*

5.1 The African Campaign

Abbott, Peter *Armies of East Africa 1914–18* Osprey, 2002.

Les Campagnes belges d'Afrique: 1914–1917. Photographic documents of the ministry for the Belgian colonies, 1919. *La Force publique au Congo Belge* Special Issue *Memo, Revue Historique* 6–81.

Hoyt, Edwin P. *The Germans who Never Lost: The most amazing story to emerge from World War One* Leslie Frewin, 1988.

Kestergat, Jean *Quand le Zaïre s'appelait Congo* Paul Legrain, Brussels, 1985.

Miller, Charles *Battle for the Bundu: The First World War in East Africa* MacDonald, London, 1974.

Pakenham, Thomas *The Scramble for Africa* Abacus, London, 1991.

Van Reybrouck, David *Congo: Een Geschiedenis* De bezige Bij, Amsterdam, 2010.

Sibley, (Major) Roger *Tanganyikan Guerilla: East African Campaign 1914–18* Pan/Ballantine Illustrated History of the First World War, 1971.

Sonck, J. P. *Les Hydravions belges du Tanganyika* Belgian Aviation History Association, 2003.

5.2 The 'Autos-Cannons' from Russia to New York…

Thiry, Marcel *Le Tour du Monde des autos-canons belges* Le Grand Miroir Editions, De Rouck, Brussels, 1965.

Thiry, August and Dirk van Cleemput 'Parade triomphale du Corps des Blindés' in *FEDRA* March 2010.

6. Occupation

Rency, Georges *La Belgique et la Guerre: Vol I. La Vie matérielle de la Belgique durant la Guerre mondiale* Editions Henri Bertels, Brussels, 1922.

6.1 Feeding the Belgians

Delmelle, Joseph *Histoire de la Navigation et des Ports belges* Paul Legrain, Brussels, 1982.

Whitlock, Brand (United States Minister to Belgium) *Belgium: A Personal Narrative* 2 vols. UCLA, 1919.

6.2 Enslaving and Robbing the Belgians

Pirenne Henri *Histoire de Belgique Vols III and IV* La Renaissance du Livre, 1907/1911.

Pirenne, Henri *Belgium and the First World War* Foreword by David Nicholas and note by Sarah Keymeulen. Brabant Press, 2014.

Rency, Georges *La Belgique et la Guerre: Vol I. La Vie matérielle de la Belgique durant la Guerre mondiale* Editions Henri Bertels, Brussels, 1922.

6.3 Dividing the Belgians

Van Everbroeck, Christine *August Borms (Zijn Leven, zijn Oorlogen, zijn Dood)* Manteau Antwerpen, 2001.

7. Resistance

Bernard, Henri *Un Géant de la Résistance Walthère Dewé* La Renaissance du Livre, Brussels, 1971.

Brown, Gordon *Courage: Eight Portraits* Bloomsbury, 2007.

Desmet, Philippe 'Margriet Ballegeer waagde haar leven om Duitsers te saboteren', *Gazet van Antwerpen* 13 March 2014.

Edith Cavell Centenary Commemorations Edited by Edith Cavell Nurses Trust, accessed at www.cavellnursestrust.org

Edith Cavell et son Réseau Lecture by Andrew Brown and Prof. Emmanuel Debruyne at the Cercle Gaulois, Brussels on 27 April 2016.

Evans, Jonathan *Edith Cavell* Royal London Hospital Museum, Whitechapel, London ,2008.

Gabrielle Petit, espionne et heroïne belge fusillée en 1916. Sarah Heynderyckx RTBF (French-speaking Belgian radio), 3 August 2014.

Resistance and Collaboration in Belgium during Wartime: difficult choices Conference led by Professor Chantal Kesteloot at the Belgian Embassy in London in 2009.

Tuchmann, Barbara *The Zimmermann Telegram* Bantam Books, 1971.

8. Belgium and the Propaganda War

De Ridder, Alfred *La Belgique et la Guerre: Vol IV. Histoire diplomatique* Foreword by Ambassador Beyens. Editions Henri Bertels, Brussels, 1921.

9. Liberation

Fredericks, Pierce G. *The Yanks Are Coming (World War One)* Bantam Books, 1964.

Johnson, J. H. *1918: The Unexpected Victory* Cassels Military Paperbacks, 1999.

Lampaert, Roger *1918: Doorbraak en Bevrijding* Uitgeverij De Krijger, Erpe, 1998.

10. Liberation Politics

10.1 Chaos in Brussels

Majerus, B. 'Bruxelles, 1918: révolution et sortie de guerre' in P. Chassaigne & J. M. Largeaud (eds), *Villes en Guerre* Armand Colin, Paris, 2004.

van Yperseele, Laurence, *Mémoire et Identité: Parcours dans l'Imaginaire occidental.* Presses Universitaires Louvain, 2008.

10.2 Lophem

Dumont, G. H. *Histoire de la Belgique* Hachette, Paris, 1977.

Van Langenhove, F. and H. Pirenne *La Politique intérieure de la Belgique après la 1ère Guerre mondiale.*

Part III: AFTERMATH

Bainville, Jacques *Les Conséquences politiques de la Paix* Paris, 1920.

Duroselle, J. B. *Histoire diplomatique de 1919 à nos jours* Dalloz, Paris, 1974.

Keynes, John Maynard *The Economic Consequences of Peace* London, 1919.

Marks, Sally *The Innocent Abroad: Belgium at the Paris Peace Conference of 1919* University of North Carolina Press, Chapel Hill, 1981.

Le Palais d'Egmont-Arenberg (Bookmaps) Inbel, Brussels, 1972.

Renouvin, Pierre *Histoire des Relations internationales: De 1914 à 1929* Hachette, Paris, 1969.

Veranneman, Jean-Michel *Belgium in the Second World War* Pen & Sword Books, Barnsley, 2014.

Westlake, Ray *Remembering the Great War: In Gloucester and Herefordshire* Brewin Books, 2002.

Willequet, Jacques 'The Belgian Luxembourg economic Union (UEBL): Problèmes économiques franco-belges en 1919 et 1920' in *Actes du Colloque de Metz Centre de Recherches des Relations internationales de l'Université de Metz: les Relations franco-belges de 1830 à 1934* Metz, 1975.

Index

Aarschot 33, 38, 121, 134
Adenauer, Konrad 40, 155
Aéronautique militaire 73, 80–1, 171
African Campaign 112–22
Albert I (King of the Belgians r.1909–1934)
 xxiii, 13–14, 22, 24–5, 30–1, 43, 49, 54,
 56–61, 66, 73, 76, 81–2, 87, 89–109,
 118, 123, 128, 132, 134–5, 144, 159, 164,
 170–1, 176, 181–2, 186–7, 194–5
 King Albert's Book 93–4
Albert, Prince (later Albert II) 82
Albert, Prince Consort to
 Queen Victoria 22
Albrechts, Sergeant xxii
Alençon, Duchess of 89
Alexandre Delcommune
 (Belgian steamer) 115
*Alles voor Vlaanderen, Vlaanderen voor
 Kristus* (AVV-VVK) 106
Alfonso XIII of Spain 132
Alsace and Lorraine 8, 94, 101–2, 144
Andenne 33, 37
Anseele, Edouard 12, 23
Antwerp xii–xii, xvi, xviii, 4–5, 9,
 11–12, 16–17, 22–3, 25–6, 30, 34–5,
 38–9, 42, 48–9, 55–9, 76, 80, 85, 97,
 101, 103, 108, 110, 139, 150, 169, 180,
 188–9, 193
Arenberg, Duke of 39–40, 129, 190
Arlosoroff, Chaïm 189
askaris 115, 120–2
Asquith, Herbert Henry 26–7, 94
Atlas V 152
Austria-Hungary 21, 102–3, 108, 124, 178
 Ambassador Clary 21
 Austro-Hungarian empire 95
 Skoda 11, 47
'auto-cannons' 123–4
Axelbrod, Pavel 23

Baden-Powell, Robert 93
BAEF *see* Belgian American Educational
 Foundation
Bainville, Jacques 178
Balfour, Arthur 94, 176
Ballegeer, Margriet 150–1
Balobanov, Angelica 23
Bamburg farm 61
Bastaardvlamingen 137
Battice 32, 36
Battle of Haelen 48–55
Battle of Merkem (1918) 162–3
Battle of Passchendaele 75, 163, 192–3
Battle of the Golden Spurs (1302)
 17, 25, 107
Battle of the Marne 48, 57
Battle of the Silver Helmets 48–55
Battle of the Somme 75–6, 96
Battle of the Yser 59–66, 91, 96
Battle of the Scarpe 125
Battle of Vimy Ridge 125
Baucq, Philippe 147–8
Baudouin of Belgium 14, 123
Bavaria 17, 147
Bavaria, Dukes in 89
Bavaria, King Ludwig of 89
Bavaria, Elisabeth of 24, 89, 186
Bavaria, Prince Rupprecht of 13, 57, 90,
 149, 167
Bavaria, Sophie of 100
BE2G (aircraft) 80
Belgian Air Component 78, 80
Belgian air force 78
Belgian American Educational Foundation
 (BAEF) 194
Belgian Catholic party 7, 8, 12, 97, 160, 171
Belgian Cavalry Division 29, 49, 164
Belgian Cenotaph Parade 195
Belgian Civic Guard (*Garde civique*) 29, 61

Index 221

Belgian Congo xviii, 6, 76–7, 90, 99, 102, 112–17, 120–2, 177, 183, 185, 195
Belgian–Dutch border 85, 127
Belgian Gendarmerie 23, 31
Belgian Jewish Consistoire 95, 109
Belgian National Day (1915) 138–9
Belgian neutrality 4–5, 7–9, 22–7, 127–8, 138, 143, 154, 159, 168, 186
Belgian Red Cross 72
Belgian Socialist Party 7, 8, 12
Belgica, polar explorer ship 11
Belpaire, *Juffrouw* 73
Benedict XV, Pope 100, 143
Bernardiston, Nathaniel 159
Bernheim, Louis 95, 109, 164, 179
Bethmann-Hollweg, Theobald von 23, 132, 135, 157
Beyens, Eugène-Napoléon 93
Bismarck, Otto von 5, 8, 21–2, 112
Bodson, Mathieu 153
Boer War 33, 114, 117
Bolshevik Revolution (1917) 95, 124
Bonar Law, Andrew 94
'Bonnot Gang' (*Bande à Bonnot*) xxi, 4, 123
Booth, William 93
Bordet, Jules 72
Borms, August 105, 109, 136–7, 187, 203
Bouko, Gendarme 23, 32
Bourbon-Parma family 91, 101–102
Boyau de la Mort 64–5
Bressoux xxii
Brialmont, Henri-Alexis 9, 33
 Brialmont forts 9, 22, 43
Briand, Aristide 101, 178
Brichard, Emile xvii
British Indian Army 116
British Military Medal 74
Brown, Gordon 139
Bruges xiii, xx, 3, 16–17, 30, 54, 72, 76, 79, 81–2, 84–8, 97, 105, 126, 141, 146, 168–70, 172, 178–9
Brussels xii–xiii, xvii, xxi, 4, 7–13, 16, 21, 23–5, 29, 31, 39–40, 49, 54–7, 73, 76–7, 80–1, 83, 89, 92, 99–101, 104–5, 113, 125, 129–30, 135–40, 144–5, 147–50, 152, 155–6, 159–60, 167, 169–70, 176, 183, 187, 189–90, 194–5

SS *Brussels*, merchant ship 146–7
Brussels–Antwerp canal 55

Caillaux, Joseph 21
Callemeyn, Victor 71
Cambon, Paul 26–7
Cantons de l'Est 183
Carabiniers 30, 35, 54, 76, 89, 157
Carabiniers Cyclistes 50–1
Carnegie, Andrew 94
Carol, King of Rumania 22
Cavell, Edith 72, 125, 139, 147–8, 153–4, 158–9
Channel ports 61, 66, 84, 95–6, 103, 163
Charlotte, Empress of Mexico 7, 129
Charlotte, Princess of Wales 4, 7
Chasseurs à Cheval 76, 104
Chisholm, Mairi 73
Churchill, Winston 56, 59, 94, 140, 146
Claes, Ernest 106
Clarendon, Lord 22
Clémenceau, Georges 101–4, 164, 168, 171, 175–7, 181–2
Cogge, Karel 63
Commission for Relief of Belgium (CRB) 130–1
Communauté Germanophone de Belgique 183
Compagnie d'Aérostiers 76
Compagnie des Aviateurs 76
Congo (as Free State and Belgian colony) 6, 13, 34, 90, 94, 99, 102, 112–17, 120–2
Cook, Frederick 11
Coppens, Willy 80–2, 165
Cooreman, Gérard 97
Coppens d'Houthulst, Willy 80–3, 165
Council of Flanders *(Raad van Vlaanderen)* 136–7, 187
Croix de Guerre 70, 81
Crombez, Henri 82
Croquet, Joseph 143
Curzon, Lord 58, 93–5, 176
Czernin, Ottokar 102

Daels, Frans 106
La Dame Blanche 142, 149, 151–2
de Becker, Jules 39
de Bettignies, Louise 147, 149

Debeuckelaere, Adiel 106, 109
de Broqueville, (Prime Minister) Charles 12, 58, 97, 186
de Croy, Marie 147–9
De Gaulle, Charles 40
de Mérode, Pauline 101
De Meulemeester, André 79, 82–3
De Mevius, Gustave 81
de Monteton, Digeon 49
de Montigny, Charles 81
de Niéport, Edouard 79
De Pillecijn, Filip 106
de Ryckel, Baron Louis 24–5
de Selliers de Moranville, Antonin 24
de Villa Lobar, Marquis 100, 130, 148
De Villiers de Waroux, Fred 71
De Vlaamsche Leeuw 140
de Weyer, Sylvain van 27
De Witte (later de Haelen), Léon 50–2, 54
Debeuckelaere, Adiel 106, 109
Depage, Antoine 72, 81, 92, 147
Depage, Marie 87, 91, 154
der blaue Teufel 80
der Lancken, Baron von 101
Derez, Mark 35
Derousseaux, Olivier xxi
Destrée, Jules 12
Deutsch Ost Afrika (DOA) 112, 114, 117, 118, 120, 183
Dewé, Walthère, 142, 151–2
Dinant xiii, 33, 40–1, 43, 48, 121, 194
DOA *see Deutsch Ost Afrika*
d'Oultremont, Henri 62
Dover Patrol 61, 84
Doyle, Arthur Conan 159
Drachen balloons 80–1
Duchène, Désiré 37
Dupérieux, Eugène 39

Elektrozaun 127
Einstein, Albert 11, 92, 95, 144, 157, 187
Elisabeth (Sissi), Empress of Austria 89
Elisabeth of Belgium (1876–1965) 24, 58, 72, 82, 89–93, 95, 100, 102–3, 186–7
Elisabethville 111
Entente cordiale agreements, 27
Erzberger, Matthias 137

Esher, Lord 27
Etappengebiet 125
Eupen 183

Fielding, Dorothie 74
Flamenpolitik 108, 132, 134–7
Flanders Army Group 164–6, 168–70
fléchettes 77
Flemish movement/Flemish 15–17, 104–9, 187–8
  frontbeweging movement 73
  ontvoogding movement 17
Foch, Ferdinand (Generalissimo) 92, 163–4, 171
Fokker, Anthony 83, 110, 180
Fonck, Cavalier Antoine 31–3
Force publique 113–16, 118, 120–1
Forts
  Barchon xx, 36, 44, 46
  Boncelles 46
  Chaudfontaine 46
  Cognelée 47
  d'Embourg 46, 153
  d'Evegnée 46
  Eben Emael 33
  Flémalle 47
  Fléron 33, 46
  Hollogne 47
  Koningshooikt 58
  Lantin 46
  Lier 46, 56, 58
  Loncin xx–xxi, xxiii, 10–11, 45–7, 58, 194
  Maizeret 47
  Malonne 47
  Marchovelette 47
  Pontisse 44, 46
  Walem 56, 58–9
Franco-Prussian war (1870) 5, 13, 22, 35, 42, 125, 157
Francqui, Emile 93, 129
francs-tireurs 34–8, 41–3, 44, 50, 64, 140, 146, 156–7
Franskiljons 137
Franz Ferdinand, Archduke 21, 102, 125, 149
Franz, Joseph 13

Frederick II 51
Friedrich of Saxe-Meiningen, Prince 47
Frontbeweging 73, 104–9
Fryatt, Charles 146–7, 158
Fulco Ruffo di Calabria 82
Fürbringer, Werner, 85–7

Galet, Émile-Joseph 23, 100
Galsworthy, John 94
Garde civique 29
Geeraert, Henry 63
George V, King of England 66, 73, 82, 92, 97, 186, 195
German war criminals 87, 155, 180, 186, 190–1
Gete River 49, 51
Gezelle, Guido 17
Ghent University 125, 136, 145
Gibson, Hugh 148
Gilkinet, Amédée 153
Goebbels, Joseph 106, 189
Goebbels, Magda (née Quandt) 189
SS *Graf von Götzen* 117
Greek neutrality 26
Grenadiers 30, 41, 45, 62, 64, 66, 75, 89
Grey, Sir Edward 25, 94
Grossetti, Paul François 61
Guderian, Heinz 53, 55
Guides 30, 50, 60, 104
Guynemer, Georges 79–80

Haber, Fritz 74
Hague Conventions (1899, 1907) 41, 131
Haig, Sir Douglas 92, 163, 176
Haldane, Lord 26
Halen, Battle of 48, 53
Hanriot 79–81, 83
Hardie, Keir 12, 23
Hardinge, Lord 94
Hearst, William Randolph 155
Heath, Edward 190
SMS *Hedwig von Wissmann* 115, 117
Henri (Hendrik) Conscience 16
Hentjens, Jules 152
Hindenburg, Paul von 101–2, 126, 133, 135, 162–3
Hitler, Adolf 6, 125, 154, 168, 187, 189

Hohenzollern-Sigmaringen 89
Hoover, Herbert 130
Hôpital de l'Océan 72, 74, 81, 87, 92
Houthulst Forest 75, 165, 168, 192, 194
Huyghé, Armand 120, 122
Huysmans, Camille 12, 23, 99
Hymans, Paul, Belgian politician 93, 97, 159, 175–7, 181–2

Ibañez, Blasco 94
Ijzerwinning farm 49–51, 52, 54
Ingenbleek, Jules 107–8
Internationale Socialiste 12, 99

Jacquet, Fernand 78, 83
Jaurès, Jean 12, 23
Jellicoe, John 93
Jettenbach, Hans zu Törring 100–1
Joffre, Joseph 60, 92
Josef, Franz 13, 102
Juarez, Benito 7, 129
Jupille 46

Kaiserliche Marinekorps 84–5, 167
Karl of Habsburg 102
Kautsky, Karel 23
Kerensky 124
Kershaw, Ian xix
Kervyn de Lettenhove, Georges 79
Kervyn de Merendree 70
Keyes, Roger 82, 84, 86, 91, 92, 95, 147, 176
Kinshasa 114
Kipling, Rudyard 93
Kitchener, (Lord) Herbert Horatio 93, 155
Klobukowski, Antony 24
Knocker, Elsie 73–4
SMS *Königsberg* 121
Kretz, Lieutenant 71
Kronprinz, Wilhelm, of Germany 43
Kruger, Paul 160
Krupp of Germany xxii, 9, 11, 29
Kück, Mathias 45
Kulturkampf 22
Künz, Charles xvii

La Belgique héroïque 140, 159
La Libre Belgique 140, 148
La Patrie 140
L'Âme belge 140
Lahaut, Julien 123
Lambert, Léon 93, 95
Lambrecht, Dieudonné 151
Lanciers 30, 36, 50, 60, 104
Landsdowne, (Lord) George 103
Lanrezac, Charles 40–1
Lansing, Robert 191
Leman, Gérard xxii–xxiii, 44, 45, 46
Leopold I (King of the Belgians r. 1831–65) 4, 22, 129
Leopold II (King of the Belgians r. 1865–1909) 5, 6–9, 13–14, 22, 58, 76, 85, 89–90, 113, 128, 159
Leopold III (King of the Belgians r. 1934–51) 50, 82, 92, 96, 187
Liebknecht, Karl 12
Liège xx–xxiii 22, 23, 30, 32, 33, 35, 110, 152
  forts 10, 22, 35, 43–7, 49, 101
Lloyd George, David 176, 181–2, 184
Lophem (Loppem) 170–2
Louvain (Leuven) 25, 30, 38–40, 42, 49, 194
Ludendorff, Erich 46
RMS *Lusitania* 40, 72, 87, 91, 154, 160
Luxemburg, Rosa 12, 23
Lyautey, Louis-Hubert 92

Maeterlinck, Maurice 17, 94
Malmédy 183
Marchand, Jean-Baptiste 45
Marx, Karl 12, 154
Maskens (Villa) 82, 91
Max, Adolphe 93, 144–5
Mercier, Désiré-Joseph 93, 108, 138, 143–4, 186
Merjay, Franz 153
Meuse River 9, 10, 32–3, 35, 37, 40, 43, 48–9, 152, 180
Michel, Victor-Constant 164
Modard, Lieutenant xxi

Naessens, Colonel xx–xxiii
Namur 9–10, 22–3, 30, 43–4, 47, 56, 77, 101, 136, 145, 187

Nansen, Fridtjof 94
Napoleon III 7, 8, 22, 154
Neuray, Fernand 108, 179
Nicolas II of Russia 123, 186
Nieuport 59, 61–2, 63, 80, 85, 91
Nieuport (aircraft) 77, 78, 79, 80, 82, 83
Nieuport-Dixmude railway 64, 70
Nivelle, Robert 92
Northcliffe, (Lord) Alfred 103, 155

Olieslagers, Jan 76–8, 80, 82, 83
Olsen, Frederick 116, 118, 120
Ostend 60 84–6, 88, 91, 141, 148, 167, 181, 193
Ourthe River 46

Pacelli, Eugenio *see* Pius XII
Pankhurst, Emily 94
Paris Peace Conference 179
Passchendaele xiii, 75, 79, 96, 162–4, 166, 192, 193
Patch, Harry xvii
Patriotism and Endurance 143
Pau, Paul 60
Pauchenne, Théodore 32
Paul Renkin (gunboat) 116
Pershing, John 60, 62
Petit, Gabrielle 149–50
Pirenne, Henri 14, 136, 138, 145
Piron, Jean-Baptiste 55
Pius XII, Pope 100, 143
Pius X, Pope 143
Planck, Max 11, 157
Plumer, Herbert 164, 166, 193
Poincaré, Raymond 66, 73, 92, 101, 102
Ponticelli, Lazare xvii
Poperinghe 75, 78
Portuguese Mozambique 119
  Prussian Line (*Preussen Stellung*) 165

Quandt (later Goebbels), Magda 189

Raad van Vlaanderen *see* Council of Flanders
Rademakers, Maximilien 53
Ramdohr, Max 190
Ramskapelle 62

Rawlinson, Henry 60
Redmond, John 94
Regiments
  Belgian: *2ème de Ligne,* 55, 64; *4ème de Ligne* xvi, 11, 30, 51, 53, 60, 64, 70, 178; *10ème de Ligne* 47, 66, 71; *12ème de Ligne* 30, 32, 66, 92; others 66
  French: 33rd Infantry 40
  German: Hanoverian Dragoons 13; Imperial Guards Uhlan 37, 51, 52, 53, 55; 89 Mecklenburg xxii, 45; others 51–2
Reigersfliet 75–6
Ribot, Alexandre 94, 101, 102, 178
Rodrigo, Don 129–30
Ronarc'h, Pierre-Alexis 61, 62, 92
Royal Flying Corps 76
Royal Marines 56, 58
Royal Naval Air Service 76, 81
Royal Navy 5, 21, 27, 56, 84, 86, 87, 91, 117, 147, 162, 172, 176
Ruanda–Urundi 118, 120, 122, 183–5
Rudolf of Austria 58, 128
Ruhleben camp 146, 158
Rupprecht of Bavaria 13, 57, 90, 149, 167

Sainte-Adresse 97, 98
São Paulo, battleship 186
Scheldt River 4, 5, 26, 56, 59, 127, 176, 180–1
Schlieffen/Moltke plan 5, 27, 32, 42–3, 48, 49
Schrek, flying boats 78, 117
Schutztruppen 115
Schwieger, Walther 87
SEDEE/DOVO xxiii, 192, 193
Sint-Margriet-Houtem 55
Soldatenräte 170
Solvay, Ernest 11, 129, 147, 154
Sopwith: Camels 78, 81, 83; Pups (*aka* Scout) 79, 83; 1½ Strutters 80, 82, 83
Spa 102, 168, 187
SPADS 76–83
Spanish-American war 155

Stanley, Henry Morton 6
Steenstraete 61, 70, 74–5, 195
Streuvels, Stijn 17

Tamines, German army 37–8
Thieffry, Edmond 77, 79, 82
Thill, Gendarme 23, 32
Thuilier, Louise 147, 149
Thys, Albert 63
Thys, Robert (son of Albert) 63
Tixhon, Axel 35
Tombeur de Tabora, Charles 115, 118–19, 122
'Treason of Flanders' 137
Treaty of London (1839) 4, 95, 158
Trésignies, Léon 55
Trulin, Leon 153

Union Économique Belgo Luxembourgeoise (UEBL) 182

Valentiner, Max 87
Van Bergen, Henri 150–1
van Cauwelaert, Frans 108–9, 136
van de Weyer, Sylvain 27
van der Smissen, Alfred 7
Van Deventer, Jacob 117
Van Overstraeten, Raoul 50, 55
Van Severen, Joris 106
Van Vlierberghe, Albert 53
Van Vollenhoven, Maurits 93, 130
Vandervelde, Emile 12, 23, 97, 175
Veranneman, Robert xvi, 11, 57, 60, 64, 70, 72, 74, 165, 178, 182
Verfaille, Emiel 74
Verhaeren, Emile 17, 91
Versailles Treaty 98, 122, 129, 155, 171, 175, 177–8, 181–6
Verschaeve, Father Cyriel 106
Villes Martyres 35
Visé 31–3, 36–8, 49, 152, 160, 168
Vlaams Nationaal Verbond (VNV) 109
Vlaamsvoelend 73, 106
von Arnim, Ferdinand 45
von Below, Nicolaus 24, 156
von Bethmann Hollweg, Theobald 23, 132, 135, 157

von Bissing, Moritz Ferdinand 54, 101, 125–7, 130, 132, 133, 136, 140, 141, 149
von Bülow, Walther 37, 43
von der Goltz, Colmar 125, 132
von der Lancken, Baron 101
von der Marwitz, Georg 49, 53–4
von Emmich, Otto xxi, xxiii, 43, 46
von Falkenhausen, Ludwig 125–6, 137
von Hausen, Max 41–3
von Kielmansegg, Johann 41
von Kluck, Alexander 43, 54
von Lettow-Vorbeck, Paul 114–15, 117–22, 184
von Moltke, Helmuth 5, 13, 28, 45
von Richthofen, Manfred 47
von Schlieffen, Alfred 54
von Schröder, Ludwig 85, 86

Wahle, Kurt 115, 118
Walput, Aloïs 74
Wavre 42
Waxweiler, Emile 100–101
Wilhelm II 8, 13, 22, 24, 28, 33, 86, 102, 132, 133, 149, 168, 190
Wilson, Woodrow 106, 132, 134, 160, 167, 177, 179, 184, 194
Withlock, Brand 40, 92, 100, 130, 148
Wurtenberg, Duke Albrecht of 43

Ypres xviii, 54, 60, 61, 75, 134, 165, 194
Yser River 59–62, 64, 66, 128

Zeebrugge 84–6, 91, 97, 141, 147, 167, 181, 186, 193
Zilliox, Joseph 152
Zimmermann telegram 141, 154, 160
Zita of Bourbon-Parme 91, 102
Zweig, Stefan 15, 24